FACULTY GUIDE

for use with

ActivePsych

**Classroom Activities Projects and
Video Teaching Modules**

FACULTY GUIDE
for use with

ActivePsych

Classroom Activities Projects and Video Teaching Modules

CD 1
ActivePsych: Classroom Activities Projects
Includes contributions from:
Richard Alexander, Muskegon Community College
Martin Bolt, Calvin College
Marian Gibney, Phoenix College
Kelly Lambert, Randolph-Macon College
Karsten Look, Columbus State Community College
Thomas E. Ludwig, Hope College
Ann Merriwether, State University of New York at Binghamton
Antoinette R. Miller, Clayton State University
Amy Obegi, Grossmont College
Andrew Peck, The Pennsylvania State University
Jennifer O. Peluso, Florida Atlantic University
Roger Sambrook, University of Colorado, Colorado Springs
Stavros Valenti, Hofstra University

CD 2 and 3
Digital Media Archive, Second Edition
Edited by Joe Morrissey, State University of New York at Binghamton (with the assistance of Ann Merriwether, State University of New York at Binghamton and Meredith Woitach, University of Rochester)

CD 4
Scientific American **Frontiers Video Collection for**
Introductory Psychology, Third Edition
Edited by Martin Bolt, Calvin College

FACULTY GUIDE
for use with

ActivePsych
Classroom Activities Projects and Video Teaching Modules

Printed in the United States of America

ISBN: Faculty Guide 0-7167-7167-5 (ISBN 13: 978-0-7167-7167-8)
     Set of 4 CD-ROMs 0-7167-7265-5 (ISBN 13: 978-0-7167-7265-1)
     CD-ROM/Faculty Guide Package 0-7167-7168-3 (ISBN 13: 978-0-7167-7168-5)
     Set of 3 VHS Tapes (Videos only) 0-7167-6144-0 (ISBN 13: 978-0-7167-6144-0)
     Set of 3 DVDs (Videos only) 0-7167-6146-7 (ISBN 13: 978-0-7167-6146-4)

Second Printing

Worth Publishers
41 Madison Avenue
New York, NY 10010
www.worthpublishers.com

FACULTY GUIDE
for use with

ActivePsych
Classroom Activities Projects and Video Teaching Modules

TABLE OF CONTENTS

PART I: Preface

PART II: Package Contents

ActivePsych CD 1: Classroom Activities Projects

Flash-Based Demonstrations: Screen-by-Screen Tab Content

Research Methods

PowerPoint-Based Demonstrations

PowerPoint-Based Demonstrations: Usage Guide and Technical Information

PowerPoint-Based Demonstrations: Descriptions and File Names

ActivePsych CD 2 and 3 / DVD 1 and 2 / VHS 1 and 2:

Digital Media Archive, Second Edition

*Edited by Joe Morrissey, State University of New York at Binghamton
(with the assistance of Ann Merriwether, State University of New York at Binghamton and
Meredith Woitach, University of Rochester)*

Digital Media Archive: Video Descriptions and Segment Lengths

Learning and Memory

Thinking, Language, and Intelligence

Emotion and Motivation

Stress and Health

Disorders and Therapy

Social Psychology

ActivePsych CD 4 / DVD 3 / VHS 3:

Scientific American Frontiers Video Collection for Introductory Psychology, Third Edition

Edited by Martin Bolt, Calvin College

Scientific American Frontiers: Video Descriptions and Segment Lengths

PART III: Video Support _(using MPEG files in PowerPoint)_

PART I: Preface

Worth Publishers would like to thank the following instructors for their generous contributions to ActivePsych:

Richard Alexander, Muskegon Community College
Martin Bolt, Calvin College
Kelly Lambert, Randolph-Macon College
Karsten Look, Columbus State Community College
Thomas E. Ludwig, Hope College
Ann Merriwether, State University of New York at Binghamton
Antoinette R. Miller, Clayton State University
Amy Obegi, Grossmont College
Andrew Peck, The Pennsylvania State University
Jennifer O. Peluso, Florida Atlantic University
Roger Sambrook, University of Colorado, Colorado Springs
Stavros Valenti, Hofstra University

In addition, we thank the following instructors for their thoughtful and considered reviews and suggestions for the classroom activities and videos presented in this work:

Marian Gibney, Phoenix College
Karsten Look, Columbus State Community College
Thomas E. Ludwig, Hope College
Ann Merriwether, State University of New York at Binghamton
Joe Morrissey, State University of New York at Binghamton
Andrew Peck, The Pennsylvania State University
Meredith Woitach, University of Rochester

Publisher
Catherine Woods

Acquisitions Editor
Kevin Feyen

Senior Media Editor
Danielle Pucci

Assistant Media and Supplements Editor
Peter Twickler

Development Editor
Elaine Epstein

Copy Editor and Associate Contributor
Paul Smaldino, The New School for Social Research

Video Producer
John Philp, Bad Dog Tales, Inc.

Video Editor
Nathan T. Ryan

Executive Marketing Manager
Katherine Nurre

Photo Researcher
Nicole Villamora

Media Production
CADRE design
www.cadre.com.au

Producer and Designer
Sonya Forrest

Technical Lead
Robert Bleeker

Managing Director
David Hegarty

For a full list of photo, video, and three-dimensional modeling credits for the ActivePsych: Classroom Activities Projects, go to the ActivePsych Main Menu and click "Credits."

System Requirements and Technical Support

Minimum System Requirements

WINDOWS:
Windows 98, 2000, XP, ME, NT; Pentium 2 Processor/266MHz or faster; 800 x 600 screen resolution or above; 64 MB RAM; 8x CD-ROM

MACINTOSH:
OSX (10.2, 10.3.9, or above); G3, G4, or faster; 800 x 600 screen resolution or above; 64 MB RAM; 8x CD-ROM

RECOMMENDED SETTINGS (MAC and PC):
1024 x 768 screen resolution or above; 128 MB RAM

ActivePsych Featured Materials

1) (CD1) **Flash-based Classroom Activities Projects:** 32 activities that combine a written overview of each topic with interactive displays, animations, videos, and specially-tailored exercises. Many activities involve input from your students and return feedback that is specific to the answers given by them.

   NOTE: These activities run in Flash. You must have **FLASH PLAYER 8** installed on your computer for the activities to run properly. Although you do not need a live Internet connection to run any component of ActivePsych, you do need to have a browser installed on your computer to launch the program.

2) (CD1) **PowerPoint-based Classroom Activities Projects:** 22 demonstrations, inventories, and surveys. These demonstrations can work easily with iClicker Classroom Response Systems.

   NOTE: These activities require **Microsoft PowerPoint** to run. In addition, many activities are accompanied by handouts provided as separate **Microsoft Word** documents.

3) (CD 2 and 3, DVD/VHS 1 and 2) **Digital Media Archive, Second Edition:** 33 short video segments and animations (some in multiple parts) that illustrate basic principles and classic experiments in psychology.

4) (CD 4, DVD/VHS 3) *Scientific American* **Frontiers Video Collection for Introductory Psychology, Third Edition:** Hosted by Alan Alda, this collection features 15 video programs with a number of prominent psychologists. Many segments include demonstrations and discussions of cutting-edge neuroimaging technology and emphasize the importance of neuroscience in modern psychology research.

   NOTE: The videos in ActivePsych are provided on DVD, VHS, and CD-ROM (in MPEG format). The MPEG video files can be easily imported into pre-existing PowerPoint lectures or run in a video player application such as QuickTime, Windows Media Player, or Real Player.

Getting Started with the CD-ROM Product

Launch Instructions for the ActivePsych Classroom Activities Projects (CD 1)

WINDOWS:
Put CD 1 in the CD-ROM drive. Double click the "My Computer" icon on the Windows desktop and then double click the "ActivePsych" CD icon. Double-click on "**ActivePsych.exe**" to launch the program.

MACINTOSH:
Put CD 1 in the CD-ROM drive. Double click the "ActivePsych" CD icon that appears on your desktop and then double click on "**ActivePsych**" to launch the program.

NOTE: These activities run in Flash. You must have **FLASH PLAYER 8** installed on your computer for the activities to run properly. Although you do not need a live Internet connection to run any component of ActivePsych, you do need to have a browser installed on your computer to launch the program.

Launch Instructions for the MPEG videos provided in Digital Media Archive, Second Edition and Scientific American Frontiers, Third Edition (CD 2, 3, 4)

WINDOWS:
Put CD 2, 3, or 4 in the CD-ROM drive. Double click the "My Computer" icon on the Windows desktop and double click the "DMA2" or "SciAm3" CD icon. Navigate to the video you have selected to show and double click on the file.

MACINTOSH:
Put CD 2, 3, or 4 in the CD-ROM drive and double click the "DMA2" or "SciAm3" CD icon that appears on your desktop. Navigate to the video you have selected to show and double click on the file.

Note: The videos in Digital Media Archive, Second Edition are broken into topic folders in which the videos for that topic are collected. You will have to navigate through the folders to find the video file you have selected to show.

Free Software Downloads

If you do not have the software required to view the materials supplied in the ActivePsych package, visit the following Web sites for free downloads.

- **Flash Player 8:** http://www.adobe.com/go/getflash

- **Apple QuickTime:** http://www.apple.com/quicktime/download

- **Windows Media Player:** www.microsoft.com/windows/windowsmedia/download/AllDownloads.aspx?displang=en&qstechnology=

- **Real Player:** www.realplayer.com

- **Acrobat Reader:** http://www.adobe.com/products/acrobat/

Download Notes

Although you do not need a live Internet connection to run any component of ActivePsych, to download the free applications listed on the previous page, you will need to be connected.

Microsoft PowerPoint and Microsoft Word are NOT free software programs. If you do not have those programs installed on your computer, you will need to purchase a copy of each program to view the .doc or .ppt files provided in the collection of PowerPoint-based Classroom Activities Projects.

Technical Support

If you have a question or comment about any aspect of the ActivePsych package, please contact technical support by E-mail at **techsupport@bfwpub.com** or by phone at **(800) 936-6899**.

Please be sure to specify the following:

1) the ActivePsych component you are using (i.e. Flash-based activities, PowerPoint-based activities, Digital Media Archive, Second Edition, or *Scientific American* Frontiers, Third Edition).

2) *(for video questions)* the format you are using (i.e. CD/MPEG, DVD, or VHS).

3) information about your computer (Mac/PC, OS version, etc.).

Introduction

Teaching an introductory psychology course is often more challenging for instructors than teaching upper level courses. The breadth of material to be covered can be overwhelming for both instructors and students alike, not to mention that many students will be unfamiliar with basic concepts and terminology. It can be tough to keep students focused while you try to make all that material engaging, with enough time to satisfactorily cover each unit and promote active participation.

With that in mind, Worth Publishers has produced ActivePsych—a suite of interactive instructor tools designed to make introductory psychology more applied and class presentations more interactive.

The Classroom Activities Projects

The ActivePsych Classroom Activities Projects includes 32 Flash-based interactive demonstrations that combine a written overview of each topic with interactive displays, animations, videos, and specially-tailored exercises. Many activities involve input from your students and return feedback that is specific to the answers given by them.

The ActivePsych Classroom Activities Projects also includes 22 PowerPoint-based demonstrations, inventories, and surveys. Designed with brevity in mind, each PowerPoint activity focuses on a single question or group of related questions. These PowerPoint-based demonstrations can easily work with iClicker Classroom Response Systems. For more information on using iClicker in your classroom, go to: http://www.iclicker.com

In addition to supplementing lessons with engaging, informative, and often entertaining video, animation, and interactive exercises, every ActivePsych activity (whether it's built in Flash or PowerPoint) concludes with one or more *"Consider This…"* screens. These screens involve open-ended questions that challenge students to consider real issues in the context of what they have just learned.

Each activity in the ActivePsych Classroom Activities Projects collection was written by a psychologist with the aim of improving his or her own classroom teaching experience. These activities span diverse topics in many areas of psychology, including development, cognition and emotion, social psychology, behavioral neuroscience, clinical psychology, and statistical analysis. Instructors can use an activity as an introduction to a unit, a topic summary, or a focused centerpiece around which complete discussion of a topic can be based. Because each spotlights a different area of study, ActivePsych activities can easily fit into almost any lesson plan or teaching style.

The Video Teaching Modules

As every instructor knows, videos are a great way to engage a class and stimulate discussion. To that end, ActivePsych also houses two exceptional collections of video teaching modules. The first, Worth Publishers: Digital Media Archive, Second Edition, includes 33 short videos and animations (some in multiple parts) that illustrate basic principles and classic experiments in psychology. The footage includes

Albert Bandura's Bobo doll experiment, Piaget's conservation experiments, Ellen Winner discussing "gifted" children, Overcoming Schizophrenia: John Nash's Beautiful Mind, and Neural Communication: Impulse Transmission Across the Synapse.

The second set of video teaching modules is the *Scientific American* Frontiers Video Collection for Introductory Psychology, Third Edition. Hosted by Alan Alda, this collection features 15 programs with a number of prominent psychologists and is an excellent way to show students how psychological research is actually conducted. Many of the segments include demonstrations and discussions of cutting-edge neuroimaging technology and emphasize the importance of neuroscience in modern psychological research.

We hope that the ActivePsych Classroom Activities Projects and Video Teaching Modules provide you with an opportunity to improve the classroom experience for both you and your students as you lead them in their first steps toward discovering the fascinating world of psychology.

Paul Smaldino
The New School for Social Research, 2006

PART II: Package Contents

ActivePsych CD 1

Classroom Activities Projects: Flash-Based Interactive Demonstrations

Flash-Based Demonstrations: Usage Guide

Using the Flash-based Demonstrations

One of the great things about the ActivePsych Classroom Activities Projects is that each activity can be used—depending on the level and time constraints of the course, as well as your personal teaching style—as an introduction to a topic, a summary, or the centerpiece of an entire lesson. The title of each activity will give you a good idea of the material it contains.

You'll want to take a good look at any activity before presenting it to a class. ActivePsych is so user-friendly, it may be tempting to just plug in your computer and improvise a class lecture around an activity. However, in order to best prepare yourself to engage the students and answer any questions that might arise from the presented material, you should go over each screen (as well as its corresponding instructions and/or explanatory material) so that, feeling more comfortable and familiar with the activity, you can present it with confidence and imbue it with your own distinctive teaching style.

Launching the Flash-based Demonstrations

You can launch any one of the ActivePsych Classroom Activities Projects (whether it's built in Flash or PowerPoint) from the **main menu**.

Click on any title to launch the demonstration in a new window.

NOTE: You must have **FLASH PLAYER 8** installed on your computer for the activities to run properly.

The ActivePsych Tabs

The Flash-based ActivePsych interface has been designed to be as easy to use as possible. Within each activity, the material you will present to your students is displayed in the main part of the window. However, you may want tips on how to present the material in class—or background information for the material being presented.

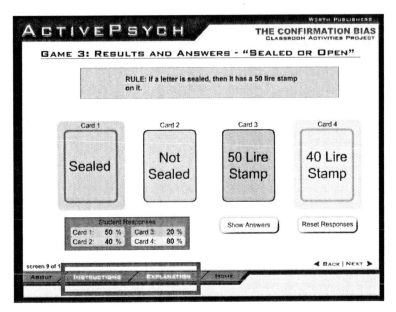

With this in mind, we have "hidden" the background material, instructions, and supplementary information behind the **About**, **Instructions**, and **Explanation** tabs.

As you can see in the example on the left, at the bottom of any activity screen an illuminated tab (that is, a tab with white text) lets you know that there is additional information available for the material being presented on that screen. You simply click the illuminated tab to view its contents.

Information on the tabs has been written in clear, concise bullet points. These points offer information that our contributors and advisors—all psychology professors themselves—feel works best with each screen in each activity. Of course, every instructor has his or her own style; you should feel free to elaborate or omit in order to make ActivePsych the best fit for *you*.

Warning: Don't open the tabs during class. You may want to have the **Explanation** or **Instructions** tab screens available for reference during a lecture. However, you probably don't want your students to see you opening and closing different screens, as this can be distracting to your students and take away from the flow of an otherwise riveting talk. As you've surely found in your own lectures, students will often focus on the bullet points displayed on the tab screens, rather than on what's happening in the activity.

So that you don't have to reference the tab information during your lecture, we have provided all the tab screens for each activity, along with the corresponding activity screen images, in this Faculty Guide beginning on page 23.

The Opening Screen and the "About" Tab

In every activity, the first screen will display the title, as well as a thought-provoking question or statement around which the activity is centered. Here is an example:

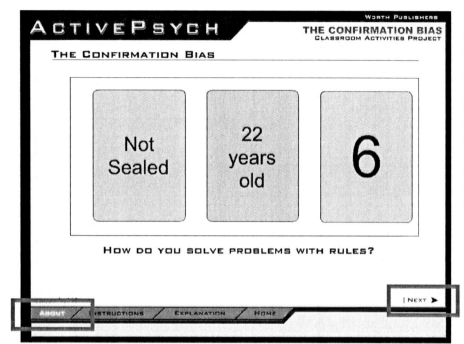

You can click the illuminated **About** tab for an overview of the activity, a summary of the topics that will be covered, and the videos, demonstrations, or procedures that will be used to advance the lesson.

On any screen you can click the "Next" button to move to the next screen.

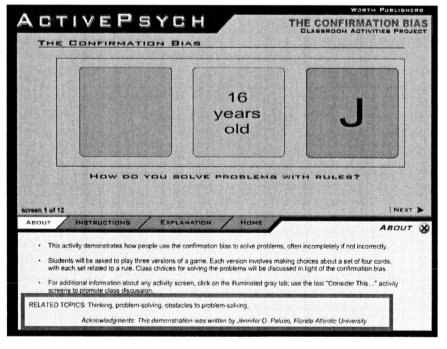

The **About** tab also offers a series of "Related Topics," as well as the name and affiliation of the academic who contributed the material.

The "Instructions" Tab

After the opening screen, each subsequent activity screen has two tabs that may be illuminated, letting you know that they contain useful information. If the screen contains a presentation, a demonstration, or an interactive classroom presentation, the **Instructions** tab will be illuminated.

The **Instructions** tab provides guidance and direction on how to utilize the interactive tools presented in the activity. It may also provide some relevant information to give to the class before beginning the activity so that they can better understand what is about to happen.

On any **Instructions** tab, you will find easy-to-follow instructions on how to use the interactive element displayed in the main part of the window. Click any illuminated **Instructions** tab to view it's contents. Here is an example:

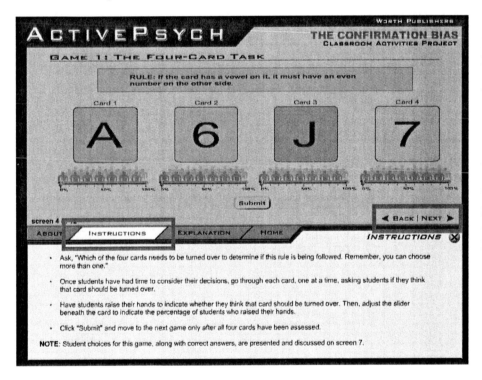

If the demonstration requires class participation, the **Instructions** tab lets you know how use the on-screen tools to best engage your students.

As with the opening screen, you can click the "Next" button to move to the next screen or the "Back" button to move to a previous screen.

The "Explanation" Tab

In addition to the **Instructions** tab, many screens have an illuminated **Explanation** tab. The **Explanation** tab provides notes that will help you to explain the activity to your students. It contains useful historical and scientific facts, evidence from research studies, interesting tangential information, and thought-provoking, open-ended questions that you can present to your students to expand their knowledge of the topic.

As the activity progresses, any screen that offers research or background information will have an illuminated **Explanation** tab. Click the illuminated tab to view it's contents. Here is an example:

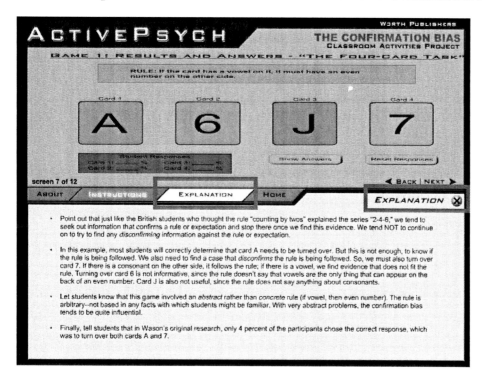

The **Explanation** tab offers supplementary information that will be helpful in explaining what is happening on screen.

You can click the "X" to close any **About**, **Instructions**, or **Explanation** tab.

The "Consider This…" Screen

Each activity ends with one or more open-ended "Consider This…" questions. You can use these critical-thinking questions to begin a class discussion, a structured in-class debate, or for any number of homework assignments.

Flash-Based Demonstrations: Technical Information

What if I can't get the demonstrations to run on my computer?

Please remember that demonstrations run in Flash and you must have **FLASH PLAYER 8** installed on your computer for the activities to run properly. If you don't have the correct Flash Player installed on your machine, please see the "Free Software Downloads" section on page 4.

Why not PowerPoint?

As a computer-savvy instructor, you've likely seen Microsoft PowerPoint used to create multimedia instructional presentations—in fact, there's a good chance you yourself have used PowerPoint to produce stimulating visual accents to your lectures. So why isn't ActivePsych made in PowerPoint?

Actually, part of it is. The ActivePsych Classroom Activities Projects includes 22 demonstrations made specifically for PowerPoint. We recognize the versatility inherent in PowerPoint software, and we have provided a number of excellent activities that take advantage of that. (For more information, see page 183.)

However, the 32 Flash-based interactive demonstrations in the ActivePsych Classroom Activities Projects are self-contained. In addition to including a large number of animations and video clips—which Flash allows us to embed directly within the activity frame—these activities often request information directly from the class (as entered by the instructor) and return visual information to specifically address the questions and viewpoints represented by your class.

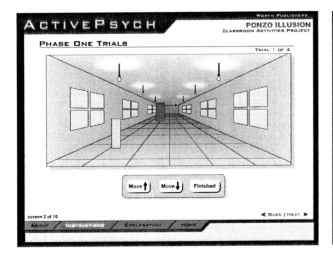
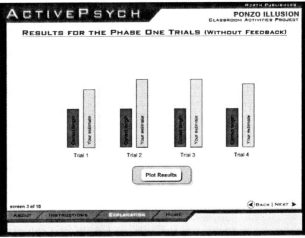

The Flash-based ActivePsych activities also include demonstrations that can be manipulated on the fly—a great way to show science at work. For example, in Fat Rats: A Simulated Experiment, students learn how electrical stimulation of different cortical regions can cause a rat to feel either insatiable or nonexistent hunger. By pointing the computer mouse to different settings on the simulated devices, students can get a sense of how working neuroscientists plan their experiments, as well as a better understanding of the relevance of the results.

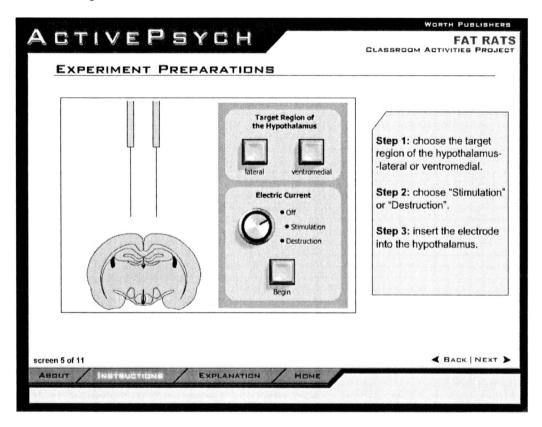

We believe that these Flash-based interactive demonstrations will offer incredibly effective educational techniques, allowing you to engage your students directly by requiring their active participation.

What if I already have a presentation CD for class?

Rather than bringing their own computer to class, some instructors work in classrooms that are already set up with a computer for the room. Because they can't use their own computer in this type of classroom, some instructors carry a personalized lecture CD containing their lesson plans, course materials, PowerPoint files, etc. That way they have all the teaching materials they need—anywhere, anytime.

If you are one of the instructors who uses a personalized lecture CD for your course materials, you may not want to have to carry around multiple CDs, let alone transfer back and forth between CDs while you're teaching. In this case, you can add ActivePsych to your pre-existing CD.

Adding the ActivePsych activities to your personalized lecture CD

***The following procedure requires you to have a CD burner in your computer.

1) Insert the ActivePsych Classroom Activities Projects disk (CD 1).

2) **WINDOWS:** Double click the "My Computer" icon on the Windows desktop and then double click the "ActivePsych" CD icon to view the CD contents.

   MACINTOSH: Double click the "ActivePsych" CD icon that appears on your desktop to view the CD contents.

3) Create an "ActivePsych" folder somewhere on your computer's hard drive.

4) Copy all the CD contents (folders, files, etc.) into the "ActivePsych" folder you've created.

   An easy way to do this is to select all the folders on the disk with your mouse (you can also choose "Select All" under the "Edit" menu). Then, drag the files into the new "ActivePsych" folder on your hard drive.

5) Once the ActivePsych CD contents have been saved to your hard drive, eject the CD.

6) At this point, if you don't have the course materials from your personalized lecture CD saved on your hard drive, you will need to import them as well. To import your personalized files, insert your lecture CD into your computer and follow steps 1 through 4.

   Note that you should create *another* folder for your pre-existing course materials, rather than putting them in your new "ActivePsych" folder.

   If you already have your personalized lecture materials saved on your computer's hard drive, go to step 7.

7) You can now burn a *new* data CD with 2 folders. The first will contain all your pre-existing lecture materials, the second will contain ActivePsych.

With both your lecture materials and ActivePsych on one CD, you will never have to spend class time switching between CDs!

Can I switch between a Flash-based ActivePsych activity and PowerPoint if they are running simultaneously?

If you are running a lecture from PowerPoint, you may want to embellish it with parts of our Flash-based demonstrations or a video from our Digital Media Archive or *Scientific American* Frontiers collections.

If you are simultaneously running an ActivePsych activity, a PowerPoint presentation, and a video (in Windows Media Player, QuickTime, RealPlayer, or some other video player), it is easy to switch between programs—even if they take up the entire screen.

Using the "Alt+Tab" technique to switch between multiple programs

1) **WINDOWS:** Hold down the **Alt** button on your computer keyboard.

   MACINTOSH: Hold down the **Command** (or **Apple**) button.

2) Press the **Tab** button.

3) You will see a small menu of all the programs you are currently running.

4) Continue to hold down the **Alt** (or **Command/Apple**) button. Each tap of the **Tab** button will select the next program in the menu.

5) Release the **Alt** (or **Command/Apple**) button when you have selected the program you want your students to see (for example, ActivePsych, PowerPoint, or Windows Media Player).

Can I launch ActivePsych from within PowerPoint?

Using the "Alt+Tab" technique described above (Command/Apple+Tab on a Macintosh computer), you may find it unnecessary to formally link any ActivePsych Flash-based activities or demonstrations to your personalized PowerPoint lecture presentations, since you can easily switch between ActivePsych, PowerPoint, Windows Media Player, or any other program running on your computer.

However, you may find it easier to launch ActivePsych from *within* your PowerPoint lecture presentation. And you can. You can even link to an individual Flash-based ActivePsych demonstration (rather than linking to the main ActivePsych menu). In the next section we will show you how to create a link to ActivePsych from within PowerPoint.

NOTE 1: For all of the following procedures, you should complete the steps BEFORE you create a new personalized lecture CD as described in the section called "Adding the ActivePsych activities to your personalized lecture CD" above.

NOTE 2: Please understand that the PowerPoint instructions on the following pages may not work with every version of PowerPoint, or every computer operating system, as all systems are different. If you have problems importing the video clips into your presentations, please see your PowerPoint Help menu, or visit Microsoft's PowerPoint home page at: http://office.microsoft.com/en-us/FX010857971033.aspx

Linking to ActivePsych

The easiest way to launch the ActivePsych Classroom Activities Projects from within PowerPoint is to create a link from your lecture presentation to the ActivePsych main menu. However, before you can create a link to ActivePsych in your presentation, you must first have the ActivePsych contents loaded on your computer's hard drive. To download the CD contents:

1) Insert the ActivePsych Classroom Activities Projects disk (CD 1).

2) **WINDOWS:** Double click the "My Computer" icon on the Windows desktop and then double click the "ActivePsych" CD icon to view the CD contents.

   MACINTOSH: Double click the "ActivePsych" CD icon that appears on your desktop to view the CD contents.

3) Create an "ActivePsych" folder somewhere on your computer's hard drive.

4) Copy all the CD contents (folders, files, etc.) into the "ActivePsych" folder you've created.

   An easy way to do this is to select all the folders on the disk with your mouse (you can also choose "Select All" under the "Edit" menu). Then, drag the files into the new "ActivePsych" folder on your hard drive.

5) Once the ActivePsych CD contents have been saved to your hard drive, eject the CD.

Once you have the ActivePsych demonstrations loaded on your hard drive you can create a link to them in your PowerPoint presentation.

Creating Hyperlinks in PowerPoint

1) Open the PowerPoint presentation you would like to edit and navigate to the slide from which you will launch ActivePsych.

2) Create a block of text that you want to represent the link to ActivePsych. You might type the word "ActivePsych" into your presentation and use that as the link.

3) Highlight the text and, under the **Insert** menu, click **Hyperlink**.

4) Under **Link to**, click **Existing File or Web Page**. From there, navigate to select the file to be linked.

5) To link to the ActivePsych main menu, navigate to the folder in which you have placed the ActivePsych contents and select the file named:

   – **ActivePsych.exe** (on a WINDOWS computer)
   – **ActivePsych** (on a MACINTOSH computer)

6) Click **OK**.

7) Once the you have created the hyperlink, you must be in "Slide Show" mode for the link to function. (To go into "Slide Show" mode, select **View Show** under the **Slide Show** menu.)

Alternately, you can use PowerPoint's own tools to create a button that, when clicked, will link to the ActivePsych Main Menu. To create a hyperlink button:

1) Open the PowerPoint presentation you would like to edit and navigate to the slide from which you will launch ActivePsych.

2) Under the **Insert** menu, select **Picture** and **AutoShapes**.

3) On the **AutoShapes** tool bar, select the object you want displayed as your button and draw the object on the slide.

4) Select the object you have drawn and, under the **Insert** menu, click **Hyperlink**.

5) Under **Link to**, click **Existing File or Web Page**. Navigate to the file to be linked.

6) Again, to link to the ActivePsych main menu, navigate to the folder in which you have placed the ActivePsych contents and select the file named:

   – **ActivePsych.exe** (on a WINDOWS computer)
   – **ActivePsych** (on a MACINTOSH computer)

7) Click **OK**.

8) Once the you have created the hyperlink, you must be in "Slide Show" mode for the link to function. (To go into "Slide Show" mode, select **View Show** under the **Slide Show** menu.)

Creating a link to an individual ActivePsych Flash-based demonstration

Rather than linking to the ActivePsych main menu, if you would prefer, you can link to an individual ActivePsych Flash-based demonstration. As with linking to the main menu, you should have copied the complete set of CD contents to your computer's hard drive (see previous instructions).

1) Open the PowerPoint presentation you would like to edit and navigate to the slide you from which you will launch ActivePsych.

2) Create a block of text or an object button that you want to represent the link to ActivePsych (see instructions for "Creating Hyperlinks in PowerPoint"). In this case, you might type the activity name into your presentation (for example, "The Ponzo Illusion") and use that as the link.

3) Highlight the text or button and, under the **Insert** menu, click **Hyperlink**.

4) Under **Link to**, click **Existing File or Web Page**.

5) From there, to link to a specific activity, navigate to the folder containing the desired ActivePsych activity (see the list on the next page), and select the file named: **index.html**.

6) Click **OK**.

7) Once the you have created the hyperlink, you must be in "Slide Show" mode for the link to function. (To go into "Slide Show" mode, select **View Show** under the **Slide Show** menu.)

Folder structure for the ActivePsych Flash-based demonstrations

Below is a list of the individual folder names, with the corresponding title, for each Flash-based ActivePsych interactive demonstration. These folders reside inside the **SWF** folder at the top level of the ActivePsych content directory.

01_ScatPlot = Scatterplots
02_BowlStats = Bowling for Statistical Significance
03_MeasureIQ = Measuring IQ
04_NerveCell = Nerve Cell Demonstrations
05_HemisPath = Hemispheric Pathways
06_SynapticTrans = Synaptic Transmission and Neurotransmitters
07_ConceptBirth = From Conception To Birth
08_PrenatalBrn = Prenatal Brain Development
09_TeenBrain = Adolescent Brain Development
10_PiagetConserv = Piaget and Conservation
11_DevTheorists = Development Theorists
12_LSTimeline = Life-Span Timeline
13_ColorSen = Color Sensation
14_McGurk = The McGurk Effect
15_Ponzo = The Ponzo Illusion
16_VisualIllusion = Some Visual Illusions
17_EEGSleep = EEG and the Stages of Sleep
18_AlcoholProg = Alcohol Progression through the Brain
19_Stroop = The Stroop Effect
20_LevelofProc = Levels of Processing
21_SerialPos = Serial Position Effect
22_AvailHeur = The Availability Heuristic
23_ConfirmBias = The Confirmation Bias
24_LangDev = Language Development in Infants and Toddlers
25_Empathy = Origins of Empathy
26_FatRat = Fat Rats: A Simulated Experiment
27_Hunger = Experiencing Hunger
28_LearnedHelp = Learned Helplessness
29_Freud = Freud Demonstration
30_ModTherapy = Some Models of Therapy
31_DisCreativity = Creative People and Psychological Disorders
32_ActorObserver = The Actor-Observer Difference in Attribution

Note that you will also find these folders on the ActivePsych Classroom Activities Projects CD by navigating to the root level of CD 1 and opening the **SWF** folder.

Notes about linking to ActivePsych from within PowerPoint

– If you are lecturing from the same computer every lecture, you can copy the complete ActivePsych contents to a folder on your computer's hard drive and there is no need for you to create a new personalized lecture CD.

– However, if you are uncertain from which computer you will be running your lecture, and usually run your PowerPoint presentations from a CD, you will want to create a new personalized lecture CD containing both your lecture materials and the complete ActivePsych contents (see instructions under "Adding the ActivePsych activities to your personalized lecture CD").

– If you bring your own computer to class, run your lecture from your own computer's hard drive, and have no need for a personalized lecture CD, you can link directly to ActivePsych CD from within your PowerPoint presentation.

– To link to the ActivePsych CD, insert the CD into your computer's drive and follow the same method described above under "Linking to ActivePsych." However, rather than navigating to a folder on your hard drive, you will navigate to the ActivePsych CD contents.

– From there, you use PowerPoint's "Hyperlink" function to link to:

1) the ActivePsych main menu by selecting the **ActivePsych.exe** file (on WINDOWS computers) or the **ActivePsych** file (on MACINTOSH computers).

2) an individual activity by selecting the **index.html** file (housed on the CD within the folder structure noted on the previous page).

Can I import an ActivePsych Flash-based demonstration into my PowerPoint presentation?

The 32 activities described in this section are self-contained, Flash-based programs, which, unfortunately, cannot be imported directly into PowerPoint. It is, however, possible to add a hyperlink within your PowerPoint presentation, which will open ActivePsych in a new window (see the instructions under "Linking to ActivePsych").

The reason we created the bulk of the ActivePsych demonstrations in Flash, rather than PowerPoint, is because we wanted to create fully interactive activities that could respond differently to each class's unique input. Our activities contain videos, animations, displays, and exercises which require software that can accommodate interactive, computational programming and sophisticated functionality. PowerPoint, while a wonderful presentation tool, lacks the ability to house truly interactive displays.

By using your students' own responses, ActivePsych enables you to better illustrate the scientific process and make psychology come alive. Using Flash, we were able to create interactive demonstrations that present psychology not merely as lessons, but as *experiences*.

However, because PowerPoint works quite seamlessly with iClicker Classroom Response Systems, we created an additional 22 PowerPoint-based demonstrations, inventories, and surveys. Designed with brevity in mind, each PowerPoint activity focuses on a single question or group of related questions.

You can learn more about using the 22 PowerPoint-based ActivePsych demonstrations beginning on page 183.

Flash-Based Demonstrations: Screen-by-Screen Tab Content

Research Methods: SCATTERPLOTS

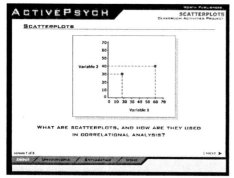

Screen 1

This demonstration was written by Thomas E. Ludwig, Hope College

About: In this activity, the class takes part in demonstrations that show how scatterplots are used as a visual indication of the strength of the relationship between two variables.

After producing a scatterplot from a table of variables, the class will have the opportunity to modify the individual points and see the impact of each change on the correlation coefficient.

For additional information about any screen activity, click on the illuminated gray tab; use the last "Consider This… " activity screen to promote class discussion.

RELATED TOPICS: The scientific method, statistics, correlation.

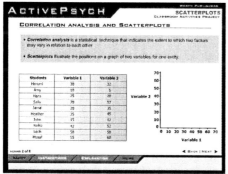

Screen 2

Instructions: To explore the relationship between the two variables for each student on the chart, click the student's name, and that person's point will then be plotted on the graph.

Explanation: Point out that correlation analysis not only indicates the extent to which two factors vary together, but it also indicates how well either factor predicts the other.

NOTE: Scatterplots that show positive, negative, or no correlation are presented on screen 3.

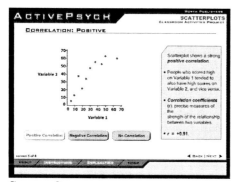

Screen 3

Instructions: To view results that show different kinds of correlations, click the "Positive Correlation," "Negative Correlation," or "No Correlation" buttons.

Explanation: Correlation coefficients (*r*) are precise measures of the strength of the relationship between two variables.

Point out that the correlation coefficient is a statistic (a number) which indicates the strength of the association between the two variables. It can take values ranging from +1.0 (the strongest possible positive correlation) through 0.0 (no correlation at all) to -1.0 (the strongest negative correlation).

Finally, make sure students understand that the appearance of the lowercase *r* is used as a symbol for the correlation coefficient.

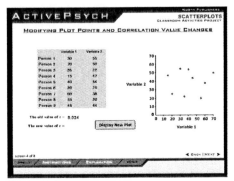

Screen 4

NOTE: If you change the variables, you must keep the data values between 0 and 70. If you enter numbers greater than 70, the data cannot regraph.

Instructions: Click on any person in the list to change that person's variable data. Once the person is highlighted in green, you can change the numeric value of either variable. (Note that when the person is highlighted, his/her plot point turns blue so that you can easily tell where each person is represented on the graph.)

Once you have finished changing the variable data, click "Display New Plot" to regraph the data and calculate a new value for **r**.

Explanation: Point out that the relationship between two correlated variables has predictive value. This means that if a strong correlation exists between two variables, then knowing a person's score on one variable allows researchers to predict a person's score on the other variable.

Note that moving an individual point closer to the "best fit" line through all the points increases the value of the correlation coefficient. ("Best fit" is shown on the next screen.)

NOTE: Predicting scores is presented and discussed on screens 5 and 6.

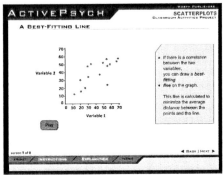

Screen 5

Instructions: Click the "Play" button to show the best-fitting line being drawn.

Explanation: Point out that a prediction is accomplished when a best-fitting line is drawn through points and then calculated in such a way as to minimize the average distance between the points and the line.

Screen 6

Instructions: Click the "Play" button to show how scores on one variable can be predicted from scores on the other variable.

Explanation: Help students understand that if you know that a person's score on Variable 1 is 41, you can predict that person's score on Variable 2—and the best estimate would be 40.

In addition, if you know that a person's score on Variable 2 is 59, the best estimate of that person's score on Variable 1 is 64.

Further point out it should be obvious that the stronger the correlation, the more accurate the prediction will be.

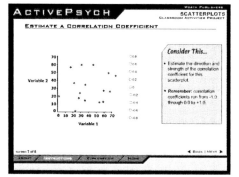

Screen 7

Instructions: In this exercise, the class will have six opportunities to estimate the correlation coefficient.

For each set of plot points, have the class come to a consensus on the estimated value of *r*. Alternately, you can ask an individual student for his/her estimate.

Once you have the estimate, click the button in the right column closest to that value. After a choice is made, the value of r will appear below the graph.

Click "Next" to move to the next graph. Once students have estimated the correlation coefficient for all six sets of plot points, move to the next screen.

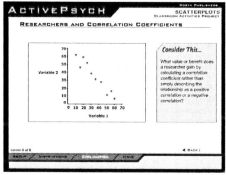

Screen 8

Explanation: Point out that visual inspection of a scatterplot gives a researcher useful information about the sample. But researchers often want more information about the strength of association between the two variables. To obtain that information, they calculate the correlation coefficient, which is a precise statistic (number).

Also point out that researchers cannot conclude *cause* based on *correlation*. For instance, a scatterplot may show that people who engage in a recreational sport show a positive correlation for positive mood. The correlation does not show that one circumstance *causes* the other; the researcher only benefits from knowing that a relationship between these two factors exists in some way.

Research Methods: BOWLING FOR STATISTICAL SIGNIFICANCE

Screen 1

This demonstration was written by Richard Alexander, Muskegon Community College

About: In this activity, students view results from a series of bowling games (each game has two participants). After they have seen the results, students will speculate on who is the better bowler. By making this judgment, students discover that they use descriptive statistics in their everyday lives.

Some screens allow instructors to record student opinions, while subsequent screens present and discuss results in light of concepts about statistics.

For additional information about any screen activity, click on the illuminated gray tab; use the last "Consider This…"activity screens to promote class discussion.

RELATED TOPICS: statistical reasoning, understanding data, experimentation.

Screen 2

Explanation: Point out that these terms are related to *statistics*. Statistics allow people to organize information and make intelligent decisions—decisions based on their analysis of the available information.

Screen 3

NOTE: Results will be presented and discussed on screen 9.

Instructions: Tell students that one day a psychology instructor invited a student to a bowling game after class. After a few games, they had a friendly discussion about who was the better bowler. Then, click "Play" to watch the instructor and student bowling together.

When the animation ends, the scores for each participant's three bowling games will appear. Students will also see each participant's average (mean) score. Tell students to consider the scores from each of the three games along with each participant's average score.

Once class members have had a minute to consider the scores, have them raise their hands to indicate which bowler they think is better, based on the scores. Adjust the sliders below each participant ("Instructor" and "Student") to show the approximate percentage of class members who chose each. Ask some students why they voted as they did or why they didn't vote at all.

Explanation: Point out that some students will say the student is the better bowler because of the higher average or because the instructor lost two games out of three.

Also point out that some students might say the instructor is the better bowler because her scores were much more consistent (or just because she's the teacher!).

Also point out that many students might decline to vote because they think the instructor may have been tired that evening or that the student was lucky.

Make sure to tell the class that in this kind of situation there will almost always be people who may not cast a vote because they feel there is not enough information to go on after only three bowling games.

Screen 4

Instructions: Tell the class that it might have been difficult to know who was the better bowler from just three games, so the instructor and student have bowled three more sets (with three games in each set). Their scores and averages (means) are shown on this screen.

Have class members raise their hands to indicate which bowler they now think is better. Adjust the sliders below each participant (instructor and student) to show the approximate percentage of class members who chose each. Ask some students why they voted as they did or why they didn't vote at all.

NOTE: Results from this screen (along with screen 3) will be presented and discussed on screen 9.

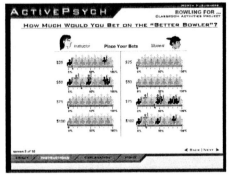

Screen 5

NOTE: The betting results are presented and discussed on the next screen (screen 6).

Instructions: Tell the class that they can bet up to $100 (in the increments shown on screen) on the very next bowling game between the instructor and the student. Then, tell each student to decide who they would bet on to win. They should choose the amount of money they are willing to risk on their bet.

Next ask students, "Who is willing to bet on the instructor?" As you list each betting amount ($25, $50, $75, or $100), ask students to raise their hands if they want to place a bet in that amount. Adjust the slider to indicate the percentage who raised their hands.

Then ask students, "Who is willing to bet on the student?" and follow the same procedure.

IMPORTANT: Be sure to explain that each student can only bet ONCE. The question is: how much money are they willing to bet, and who are they betting for? The analysis to follow will compare average bets for each participant.

Also, when you are entering student results, be sure that the total class bets on both the instructor and the student does not total more than 100 percent.

Screen 6

NOTE: The next screen (screen 7) discusses factors that helped in making this decision.

Instructions: Click "Instructor" to see a graph that shows the distribution of bets for the instructor made on screen 5.

Each RED bowling ball indicates that 10 percent of your students were willing to bet that amount ($25, $50, $75, or $100) on the instructor winning the next bowling game. (Note that you will also see the average dollar amount bet on the instructor.)

Click "Student" to see to see a graph that shows the distribution of bets for the student made on screen 5.

Each GREEN bowling ball indicates that 10 percent of your students were willing to bet that amount ($25, $50, $75, or $100) on the student winning the next bowling game. (Note that you will also see the average dollar amount bet on the student.)

Explanation: Point out that each set of bars represents the distribution of betting amounts made by class members on the instructor and the student. (Again, bets on the instructor are represented by RED bowling balls; bets on the student are represented by GREEN bowling balls.)

Encourage class members to discuss how and why they made their betting decisions.

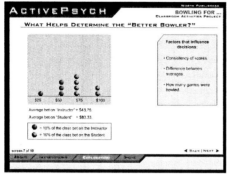

Screen 7

Explanation: Point out that deciding who's the "better bowler" is exactly the same as deciding (in a research experiment) if the experimental group or the control group—or neither—is the "better" group.

Also explain that research psychologists use the same three factors when analyzing data (consistency of scores; difference between averages; how many times the experiment was performed). However, a variety of mathematical formulas are applied in place of a simple mental estimate. The use of mathematical methods creates a common standard, enabling researchers to compare results from different studies with one another.

Finally, help students appreciate that when they make generalizations from samples they should avoid being overly impressed by a few anecdotes. Generalizations based on a few unrepresentative cases are unreliable. Representative samples are better than biased samples; less-variable observations are more reliable than those that are more variable; more cases are better than fewer.

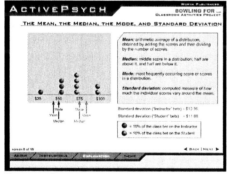

Screen 8

Explanation: On this screen the *mean, mode, median,* and *standard deviation* for the distribution of "Instructor" and "Student" bets (from screen 5) are calculated and indicated on the graph.

Point out that *standard deviation* gauges whether scores are packed together or dispersed, because it uses information from each score. (The computation assembles information about how much individual scores differ from the *mean.*

As an example of how standard deviation works, point out that the more homogeneous the population, the smaller the standard deviation tends to be. For example, when analyzing high school math achievement scores, a sample drawn from the math club will likely have a smaller standard deviation than one drawn from the entire school.

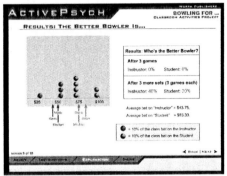

Screen 9

Explanation: The results presented beside "Instructor" and "Student" represent the percentage of class members who thought that participant was the "Better Bowler" after 1) only three games were played and 2) after three additional sets of three games were played. (Remind students that these percentages were gathered earlier on screens 3 and 4.)

Tell the class that they have just covered the basic essentials of statistical analysis, without using any math beyond a bowling average. Point out that statistical analysis just adds some structure to what students already intuitively know.

You might ask bettors if, after deciding to wager a lot of money on the "better bowler," there still was a sliver of doubt over who was the better bowler.

Further point out that just like with the bowling example, researchers are never 100 percent confident—there's always a possibility that the difference between the experimental and control groups happened just by chance or because of an uncontrolled variable that was overlooked. However, researchers have a common standard that allows for that very slight bit of doubt.

Screen 10

Explanation: Point out that when averages from two samples are each reliable measures of their respective populations (as when each is based on many observations that have small variability), then their difference (sometimes even a very small difference) is likely to be reliable as well. But when the difference between the sample averages is large, there is even more confidence that the difference between them reflects a real difference in their populations.

Further point out that when the sample averages are reliable and the difference between them is relatively large, we say the difference has *statistical significance*; that is, the difference observed is probably not due to chance variation between two samples.

Also point out that psychologists are conservative, like juries that must presume innocence until guilt is proven. Most psychologists don't make much of a finding unless the odds of its occurring by chance are less than 5 percent (an arbitrary criterion).

Research Methods: MEASURING IQ *(also in Thinking, Language, and Intelligence unit)*

Screen 1

This demonstration was written by Thomas E. Ludwig, Hope College

About: In this activity students explore cross-sectional, longitudinal, and sequential studies as ways of measuring how intelligence changes with age.

Animated illustrations demonstrate how confounding factors can bias or distort results in the different studies.

For additional information about any screen activity, click on the illuminated gray tab; use the last "Consider This…" activity screen to promote class discussion.

RELATED TOPICS: intelligence, adult cognitive development, research methods, experimental design.

Screen 2

Instructions: Ask students to respond to the statement presented on screen: "PREDICT: As adults age, intelligence _____."

Once students have had the opportunity to consider the statement, have them raise their hands to indicate their choice.

Adjust the sliders beneath each option to reflect the approximate percentage of students who selected each response choice.

NOTE: Results of student predictions will be presented and discussed on the next screen.

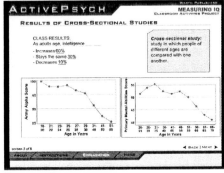

Screen 3

Explanation: These graphs show results from typical cross-sectional studies of intelligence. The left graph (Jones, 1959) summarizes scores on the *Army Alpha Test* used in World War I as a quick way of determining aptitude for officer training. Most men who took the test were in their late teens or early 20s, but some were older—up to 60 years old.

The *Army* results prompted a boom in research. The right graph (Schaie, 1988) shows the results from a different intelligence test called the Primary Mental Abilities Test. By the 1950s, hundreds of cross-sectional studies had been published on adult intelligence, and most of them showed a dramatic drip in intelligence after age 30 or 35.

After students have had time to examine the graphs and compare them with predictions from screen 2, make sure they understand that in these studies men in their 20s performed much better than men in the 30s, 40s, or 50s. These results suggest that intellectual ability peaks during late adolescence or early adulthood and then declines steadily.

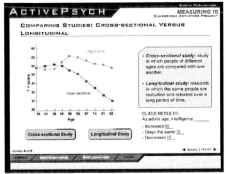

Screen 4

Instructions: Explain to students how cross-sectional and longitudinal studies differ. Then, ask them to predict the intelligence testing results using the two study methods. After students have had the opportunity to discuss the differences, show them the results.

To view the results of *cross-sectional* studies on intelligence, click "Cross-sectional Study." To view the results of *longitudinal* studies on intelligence, click "Longitudinal Study."

Explanation: Point out that by the 1950s, some researchers had begun using longitudinal studies to determine whether intelligence changes with age across the adult years.

Remind students that cross-sectional studies showed a drop in intelligence after age 30 to 35 (Schaie & Geiwitz, 1982). Then, explain that the results on this new graph disagree with the cross-sectional research—in longitudinal studies, intelligence was shown to hold steady or improve with age (Schaie, 1994).

Point out that by the late 1960s, researchers thought they had the answer: cross-sectional studies exaggerated the effects of aging. With these findings, researchers began to lean more heavily on the longitudinal results.

Before you move to the next screen, let students know that each type of study has flaws. On screens 5 and 6, you will examine the confounding factors in both cross-sectional and longitudinal studies on adult intelligence.

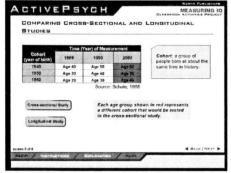

Screen 5

Instructions: Ask students to identify a group of cells in the table that would represent a *cross-sectional study*.

After students have responded, click the "Cross-sectional Study" button. The cells representing one possible cross-sectional study (in the year 2000) will be shown in red. Note that the cohorts born in 1940, 1950, and 1960 are all tested.

Next, ask students to identify a group of cells in the table that would represent a *longitudinal study*.

After students have responded, click the "Longitudinal Study" button. The cells representing one possible longitudinal study (using the cohort born in 1940) will be shown in blue. Note that these cells show the different times (years) in which the cohort would be tested. If the cohort born in 1950 or 1960 were being tested, those rows would be displayed in blue.

Explanation: This table represents the different cohorts and years that could have been used in cross-sectional and longitudinal intelligence studies. In the table, the three different cohorts are shown in the far left column—people born in 1) 1940, 2) 1950, and 3) 1960.

Point out that a cross-sectional study will confound (mix the effects of) age and cohort by studying people from different cohorts. Using this table, a researcher doing a cross-sectional study in the year 2000 would test subjects from all three cohorts (as shown by the red cells). However, explain that it is impossible to tell whether the performance difference is due to age or *other* differences among the three cohorts tested.

Further point out that a longitudinal study will confound age with historical time. Using this table, a researcher doing a longitudinal study would test subjects from the same cohort across three decades (as shown by the blue cells). However, explain that this makes it impossible to tell whether a specific difference in performance is due to the test-taker's age or to some other differences between the years in which the subjects were tested. For example, performance may differ because of practice; when people take the same tests again and again over many years, their performance tends to improve.

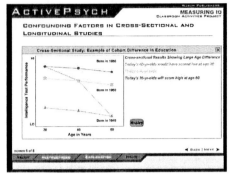

Screen 6

Instructions: These animated graphs present examples of confounding factors that can distort results in cross-sectional and longitudinal studies on adult differences in intelligence.

Click "Play" beside each title to view a presentation of the data from that study. Click the "X" to close the box and display another study.

The cross-sectional study graph will show how each cohort might be affected by differences in education (in general more recent cohorts—people born in 1960 vs. 1940—have had more and better education).

The longitudinal study graph will show the effect of *selective attrition* (when people withdraw or die during the course of a study) on a single cohort.

Explanation: Point out that in cross-sectional studies of intelligence, the key difference between groups of cohorts is *education*. In general, more recent cohorts—people born in 1960 vs. 1940—have had more and better education, which might explain the difference in performance on the intelligence tests.

Explain that in the 1970s researchers realized that longitudinal studies had serious flaws, such as *selective attrition*—the nonrandom loss of subjects in longitudinal studies, as a result of withdrawal or death. The subjects who drop out tend to be those who initially have the lowest IQ scores; those who remain are usually the most stable, well-functioning adults. The continuing presence of high-scoring adults artificially inflates the group scores over time.

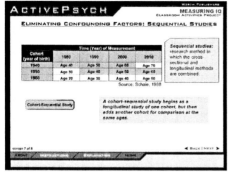

Screen 7

Instructions: This screen examines *sequential studies*—a type of study which could eliminate the effects of confounding factors in intelligence testing (as well as other types of research).

Ask students to identify a group of cells in the table that would represent a *cohort-sequential study*.

After students have responded, click the "Cohort-Sequential Study" button. The cells for one possible cohort-sequential study will appear in yellow.

Explanation: Point out that a researcher named K. Warner Schaie proposed that confounding factors could be disentangled, at least in part, by using a more complex research method that he called a *sequential study*. A *cohort-sequential study* is a kind of sequential study.

Explain that a *sequential study* is a research design that combines cross-sectional and longitudinal research. Groups of people of different ages are studied over time, to distinguish differences related to age from differences related to historical period.

Let students know that sequential studies are relatively rare since they take more years to complete and cost more than the other types of developmental research.

To this effect, make sure students expand their understanding by explaining that this study begins in 1980 with the cohort born in 1940. If one follows the pattern shown, and continues testing with the cohort born in 1960, that cohort would begin testing in the year 2000, and would complete testing in 2020. Testing all three cohorts, the study would take 40 years.

Screen 8

Instructions: Before students discuss the "Consider This…" question, remind them that cross-sectional studies showed a drop in intelligence after age 30 to 35, whereas longitudinal studies showed that intelligence held steady or improved with age.

Explain that the reality is somewhere in between—once researchers realized the confounding factors in both types of studies, they began to take a more balanced view of the whole process of cognitive aging. Most researchers now believe that the average person's intellectual performance across adulthood will fall somewhere between the typical results from the two types of studies.

Explanation: After students have expressed their preferences, point out that at age 70, John Rock developed the birth control pill; at 78, Grandma Moses took up painting—and was still painting after 100; and at 89, architect Frank Lloyd Wright designed New York City's Guggenheim Museum.

Explain that research about intelligence is about more than one trait. Intelligence tests that assess speed of thinking place older adults at a disadvantage because of slower neural mechanisms for processing information. But slower doesn't necessarily mean less intelligent. When given tests that assess general vocabulary, knowledge, and ability to integrate information, older adults usually fare well (Craik, 1986). Add that, in four studies, the highest average performance on *New York Times* crossword puzzles (given 15 minutes to fill in words) was achieved by adults in their fifties, sixties, and seventies (Salthouse, 2004).

Finally, explain that *crystallized intelligence*—accumulated intellectual knowledge as reflected in vocabulary and analogies tests—increases up to old age. *Fluid intelligence*—the ability to reason speedily and abstractly, as when solving logic problems—decreases slowly up to age 75 or so, then more rapidly, especially after 85 (Cattell, 1963; Horn, 1982).

Neuroscience and Behavior: NERVE CELL DEMONSTRATIONS

Screen 1

This demonstration was written by Karsten Look, Columbus State Community College

About: After students view animations, they will participate in demonstrations in which they will enact neural transmission of an impulse by playing the roles of either the dendrite, soma, axon, or axon terminal of a nerve cell (neuron).

You will initiate the demonstration by sending a signal (an electrical impulse) and instructing students how to play their assigned roles.

For additional information about any activity screen, click on the illuminated gray tab; use the last "Consider This…" activity screen to promote class discussion.

RELATED TOPICS: The central nervous system, neural communication, neurons, the synapse, drugs/chemicals and neurotransmission, sensation and pain.

NOTE: This activity can be use in conjunction with the ActivePsych activity "Synaptic Transmission and Neurotransmitters."

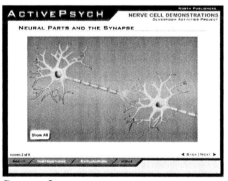

Screen 2

Instructions: Labels for each part of the neuron will appear as you roll your mouse over the illustration.

To show all labels and have them remain on screen, click "Show All."

Explanation: You may want to point out the differences among neurons: some may not have axons; some may have multiple axons or dendrites; or the synapse may be on a dendrite, soma, or axon rather than at the terminal buttons.

Extend students' understanding by telling them that impulses jump across the nodes of Ranvier, speeding up communication. Furthermore, in diseases like multiple sclerosis (MS), damaged myelin prevents axons from sending communications correctly.

Tell the class that they will enact the role of basic neural parts during neural transmission.

NOTE: Students will view an animation about neural transmission on screen 3 before receiving detailed demonstration guidance on screens 4 and 5.

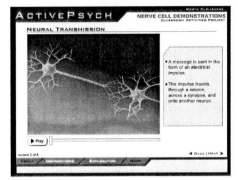

Screen 3

Instructions: Click "Play" to view the animation of neural transmission.

Explanation: Tell students that when an impulse (neural information) is successfully transmitted, it passes from nerve cell to nerve cell by crossing a *synapse* (a small gap, or cleft, between neurons).

Point out that the *synaptic gap*, or *cleft*, is less than one millionth of an inch wide.

When the impulse reaches the axon terminal, it triggers the release of neurotransmitters, which cross the synaptic gap and bind to the receptor sites on the receiving neuron.

To extend their understanding, tell students that there are three basic types of neurons: *motor neurons*, *interneurons*, and *sensory neurons*. Depending on the type of neuron, an impulse can originate in either the dendrite or the *soma* (cell body).

NOTE: The actual student demonstration procedure of neural transmission is animated and explained, step-by-step, on screen 4.

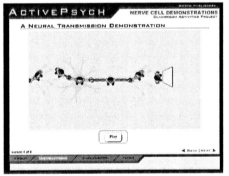

Screen 4

Instructions: Click "Play" to view an animated version of the demonstration for neural transmission.

Select four volunteers to act as the parts of a nerve cell. Assign neural parts to each group member (dendrite, soma, axon, axon terminal). Although the animation shows an impulse transmitted across one neuron and synapse, you can organize multiple groups of four to enact a transmission along multiple nerve cells.

Explain that you will initiate a signal (whisper a number from one to five to the student acting as dendrite). In succession, the group members squeeze hands to represent the signal you've initiated. The student acting as axon terminal whispers the number of squeezes he received and the last, solo student records the message number on the chalkboard.

Feel free to repeat the demonstration with students changing roles and you changing the signal number.

NOTE: The next screen (screen 5) presents an animation of a mnemonic that students might find useful as they enact the role of axons and dendrites in neural transmission.

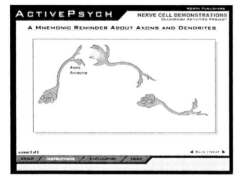

Screen 5

Instructions: Before student demonstrations begin, show them this animation as a mnemonic reminder about the roles of axons (at terminals) and dendrites during transmission.

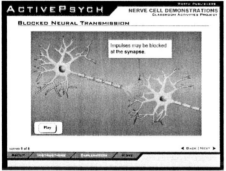

Screen 6

Instructions: Click "Play" to view an animation of blocked neural transmission.

Explanation: Unlike successful neural transmission, this illustration shows an impulse blocked at the synapse, unable to reach another neuron.

Remind students that the synaptic gap, or cleft, is less than one millionth of an inch wide.

Again, point out that in order to cross the synaptic gap, or cleft, the impulse is carried by chemical messengers, called *neurotransmitters*, which are released from the axon terminal.

Certain chemical interactions may block neural transmission. The interactions may occur between neurotransmitters due to either chemicals produced within the body or substances introduced from the outside, such as drugs.

Explain that blocked transmissions are just as vital to the operation of the nervous system as successful transmissions and that they occur with a comparable level of frequency.

NOTE: An animation with detailed guidance for a student demonstration of blocked neural transmission appears on screen 7.

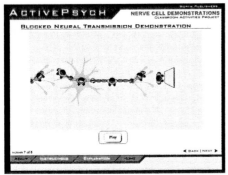

Screen 7

Instructions: Click "Play" to view an animated version of the demonstration for blocked neural transmission.

As you did on screen 4, select volunteers to act as the parts of a nerve cell. Have group members represent each neural part (dendrite, soma, axon, axon terminal) and review each group member's role.

Explain that you will initiate a signal (whisper a number from one to five to the student acting as dendrite). In succession, the group members squeeze hands to represent the signal you've initiated.

However, as the axon terminal whispers the number of squeezes he received, dramatically impose yourself in the gap so that the last, solo student cannot see or hear the message. This shows that the impulse cannot travel cross the synapse and the message is blocked.

In this animation, the last student covers his ears to block the message.

Explanation: Present the following analogy for students: you have just acted as aspirin in someone who is experiencing a fierce headache.

Using the aspirin model, elicit from students that the message from the impulse that traveled through the nerve cell and then became blocked at the synapse was pain.

You might want to challenge students to come up with other possible real-life examples of neural impulses that become blocked. For each instance, ask: What does a person experience from the initial impulse? What blocks the impulse? What is the result of the blockage?

Point out that many drugs work by affecting neurotransmitters that have the ability to allow impulses to cross the synaptic gap from nerve cell to nerve cell.

Extend students' understanding by telling them that when an axon is severed from the soma (cell body), it experiences Wallerian degeneration—that is, the axon dies. When a neuron dies, other support cells in the nervous system consume it; this process is called *phagocytosis*.

Screen 8

Explanation: If an impulse of pain is traveling the neural path and a different impulse is suddenly introduced on that same path, the neurons essentially receive a confused, or mixed, message.

Specifically, several signals confuse the receiving dendrite, thereby dulling the pain impulse message.

Small Group Idea: If students take up the challenge of demonstrating the answer to this question, several students in the roles of the parts of one neuron should hold up a different number of fingers (and/or call out different numbers) at the synapse in order to present a confused, or mixed, message being transmitted to another nerve cell.

Here are some interesting facts: 1906 Nobel prize winner Santiago Ramón y Cajal established the neuron as a basic but independent unit in the Central Nervous System. Sir Charles Sherrington (1857–1952) observed interruptions in transmission—he called this junction the *synapse*, and the gap is called the *synaptic gap* or *cleft*.

Neuroscience and Behavior: HEMISPHERIC PATHWAYS

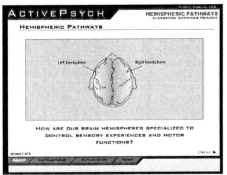

Screen 1

This demonstration was written by Thomas E. Ludwig, Hope College

About: This activity illustrates the pathways through which the hemispheres of the brain receive information and control sensory experiences (including touch, sight, and vision) and motor functions.

On some activity screens, students will activate animations and view the areas of the brain hemispheres that correspond to touch, sound, or visual experiences as well as voluntary muscle movement.

For additional information about any screen activity, click on the illuminated gray tab; use the last "Consider This…" activity screen to promote class discussion.

RELATED TOPICS: Neuroscience and behavior, the brain, hemispheric lateralization.

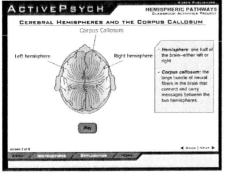

Screen 2

Instructions: Click "Play" to view an animation that shows the left and right hemispheres of the brain as well as the location of the corpus callosum.

Explanation: Point out that when viewed from above (in a top view) the human brain resembles a walnut.

Also point out that if students could look at a human brain, both hemispheres would appear to be symmetrical. But the left and right hemispheres are not exactly identical—one may be a slightly different size than the other; there are differences in the sizes of particular structures within each hemisphere; there may be a difference in the distribution of white and gray matter as well as in the patterns of folds, grooves, and bulges on the surface of the cerebral cortex. [Note that gray matter corresponds to the neuron cell bodies, whereas white matter is made up mostly of myelinated axons.]

Further point out that people rely on the smooth, integrated functioning of both hemispheres to accomplish most tasks—especially demanding cognitive tasks. On the other hand, each hemisphere appears to be somewhat specialized for different abilities.

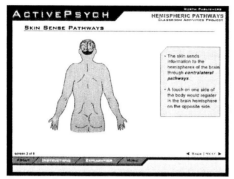

Screen 3

Instructions: Students should come to agreement about which hemisphere registers the touch. As you roll your mouse over the brain, each hemisphere will be illuminated. Click the brain hemisphere that represents the class response.

When you click each hemisphere, students will view the message pathway and read feedback about their chosen response. Click "Reset" to start the animation again.

Explanation: Point out that the word *lateral* means "relating to the side" and the prefix *contra-* means "opposite." Hence, with contralateral pathways, each brain hemisphere is primarily connected to the opposite side of the body.

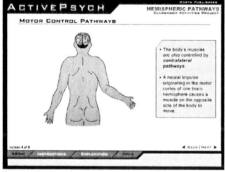

Screen 4

Instructions: Ask students which hemisphere causes the right arm—indicated by the flashing light—to move.

Students should come to an agreement about which hemisphere originates the message to move the arm. As you roll your mouse over the brain, each hemisphere will be illuminated. Click the brain hemisphere that represents the class response.

When you click each hemisphere, students will view the motor control pathway and read feedback about their chosen response. Click "Reset" to start the animation again.

Explanation: Students might be interested to learn that all *chordates* (animals that have both a brain and a spinal cord—a group to which humans belong) have nervous systems in which the brain sends motor movement commands to the opposite side of the body.

The reason for contralateral pathways in chordates is not fully understood, but it is possible that crossed pathways allow for greater movement in the limbs than the trunk.

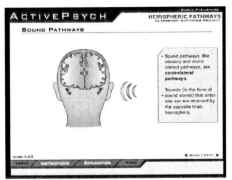

Screen 5

Instructions: Ask students which hemisphere registers the sound waves at the right ear—indicated by the illustrated sound waves.

Students should come to an agreement about which hemisphere registers the sound. As you roll your mouse over the brain, each hemisphere will be illuminated. Click the brain hemisphere that represents the class response.

When you click each hemisphere, students will read feedback about their chosen response. Click "Reset" to start the animation again.

Explanation: Point out that the brain "hears" when sound waves cause the tiny bones in the middle ear to vibrate. These vibrations are then detected by the *cilia* (tips of hair cells embedded in the inner-ear cochlea) and transmitted as messages to the brain.

Surgically implanted electronic devices called *cochlear implants* are processors with microphones that detect frequencies of sound waves that enter the ear and then transmit the detected sound wave information to the brain, thus allowing those who are nerve deaf to experience sound.

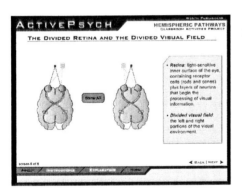

Screen 6

NOTE: The next screen (screen 7) provides an animation to further illustrate the divided visual field as well as the visual pathways to the brain hemispheres.

Instructions: With your mouse, roll over the yellow and blue boxes as well as each eye shown in the illustration.

Brief descriptions will appear for the retina of each eye explaining how the retina responds to objects taken in from the right or left visual fields.

Click "Show All" to display all labels. Click "Reset" to hide all labels.

Explanation: Point out that each hemisphere of the brain receives information from both eyes, but only the information that comes from the opposite visual field.

Make sure students understand that **each retina is divided in half**. This means that an object viewed in the left visual field is registered as information on the right half of the retina of both eyes. An object viewed in the right visual field is registered as information on the left half of the retina of both eyes.

Then, from the right half of each retina, the visual information travels to the right hemisphere of the brain. Likewise, from the left half of each retina, the visual information travels to the left hemisphere of the brain.

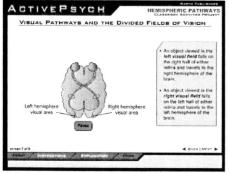

Screen 7

Instructions: Click "Play" to view an animation of an object moving from the left and right visual fields along the visual pathway from the eye to the brain.

Explanation: Help students understand that the visual pathway from the eye to the brain is quite different than the pathway for touch or motor control.

By viewing the animation, it becomes clear that each eye is not connected to one hemisphere only. Rather, an object on either side of the visual field is projected along the visual pathway to the opposite hemisphere of the brain.

Screen 8

Instructions: Present the class with the question shown on the screen. After students have had a moment to consider the question, click "Show Pathways" to display the brain's hemispheres and visual pathways.

Have students discuss the possible answers to the question. When students have come to agreement about which hemisphere would receive the visual information presented on this screen, click "Show Answer." Click "Reset" to start the animation again.

Explanation: Point out that because the retina is divided into two parts, an image is seen with both hemispheres of the brain.

Even if we cover a person's eye, whatever appears in the *right* half of the left eye's visual field will fall on the left half of the retina and will go to the left hemisphere (yellow pathway).

Whatever appears in the *left* half of the left eye's visual field will fall on the right half of the retina and will go to the right hemisphere (blue pathway).

Therefore, both brain hemispheres will be involved in the person seeing through just the left eye.

Neuroscience and Behavior:
SYNAPTIC TRANSMISSION AND NEUROTRANSMITTERS

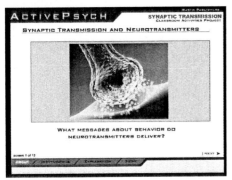

Screen 1

This demonstration was written by Karsten Look, Columbus State Community College

About: In this activity, students learn about various neurotransmitters and their effect on a person's ability to perceive, feel, think, move, act, and react. To better understand neurotransmitters, a brief explanation of *action potential* and *synaptic transmission* begins the activity.

Some activity screens present neurotransmitter "level" meters. When a meter level is chosen, photographs or illustrations indicate the effect of that level of neurotransmitter on a person.

For additional information about any screen activity, click on the illuminated gray tab; use the last "Consider This…" activity screen to promote class discussion.

RELATED TOPICS: the neuron, neuroscience and behavior, physical effects of stress, psychological disorders.

NOTE: This activity can be use in conjunction with the ActivePsych activity "Nerve Cell Demonstrations."

Screen 2

Instructions: For a detailed illustration of communication along a neuron's axon, click "View Close Up."

Once the animation has zoomed into a close-up image of the interior of an axon, click the "Stimulus arrives" or "Stimulus continues" arrows to show what happens to sodium and potassium ions and channels when a neuron is stimulated.

Explanation: The function of neurons is to transmit information throughout the nervous system. Messages are gathered by the dendrites and cell body and then transmitted along the axon as a brief electrical impulse (an *action potential*).

Point out that the neuron at rest is *polarized*—that is, the fluid outside the neuron is more positively charged than the fluid inside. At this point, the difference in electric charge between the inside and outside of the neuron is called the resting potential. As the neuron receives signals from elsewhere in the nervous system its potential may rise and fall as positively and negatively charged ions pass in and out of the cell body in response to those signals.

With sufficient stimulation (the *stimulus threshold*), the neuron *depolarizes*, beginning the action potential. The *all-or-none* law says that there are no gradient levels of neural firing—either an action potential occurs, or it does not. The action potential sets off a chain reaction. Depolarization causes ion channels along the axon to open, allowing positively charged sodium ions to enter and further depolarize the axon, thereby opening more channels further along the axon until the signal reaches the axon terminal.

For about a millisecond after an action potential, a neuron does not fire (the *refractory period*). It *repolarizes*, re-establishing the ion balance inside and outside the neuron.

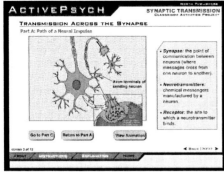

Screen 3

Instructions: This screen offers a three-stage detailed illustration of the synaptic transmission process.

After students have fully absorbed the material presented in Part A, click "Go To Part B" to move to the next stage.

Again, after students have fully absorbed the material in Part B, click "Go To Part C" to move to the final stage.

When you have finished with Part C, click "View Animation" to view an animation of an action potential as it moves along the axon across the synaptic gap and causes the release of neurotransmitters.

Once the animation has loaded, click "Play."

Explanation: Remind students that stimulation activates the presynaptic neuron and generates an action potential that travels to the end of the axon (where the axon terminals are located). Arrival of an action potential causes the tiny sacs called synaptic vesicles (which float in the *axon terminals*) to release *neurotransmitters* (chemical messengers manufactured by neurons) into the synaptic gap.

Point out that a neurotransmitter molecule released into the synapse binds with receptor sites on the receiving neuron like pieces of a jigsaw puzzle that fit together perfectly.

Finally, explain that after neurotransmitters bind to receptor sites, some excess neurotransmitters are reabsorbed by the sending neuron in a process called *reuptake*. Other excess neurotransmitters are broken down by enzymes released by the postsynaptic neuron (such as MAO—monoamine oxidase. This particular enzyme is inhibited in its function by drugs acting as MAO inhibitors, or MAOIs).

To extend their knowledge, have students speculate how long it takes a neurotransmitter molecule to cross the synaptic gap (ANSWER: within 1/10,000 of a second). Then, further point out that the amount of neurotransmitters present in the human brain is analogous to a pinch of salt in an Olympic-sized swimming pool.

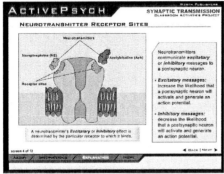

Screen 4

Explanation: Explain that each neurotransmitter has a distinct molecular shape. For a neurotransmitter to communicate its message, its shape must exactly match the postsynaptic neuron's receptor site (like a key in a lock).

Point out that the postsynaptic neuron can have many differently shaped receptor sites (to accommodate many different types of neurotransmitters). The message sent by a neurotransmitter is dependent upon the particular receptor site to which it binds. On one site, a neurotransmitter might send an inhibitory message; on another site, its message might be excitatory. If a postsynaptic neuron receives excitatory and inhibitory messages simultaneously, they may effectively cancel each other out.

The likelihood that a postsynaptic neuron will fire depends on the number and type of neurotransmitters that bind to the receptor sites along the dendrites and cell body, released by *adjoining* presynaptic neurons. With a sufficient number of excitatory messages, the postsynaptic neuron depolarizes—generating an action potential and releasing its own neurotransmitters.

On average, each neuron in the brain communicates directly with 1,000 other neurons. So, a human brain can have up to 100 trillion synaptic interconnections (Greengard, 2001).

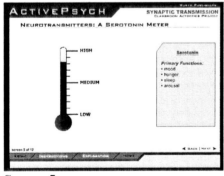

Screen 5

Instructions: First, have students speculate about the effects of high and low levels of serotonin. Then, to show students the effects of different levels of serotonin in the brain, click "High," "Medium," or "Low" on the meter.

For each meter level, a corresponding illustration and description of the effects of serotonin will appear.

Explanation: Serotonin along with dopamine and norepinephrine make up the *monoamines*, which are neurotransmitters that regulate many aspects of everyday human behavior.

Point out that anti-depressant drugs, like Prozac, affect serotonin levels. Prozac belongs to a class of drugs called *selective serotonin reuptake inhibitors* (SSRIs) that slow the reuptake process of serotonin at synapses.

In animals, research shows that neural circuits using serotonin moderate aggressive behavior; the most aggressive animals had the lowest levels of serotonin (Bouwknecht et. al., 2001). Some evidence points to a link between serotonin levels and aggressive as well as impulsive behavior in humans (Dolan, Anderson, & Deakin, 2001; Nelson & Chiavegatto, 2001).

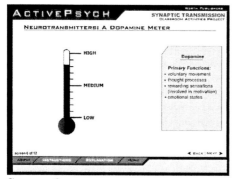

Screen 6

Instructions: First, have students speculate about the effects of high and low levels of dopamine. Then, to show students the effects of different levels of dopamine in the brain, click "High," "Medium," or "Low" on the meter.

For each meter level, a corresponding illustration and description of the effects of dopamine will appear.

Explanation: Explain that the *dopamine hypothesis* is the view that schizophrenia is related to excessive dopamine activity in the brain. Antipsychotic drugs (ex. Haldol or Thorazine) that reduce or block dopamine activity can reduce schizophrenic symptoms. In addition, drugs like amphetamines and cocaine encourage dopamine production and, in normal adults, can produce schizophrenia-like symptoms (Walker et. al., 2004).

However, this hypothesis is somewhat misleading. Not all individuals experience a reduction in schizophrenic symptoms when they use drugs that reduce dopamine activity (Heinrichs, 1993).

Tell students that the drawing shown for the "High" dopamine level was made by a young man who was hospitalized for schizophrenia. At the time he made the drawing, he was hallucinating and very paranoid. It represents the distorted perceptions that occur during schizophrenic episodes—the smaller face superimposed on the larger face might represent hallucinated voices.

Finally, point out that *L-dopa*, a drug that increases dopamine levels, has been used to treat people with Parkinson's disease. Michael J. Fox, who suffers from Parkinson's has said, "…I am a bunch of neurotransmitters that may or may not work."

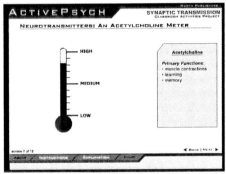

Screen 7

Instructions: First, have students speculate about the effects of high and low levels of acetylcholine. Then, to show students the effects of different levels of acetylcholine in the brain, click "High," "Medium," or "Low" on the meter.

For each meter level, a corresponding illustration and description of the effects of acetylcholine will appear.

Explanation: Explain to students that acetylcholine was the first neurotransmitter discovered. Every time you click a mouse, or make other muscle-prompted movements, your brain releases acetylcholine from motor neurons into your muscles (Kandel & Sigelbaum, 2000). *Nerve gas* is a substance that kills by causing an overproduction of acetylcholine. This overproduction causes muscle spasms so severe its victims cannot breathe and quickly suffocate.

Point out that hunters in some native South American cultures placed a substance called *curare* on arrow tips. Prey struck by these arrows became paralyzed when the curare blocked acetylcholine at neural receptor sites, preventing the animals' muscles from activating.

Further point out that acetylcholine is important in learning, memory, and general intellectual functioning. Research links the amount of acetylcholine released in different neural systems with the regulation of the relative contributions of these systems to learning (Gold, 2003).

Finally, people suffering from Alzheimer's disease (characterized by progressive memory loss and reduced intellectual functioning) have a severe depletion of several neurotransmitters, most notably acetylcholine (Neuron art reference, Scheibel 1982).

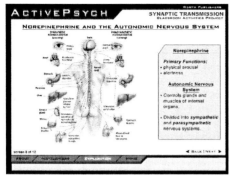

Screen 8

<u>Explanation</u>: Explain to students that the autonomic nervous system is a branch of the peripheral nervous system that regulates involuntary functions (heartbeat, blood pressure, breathing, etc.). It is further divided into the sympathetic and parasympathetic nervous systems. The *sympathetic* nervous system produces rapid physical arousal. The *parasympathetic nervous system* calms you down after a period of arousal or excitement.

Further point out that adrenal glands are commanded into action by the *autonomic nervous system* and that *norepinephrine* helps the body prepare to face dangerous or threatening situations. At a time of threat, the adrenal glands release epinephrine (adrenaline) and norepinephrine (noradrenaline). These hormones provide a surge of energy by increasing heart rate, blood pressure, and blood sugar.

Related fact: Goose bumps are a response related to the release of norepinephrine in the sympathetic nervous system. Goose bumps are similar to responses in other mammals—for instance, a cat whose fur or hair bristles stand up when confronted with possible danger.

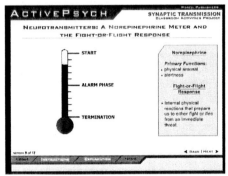

Screen 9

Instructions: First, have students speculate about the effects of high and low levels of norepinephrine. Then, to show students the effects of different levels of norepinephrine in the brain, click "Start," "Alarm phase," and "Termination" on the meter.

For each meter level, you will be presented with a corresponding illustration and description of the effects of the fight-or-flight response as related to norepinephrine.

Explanation: Remind students that, when faced with threatening situations, the *autonomic nervous system* commands the adrenal glands to release the stress hormones epinephrine (adrenaline) and norepinephrine (noradrenaline)—providing a surge of energy by increasing heart rate, blood pressure, and blood sugar.

Explain that noted psychologist Walter Cannon confirmed that the stress response is part of a unified mind-body system in which threatening situations trigger the release of stress hormones—what he called the *fight-or-flight* response (Cannon 1929). But since then, physiologists have found an additional stress response system. The cerebral cortex (via the hypothalamus and pituitary glands), tells the adrenal gland to secrete glucocorticoid stress hormones like *cortisol*. Biologist Robert Sapolsky says that "…epinephrine is the one handing out guns but glucocorticoids are the ones drawing up blueprints for new aircraft carriers needed for the war effort" (Sapolsky 2003).

Finally, point out that, like the other monoamines (dopamine and serotonin), norepinephrine is implicated in depression and other mental disorders (Holden, 2003). The main effects of most antidepressant drugs are at the norepinephrine and serotonin synapses (Garlow, Musselman, & Nemeroff, 1999).

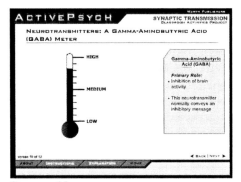

Screen 10

Instructions: First, have students speculate about the effects of high and low levels of gamma-aminobutyric acid (GABA). Then, to show students the effects of different levels of gamma-aminobutyric acid (GABA) in the brain, click "High," "Medium," or "Low" on the meter.

For each meter level, a corresponding illustration and description of the effects of gamma-aminobutyric acid (GABA) will appear.

You may want to point out to your students the following paradox: high levels of an *inhibitory* neurotransmitter lead to behavior that we call "uninhibited."

Explanation: Point out that GABA is a neurotransmitter that usually communicates an inhibitory message to other neurons. It offsets excitatory messages and helps people keep their emotional balance.

Increased GABA (which reduces brain activity) makes people who have ingested alcohol feel relaxed and less inhibited.

Medications that treat anxiety, such as Xanax and Valium, work by increasing GABA—inhibiting action potentials that produce feelings of anxiety. The most often prescribed sedative used to treat insomnia (benzodiazepine medications) affects GABA synapses.

Point out that studies implicate GABA in the expression of seizures (Charney et al., 1996; Shank, Smith-Swintnosky, & Twyman, 2000).

Also point out that fatalities from a combination of sedatives and alcohol may be explained by the *synergistic* effect of both drugs on GABA (that is, the combined effect is greater than either drug's individual effect).

Screen 11

Instructions: First, have students speculate about the effects of high and low levels of endorphins. Then, to show students the effects of different levels of endorphins in the brain, click "High," "Medium," or "Low" on the meter.

For each meter level, a corresponding illustration and description of the effects of endorphins will appear.

Explanation: Point out that endorphins are similar in structure and effect to opiates (e.g. morphine, heroin, codeine) and are produced in response to stress or trauma. The word "endorphin" is actually a contraction of "endogenous (meaning produced in the body) morphine."

The finding that endorphins and opiates are similar was made by neuroscience graduate student, Candace Pert, whose research was prompted by a personal experience—as a hospital patient in 1970, she was given morphine injections to relieve pain from a horseback riding accident. In later research, she and Solomon Snyder attached a radioactive tracer to morphine injected into an animal. They found that the morphine traveled to areas of the brain linked with mood and pain sensations. This discovery showed that effects of morphine occur when it binds itself to specialized receptors in the brain (Pert & Snyder, 1973).

Explain that research with endorphins is relatively new. But so far mice have been noted to release endorphins in *anticipation* of receiving a shock (even when they did not receive the anticipated shock). It is conjectured that people who experience everyday stress and fear to an extreme degree (including those with phobias like *claustrophobia*, a fear of enclosed, elevator-like spaces) may not release endorphins to help regulate the extreme arousal they experience (Bloom, Nelson, Lazerson, 2001).

Screen 12

Explanation: Explain that "runner's high" is associated with an increase of endorphins, which encourages positive feelings, during aerobic exercise. Marathon runners have been found to exhibit four times the normal levels of endorphins (Mahler & others, 1989).

The release of endorphins, creating pain-relieving effects, may also be linked to the *placebo effect*—that is, ineffectual, fake, or empty treatment that produces the experience of change due to a patient's expectations (Fields & Levine, 1984).

Point out that endorphins are implicated in *acupuncture*—an ancient Chinese practice in which needles inserted in the body at certain points rid people of pain (Ulett & Han, 2002).

Development: FROM CONCEPTION TO BIRTH

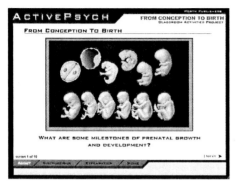

Screen 1

This demonstration was written by Thomas E. Ludwig, Hope College

About: In this activity students observe prenatal growth and development in an animation, shown in segments throughout the activity and then shown in full on the final activity screen.

On some activity screens, students will have the opportunity to review their understanding of prenatal development with illustrated timelines.

For additional information about any screen activity, click on the illuminated gray tab; use the last "Consider This..." activity screen to promote class discussion.

RELATED TOPICS: Prenatal development, prenatal brain development.

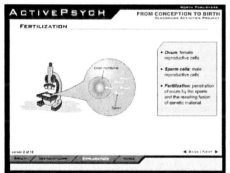

Screen 2

Explanation: Point out that the journey to fertilization begins with the release of the ovum (the female reproductive "egg" cell) from the woman's ovary into one of her fallopian tubes.

If intercourse occurs within a few days before or after this release, conception may occur if a sufficient number of sperm cells survive the journey to the ovum.

Also point out that anywhere from five to 200 sperm cells make it to the ovum in a typical ejaculation, but only one may eventually penetrate the ovum membrane and enter the ovum.

Help students understand that with the fusion of the mother's ovum and father's sperm, the journey to life begins in the one-celled zygote that has been formed.

Screen 3

Click "Play" to start the animation. To replay the animation, click "Play" again.

To return to the view with definitions of the prenatal structures, click "Reset."

Instructions: You can use your cursor to roll over the images of the zygote, morula, and blastocyst for definitions of those prenatal structures.

If you would like to see all the definitions at once, click "Show All Definitions."

Once students have an understanding of the earliest prenatal structures, click "Show Animation" to launch an animation of prenatal development from conception through eight weeks.

Explanation: Point out that the zygote is the first cell of a new individual, formed when a sperm cell makes contact with an ovum (egg cell). Cell division begins within a day. Fewer than one half of all zygotes survive the first two weeks, but all zygotes begin as one cell that divides into two, and so on. As the cells begin to differentiate, they become specialized in both structure and function.

The morula forms by day three and begins its journey through the fallopian tube to the uterus, where it transforms into the blastocyst and becomes implanted in the mother's uterine wall (around day 10).

The outer blastocyst cells develop into the baby's portion of the placenta (an organ made up of tissue from mother and fetus that serves as a barrier and a filter between their bloodstreams and provides nourishment for the fetus). The inner part of the blastocyst forms the embryo.

Point out that the embryo is enclosed in and cushioned by a fluid-filled *amniotic sac*.

Help students identify the *neural tube* (the thin line seen down the middle of the embryo in the animation), and tell them that this becomes the central nervous system, which includes the brain, spinal column, and nerves in neural networks.

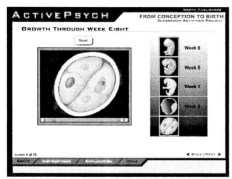

Screen 4

NOTE: By viewing the still timeline of images alongside the animation, students can better gauge growth and development from conception through the *germinal period* (the first two weeks) and *embryonic period* (weeks three through eight).

Instructions: Roll over each image on the timeline for a closer look at that structure. Each image represents a segment of embryonic growth through eight weeks. Once students understand the structural differences in development, click "Show Animation" to review prenatal growth through eight weeks. (Note that this animation was also displayed on the previous screen).

Click "Play" to start the animation.

Explanation: Point out that during the *embryonic period* (weeks three through eight), the organs, skeletal system, and bone cells begin to form; also, the organism takes on recognizable human features. The embryo grows to about 2.5 centimeters (one inch) long and one gram (1/30 ounce) in weight.

Further point out that by week four, eyes, ears, nose, and mouth start to form; also, a tiny blood vessel begins to pulse—a structure that will develop into the heart. By week five, buds that will become arms and legs appear, as well as a tail-like appendage that will become the spine.

Finally point out that by the end of the embryonic period, the organism has all the basic body parts and organs of a human being except for knees, elbows, and sex organs.

RELATED TOPICS: *Teratogens* are substances that can cause birth defects or even death. They come from diseases, pollutants, radiation, medicinal drugs, psychoactive drugs, and social and behavioral factors. The embryonic period is a time when the organism is particularly vulnerable to teratogens.

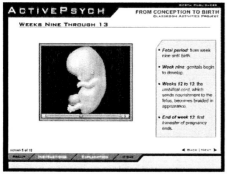

Screen 5

Instructions: Click "Play" to view an animation of fetal development between weeks nine and 13.

Explanation: Point out that between weeks nine and 11, the fetus grows from about the size of the first joint of a thumb to the length of a thumb, about six centimeters (2 1/2 inches).

Also point out that by week 11, the brain has formed (having developed from the neural tube, as seen in the animation segment on screen 3 and 4). At this time, the vocal cords are formed but soft, and fetal sounds cannot be detected.

Further point out that by weeks 12–13, the lungs of the fetus inflate, and a heartbeat can be detected with the proper instruments.

As for the mother, she can't yet feel the fetus moving. But, inside the womb, the fetus has gone from making twitches to larger movements of its legs and arms.

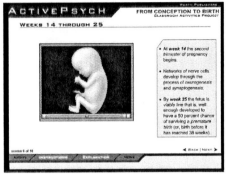

Screen 6

Instructions: Click "Play" to view an animation of fetal development between weeks 14 and 25.

Explanation: Point out that by week 17, the head is erect; the eyes are close together, and they blink.

Also point out that by week 17, an insulating substance called *myelin* coats the *axons* (the part of the nerve cell that transmits messages). Myelin helps to speed neural communication.

Further explain that between weeks 18 and 25 the fetus experiences sleep and wake cycles (and finds sleep positions). Also, it might suck its thumb and it can respond to sounds (because the middle ear bones harden and conduct sounds). Overall, the fetus experiences a surge in body and brain growth and, by the end of this period, the womb becomes cramped.

As for the mother, point out that by the beginning of the second trimester, at week 14, most women no longer experience morning sickness (the nausea that often accompanies the first trimester period of pregnancy).

The second trimester ends at week 25. At this point, the fetus may be viable. But with an approximate weight of two to three pounds it has what is considered very low birthweight (VLBW) and has only a 50 percent chance of survival.

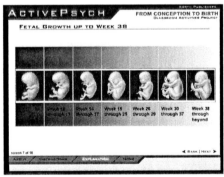

Screen 7

Explanation: Point out that at nine weeks, the fetus is about 2.4 centimeters (one inch) and by week 38 (and birth), it measures around 50 centimeters (20 inches).

You might want to present a yard/meter ruler to allow students to visually gauge the growth (in length) of the fetus from week nine to week 38.

Review milestones students have already learned about fetal growth and development by encouraging volunteers to correlate each illustration of a fetus with a description of body, organ, and brain growth as well as development of human function (breathing, heartbeat, sleep) and movement.

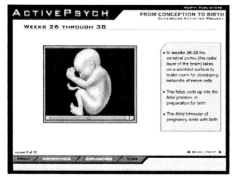

Screen 8

Instructions: Click "Play" to view an animation of fetal development between weeks 26 and 38.

Explanation: Point out that in the third trimester, the cerebral cortex becomes covered in wrinkles called *sulci* and *gyri* (the brain's troughs and peaks, respectively).

By this time, the brain controls temperature and rhythmic breathing of amniotic fluid. If an instrument (an *encephalograph*) could be placed on the scalp of the fetus, fetal brain waves could be recorded. The fetus also opens and closes its eyes according to sleep cycles.

Explain that, toward the end of this trimester, the skin smoothes as white fat accumulates beneath the skin of the fetus. This fat will be used as an energy source after birth as the fetus makes the transition from the placenta to milk for its nourishment.

As for the mother, she often speaks to her fetus and/or pats her belly to communicate with the fetus as it moves and responds to her sounds, movements, and functions.

Finally, point out that in the fetal position (the position preferred for birth), the fetus wedges its head against the mother's cervix—the ring of muscle at the opening of the mother's uterus.

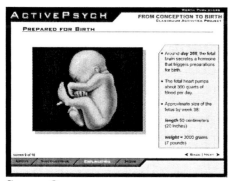

Screen 9

Explanation: Students should understand that at this point the fetus' lungs are finally reaching maturity. Its bones have become more rigid, but the skull is not yet solid.

As the fetus prepares for birth, five bony plates in the skull—*fontanels*—compress into a bullet shape with a reduced diameter, making the journey through the mother's birth canal possible. After birth, the newborn's head returns to a rounded shape.

Point out that, at around day 266, the fetus makes itself and its mother ready for the birth process. Its brain secretes a hormone that prepares it to breathe outside of its mother's womb and also prepares the mother's uterus for labor.

Finally, explain that the fetus does not always assume the preferred fetal position (head wedged against the mother's cervix). Sometimes, due to a problem with space and positioning of the umbilical cord, the fetus assumes a more difficult birth position, called a *breech* position, in which the legs and buttocks of the fetus are down.

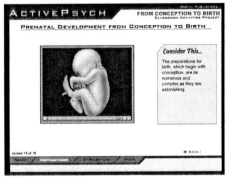

Screen 10

Instructions: Click "Play" to view an animation of the complete process of prenatal development—from conception through week 38.

Development: PRENATAL BRAIN DEVELOPMENT

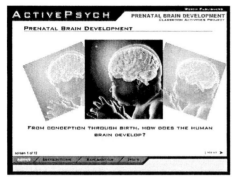

Screen 1

This demonstration was written by Stavros Valenti, Hofstra University

About: In this activity students follow animations that depict brain development from the beginning of life to week four, then week eight, week 26, and finally to the newborn at about week 40. Students will also have the opportunity to view the full animation from conception through birth on the activity's last screen.

For additional information about any activity screen, click on the illuminated gray tab; use the last "Consider This" screen to promote class discussion.

RELATED TOPICS: Neuroscience and behavior, neural communication, the brain, the cerebral cortex, conception, prenatal development.

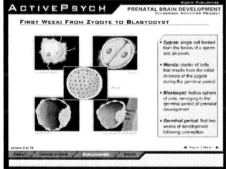

Screen 2

Explanation: Point out that the zygote is the first cell of a new individual, which forms within a woman's fallopian tube when a sperm cell makes contact with an ovum (egg cell). Cell division begins within a day; the morula forms by day three and begins a journey through the fallopian tube to the uterus, where it transforms into the blastocyst.

Also point out that the germinal period is characterized by rapid cell division and differentiation.

Students should understand that the blastocyst becomes implanted in the uterine wall. The outer blastocyst cells develop into the baby's portion of the *placenta* (the organ made up of tissue from mother and fetus that serves as a barrier and a filter between their bloodstreams). The surrounding membranes develop into the *amnion* (membrane that holds the amniotic fluid and surrounds the developing fetus) and *chorion* (membrane that forms the fetal component of the placenta).

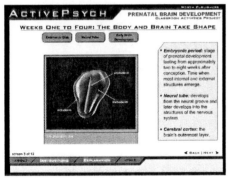

Screen 3

To view animations of the neural tube and early brain development, click the corresponding buttons. When you see "View Close Up," click that button for a 3-dimensional rotating view of that structure.

Instructions: Click the "Embryonic Disk" button to view an illustration of that structure. You can roll your mouse over the labels for additional definitions.

Explanation: Point out that once the blastocyst is implanted in the uterus and the inner cell mass begins to take nourishment, the embryonic period begins. Soon after the organism resembles a disk with three layers: the *mesoderm* (cells of the inner cell mass that give rise to the muscles, bones, circulatory system, and inner layers of the skin), *endoderm* (cells of the inner cell mass that develop into the digestive system and lungs), and *ectoderm* (cells of the inner cell mass that develop into the outer surface of the skin, nails, part of the teeth, lens of the eye, the inner ear, and the central nervous system).

Further point out that a groove in the ectoderm transforms into the neural tube; over the course of two to three weeks, the neural tube thickens and differentiates at one end, giving rise to three distinct brain structures: the *forebrain* (develops into the cerebral cortex, which translates sensory stimulation, controls complex behaviors, thoughts, memories, and problem solving), *midbrain* (develops into neural relay station for sending messages between the body and the sites in the brain), and *hindbrain* (develops into part of the brain that controls basic physiological processes, such as breathing and heart rate).

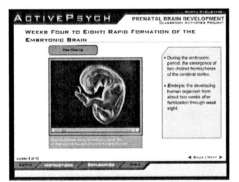

Screen 4

For a closer look, click "View Close Up" and then drag your cursor across the window to rotate the image.

Instructions: Click "Play" to view the animation showing the emergence of distinct hemispheres in the cerebral cortex as the brain develops during the embryonic period.

Explanation: Point out that in the brief time between four and eight weeks, the embryo increases five-fold in length—from about 5mm to 26mm—from crown to rump (that is, from less than one quarter inch to about one inch).

Also point out that during this period, the embryo's face begins to look distinctly human, but the eyes are still located on the sides of the head. They will continue to migrate forward in the weeks ahead.

Further point out that the cerebral cortex integrates information from several sensory sources with memories of past experiences, processing them in a way that results in human forms of thought and action. During this time, brain development is particularly rapid, with the emergence of two distinct hemispheres of the cerebral cortex, brain waves, and body movements that are controlled by the brain's activity.

Screen 5

For a closer look, click "View Close Up" and then drag your cursor across the window to rotate the image.

Instructions: Click "Play" to view the animation of brain development during the fetal period: Rapid growth of the cerebral cortex.

Explanation: Help students distinguish the fetal period by explaining that whereas the embryonic period is when most body and brain structures first emerge, the fetal period is when organs enlarge and mature. The brain is no exception.

Further point out that the most dramatic changes involve the cerebral cortex that enlarges and rapidly covers the midbrain. At this point, the cortex is a relatively thin and smooth sheet of densely packed neurons.

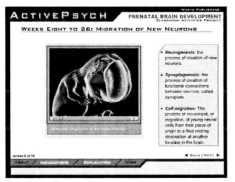

Screen 6

Instructions: Click "Play" to view the animation of cell migration and growth in the outer layers of the brain.

Explanation: Point out at the beginning of the fetal period, the structures of the brain are already in place, but the amount of tissue rapidly increases due to neurogenesis and synaptogenesis.

To better understand neural networks, point out that with synaptogenesis, synapses are created between neurons' *axons* (main protruding branches of a neuron that carry messages to other cells in the form of electrical impulses) and *dendrites* (protruding part of a neuron that receives messages from the axons of other cells).

Also point out that in cell migration, various parts of the central nervous system take shape with the movement of immature (undifferentiated) cells from the innermost layers to other locations, such as the cerebral cortex.

Further point out that the migration occurs in waves. Most of the early migrants rest closer to their starting point; later migrants move past the first ones to more distant, outer layers. In this way the brain grows, adding layers to itself like skins of an onion.

Screen 7

Instructions: Click "Play" to view the animation of migrating cells that follow glial fibers.

Explanation: Point out that, like gymnasts climbing ropes, immature neurons are guided to their final destination by fibers from another type of cell, called the radial glial cell.

Students may be interested to know that the term glial cells means "glue cells."

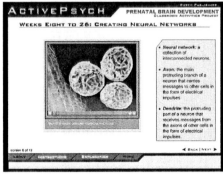

Screen 8

Instructions: Click "Play" to view the animation of the growth of axons and dendrites within neural networks.

Explanation: Make sure students understand that neural networks in the central nervous system integrate information from different sources and control various functions of the body.

Point out that when immature neurons reach their final destination, they acquire specific characteristics of neurons of that particular brain region. The neurons sprout extensions: dendrites (multiple, short, thin, antenna-like extensions for receiving incoming messages) and axons (a single larger extension which carries outgoing messages to other neurons).

Further point out that an axon can be as short as a few millimeters (for carrying signals to its close neighbors) or as long as a few centimeters (for carrying signals to the opposite side of the brain). Some axons that carry signals between the brain and lower parts of the body can reach more than a meter in length.

Screen 9

Instructions: Click "Play" to view the animation of a close-up view of a neural impulse as it crosses the synapse.

Explanation: Remind students that the junction where one neuron communicates with another is the *synapse*.

Point out that this communication occurs when a neural impulse reaches the end of an axon, stimulating the release of a chemical, called a *neurotransmitter*, across the synapse to the receiving *dendrite* of the second neuron.

Further point out that the neurotransmitter communicates with the second neuron in various ways—for example, by stimulating it to begin a new neural impulse.

Related term: Because the rate of synaptic formation, or *synaptogenesis*, is so rapid during the prenatal period and into the first year, researchers often use the term *exuberant synaptogenesis*.

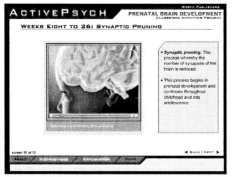

Screen 10

Instructions: Click "Play" to view the animation of synaptic pruning, which customizes neural networks.

Explanation: Students should understand that an overabundance of synapses form during the prenatal period and the first year after birth, creating a brain of great flexibility for learning. At one year old, an infant's brain is estimated to have more than four times the number of synapses than the mature adult brain.

Point out that "pruning" is a term borrowed from gardening, where it means "removing dead or unwanted twigs and branches in the interest of obtaining better health for a plant." Similarly, for a brain to work rapidly and efficiently, many of the early synapses need to be removed or "pruned."

Further point out that synaptic pruning occurs at different times in different places throughout the fetal period, infancy, and childhood. Although the mechanism is not entirely understood at present, it is believed that one purpose of pruning is to "customize" an individual's nervous system in response to that individual's life experiences.

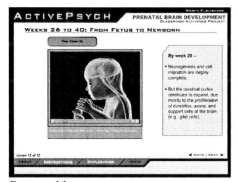

Screen 11

Instructions: Click "Play" to view the animation of the expansion of the cerebral cortex. For a closer look, click "View Close Up" and then drag your cursor across the window to rotate the image.

Explanation: Point out the major structural change that occurs during this time: The cortex, a sheet of cells only 2mm thick, expands greatly in surface area and becomes wrinkled and folded inside of the skull. These "hills and valleys" (*gyri* and *sulci*, respectively) start to form at approximately week 28; they become more prominent over time.

Further point out that the purpose of the folds and wrinkles is to permit more points of contact among neurons (synapses). This contributes to the ability of each neuron to connect to and influence hundreds, even thousands, of neighboring cells. These vast neural networks allow the brain to become a highly flexible and precise control center and processor of information.

Related information: Students may be interested to know that researchers estimate that a baby's brain contains about 100 billion neurons, with more than 100 trillion (100,000,000,000,000) synaptic connections.

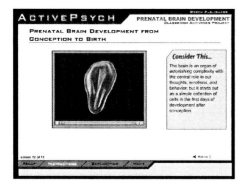

Screen 12

Instructions: Click "Play" to view the full animation of prenatal brain development from conception to birth.

Development: ADOLESCENT BRAIN DEVELOPMENT

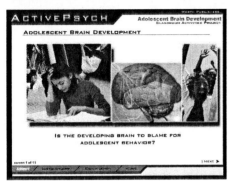

Screen 1

This demonstration was written by Stavros Valenti, Hofstra University

About: In this activity, illustrations and animations help students explore how the brain develops during the teen years and the relationship between brain development to adolescent behavior.

Early in the activity students will respond to a survey question about the cause(s) of adolescent behavior. That question will be asked again, later in the activity, in light of what students have learned about brain development.

For additional information about any activity screen, click on the illuminated gray tab; use the last "Consider This…" activity screen to promote class discussion.

RELATED TOPICS: Neuroscience and behavior, the brain, adolescence, cognitive development.

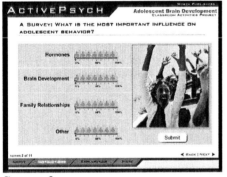

Screen 2

Instructions: Have students choose the one response that best answers the question for them. Use the slider beneath each response to show the estimated percentage of students who chose it.

If it appears that the class feels the causes of adolescent behavior go beyond the three options given, choose "Other."

After all sliders have been adjusted, click "Submit," and go on to the next screen.

NOTE: The responses to this question will be shown and discussed on screen 10, in relationship to material presented about brain development and adolescent behavior.

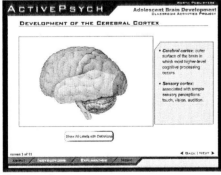

Screen 3

NOTE: The frontal cortex is presented in detail on screen 6.

Instructions: Roll over the illustration to highlight and identify each region of the cerebral cortex. To view all the labels and definitions, click "Show All Labels with Definitions."

Explanation: Point out that a general back-to-front pattern can be seen in the development of the cerebral cortex.

The control centers for sensation and perception (sensory cortex areas located in the occipital, parietal, and temporal lobes) show early and rapid development.

Neural networks that control voluntary, planned behavior (located in the frontal lobe) develop much more slowly.

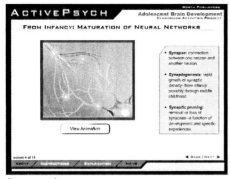

Screen 4

Instructions: Click "View Animation" to view an animation showing the development of neural networks, synaptogenesis, and synaptic pruning.

Explanation: In this animation, students will watch as nerve cells expand and grow. As they expand, they reach out and form connections with other nerve cells. As the process continues, the nerve cells that are not used contract, and those connections are eliminated.

Point out that during the fetal period, before birth, nerve cells in the brain multiply and form connections—or *synapses*—with other nerve cells, usually between the axon terminal of one neuron and the dendrite of another neuron. Remind students that in neural communication the *axon* is the part of the neuron that "announces" messages and the *dendrites* "receive" messages.

The formation of neural networks is known as *synaptogenesis*. The networks are shaped not only by genetically controlled biological processes, but also by life experiences.

The elimination of synapses is known as *synaptic pruning*. Both the creation and removal of synapses occur in response to specific experiences, thereby allowing the brain to become a custom-tailored organ for controlling a person's thoughts, behaviors, and emotions.

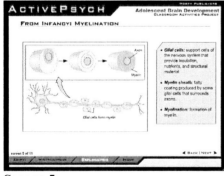

Screen 5

Explanation: Point out that the illustration shows glial cells that envelop axons, forming the myelin sheath; the close up view shows the myelin sheath.

Further point out that the glial cells that form the myelin sheath act as the supporting structure in the brain; they also provide nourishment for neurons.

Myelin not only insulates nerve fibers and speeds up transmission of neural impulses from one neuron to the next, it also improves the efficiency of the signal communication within neural networks.

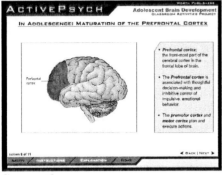

Screen 6

Instructions: Roll over the illustration to highlight and label the *prefrontal cortex*, *premotor cortex*, and *motor cortex*.

Explanation: Unlike centers for sensation and perception, the frontal lobe of the cortex (in particular, the prefrontal cortex) changes significantly from mid-childhood through the early 20s.

Throughout childhood, the number of synaptic connections continues to rise in the frontal cortex until puberty (11–13 years), after which a gradual pruning begins. Synaptic overproduction and pruning is thought to increase the efficiency of information processing in these brain circuits.

Remind students that myelin in the brain coats and insulates the neural fibers, thereby enhancing communication between neurons. With this in mind, point out that there is evidence that a relatively high degree of myelination occurs in the frontal cortex during adolescence and early adulthood.

Screen 7

Explanation: Point out that *metabolism* is the physical and chemical processes by which some substances are produced or transformed into energy or products for uses by the body, while others (e.g., waste products and other toxins) are produced and excreted from the body.

Brain research has found that heightened level of brain activity is sustained until approximately age 10, after which it steadily declines until approximately age 20. The full significance of the slowing of brain metabolism in adolescence is unclear, but it could simply be an indication of fewer synapses (hence less brain activity) and more efficient brain functioning.

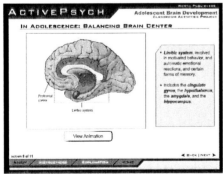

Screen 8

Instructions: Click "View Animation" for a close-up view of the brain structures in the limbic system.

To view definitions for the brain structures, click "Show Definitions." To continue the animation, click "Continue".

Explanation: Point out that recent studies have suggested that there is a change in the balance of activity between the limbic system and the prefrontal cortex. This change may be responsible for the gradual increase in deliberate and thoughtful behavioral control that occurs across the adolescent years.

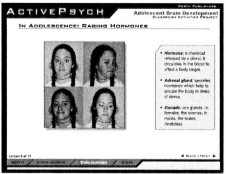

Screen 9

Explanation: Point out that along with other brain changes in adolescence there is a rise in hormone levels in the bloodstream from the adrenal glands and gonads.

Adrenal hormone levels begin to rise around age 7 and reach a plateau in late adolescence.

Gonadal hormones, responsible for the bodily changes of puberty, are related to moodiness, aggressive behavior, and aggressive thoughts in both boys and girls (Spears, 2000).

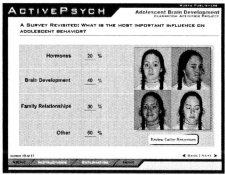

Screen 10

Instructions: Now that you have gone through the information on brain development as it relates to adolescent behavior, ask students to rethink their opinion regarding the most important influence on adolescent behavior in light of this activity.

Then, click "Review Earlier Responses" so the students can see how their opinions have changed." Ask students to discuss how and why their responses changed.

Explanation: Remind students that "correlation is not causation." While the brain *is* changing, that doesn't necessarily mean these changes are the cause of unique adolescent behaviors.

Recent research has shown that there is little support for the idea that risky adolescent behavior is *primarily* caused by "raging hormones." Certainly, stress from hormonally-induced body changes (increases in sex drive and aggression) plays a role in adolescent behavior. However, hormonal changes may be subservient to the changes in the brain structures governing emotions and decision making.

In studying the way the brain experiences "reward" and "pleasure," researchers have observed that the shift in the balance of activity between the limbic system and the prefrontal cortex may be responsible for the decline in mood often observed in early adolescence.

Point out that some researchers have described adolescents as having a "mini reward-deficiency syndrome," leading some teens to seek increased levels of stimulation through more interaction with peers, risky behavior, and drug or alcohol abuse.

Explanation: Point out that some researchers stress that the roots of adolescent risk taking and impulsive behaviors are more likely to rest in a teenager's lack of relevant experiences and skills. Adults, after all, have many more years of experience with both the short-term and long-term consequences of risky behavior.

Screen 11

Development: PIAGET AND CONSERVATION

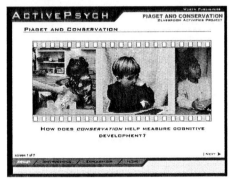

Screen 1

This demonstration was written by Thomas E. Ludwig, Hope College

About: This activity demonstrates the principle of conservation—the understanding that changing the shape or form of an object or group of objects doesn't change the amount.

Students will view videos of children at different ages engaged in either a number or liquid conservation task; students will also speculate on the responses of child participants—ages 4, 7, and 13, respectively, in the *preoperational, concrete operational,* and *formal operational* stages of cognitive development—in a simulation of another conservation-based task (checkers task).

For additional information about any screen activity, click on the illuminated gray tab; use the last "Consider This…" activity screens to promote class discussion.

RELATED TOPICS: The developing person, continuity and stages in development, Piaget, cognitive development.

Screen 2

Instructions: Click Play to view a video of "Aliyah" (age 5) responding to a liquid quantity question.

Have students speculate about the reasons for Aliyah's answer.

Explanation: After students have had time to speculate about Aliyah's response, point out that in Piaget's theory of *cognitive development,* children (from about age 2 to 6) cannot use concrete logic to comprehend when they are in the *preoperational stage.* For Aliyah, this means she cannot understand that, though the level appears "higher," there is the same amount of liquid in the cup.

Further explain that children (from about age 7 to 11) can think logically about *concrete events* in the *concrete operational stage* and children (from about age 12 and above) can think logically about abstract concepts in the *formal operational stage.*

Explain that Piaget measured a child's stage by posing problems that challenged the child's ability to think with concrete logic. Some of these tasks tested a child's comprehension of the principle of *conservation.*

Students might be interested to know that Piaget—a Swiss psychologist (1896–1980)—tested his theory of cognitive development on his own three children.

Screen 3

Instructions: The checkers task is a conservation-of-number simulation. In it, three children will answer the question posed on the screen. In step 1, the checkers are displayed in equal rows. In step 2, they are spaced farther apart. (Note that the question is the same for both steps in this simulation.)

First, ask students to speculate how each child (Lisa age 4, Juan age 7, Keiko age 13) would answer the question. To find out each child's response, click the "Step 1" button beneath each photograph.

To activate step 2 of the simulation, click "Play." (The Step 1 buttons will disappear and the red checkers will move.)

After the checkers have moved, to find out each child's response to the question, click the "Step 2" button beneath each photograph.

On the next screen (screen 4) you will be presented with the final two steps of the checkers task.

To begin this task again, click "Reset."

Explanation: Point out that in a genuine experiment, each child would be tested individually to avoid the possibility that one child's responses would influence the others. But in these simulations the three children's responses are shown on one screen to help students make comparisons.

After students speculate how each child's response relates to a particular stage of cognitive development, make sure students connect Lisa's response in Step 2 (as a four-year-old) to *preoperational thinking*, Juan's response (as a seven-year-old) to the *concrete operational* thinking of a child who may not yet be quite sure of his ability to think with concrete logic; and the tone of Keiko's thirteen-year-old response to a child with established logical thinking—someone who has probably entered the *formal operational* period.

Finally, point out that Piaget measured the formal operational period by a child's ability for *formal thought*—that is, the type of thinking in which *volume* remains the same despite a change in the *form* of an object (or objects).

Screen 4

Instructions: Next, you will ask students to speculate on how each child (Lisa age 4, Juan age 7, Keiko age 13) would answer the question posed in steps 3 and 4 of the checkers task. Note that the screen opens with the red checkers moving back together so that they are spaced evenly with the gray checkers. This is step 3.

To find out each child's response to the question (with the checkers again evenly spaced), click the "Step 3" button beneath each photograph.

To activate step 4 of the simulation, click "Play." (The Step 3 buttons will disappear and the gray checkers will move.)

After the checkers have moved, to find out each child's response to the question, click the "Step 4" button beneath each photograph.

As with steps 1 and 2, the task question is the same for both Steps 3 and 4.

To begin this task again, click "Reset."

Explanation: If students do not understand the link between the preoperational, concrete operational, and formal operational stages of cognitive development and each participant's responses, point out that Piaget believed that simple objects, such as checkers (among other objects) can be used to test logical thinking in children. Both the answers the children give and the errors they make provide clues to each child's mental growth.

Further point out that, in the preoperational stage (ages 2 to 6, which would include Lisa), concrete logic is not used for comprehension. However, concrete logic is used in the concrete operational stage (ages 7 to 11, which would include Juan) and in the formal operational stage (ages 12 and above, which would include Keiko).

Finally, point out that Piaget believed that each stage builds on the accomplishments of the previous one and allows a child to overcome some of the limitations of the previous stage.

Screen 5

Instructions: Click Play to view a video of two children responding to questions in a conservation-of-number task.

Explanation: Make sure students apply the principle of *conservation* when they answer the questions. (Remember, changing the shape or form of an object, or group of objects, doesn't change the amount.)

Further, make sure that students connect the boy's cognitive development to Piaget's ideas about the *preoperational stage* (between ages 2 and 6, when children do not yet use concrete logic to comprehend) and the girl's cognitive development to Piaget's ideas about the *concrete operational stage* (between ages 7 and 11, when children use concrete logic).

Finally, have students connect the boy's response with Lisa's (from the checkers task) and the girl's response with Juan's (also from the checkers task).

Screen 6

Instructions: Click Play to view a video of "Ashley" responding to questions in a conservation-of-liquid task.

Explanation: Again, make sure students apply the principle of *conservation* when they answer the question. The same principles that apply to number problems also apply to liquid problems. Changing the shape or form of an object, or group of objects, doesn't change the amount.

Students should connect Ashley's age to Piaget's ideas about the preoperational stage of cognitive development. (Between the ages of 2 and 6, children do not yet use concrete logic to comprehend.)

Finally, have students connect Ashley's response in the conservation-of-liquid task with Lisa's responses (from the checkers task) and with the boy's responses (in the candy-counting task). Students should understand that all three children are around the same age and at the same stage of cognitive development.

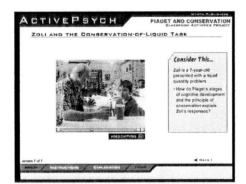

Screen 7

Instructions: Click Play to view a video of "Zoli" responding to questions in Piaget's conservation-of-liquid problem.

Explanation: For the last time, have students apply the principle of *conservation* to the liquid quantity problem. Again, the same principles that apply to number problems also apply to liquid problems. Changing the shape or form of an object, or group of objects, doesn't change the amount.

Make sure that students connect Zoli's age to Piaget's ideas about the concrete operational stage of cognitive development. (Between ages 7 and 11, children use concrete logic to comprehend.)

Finally, have students connect Zoli's response in the liquid quantity problem with Juan's response (from the checker's task) and with the girl's responses (in the candy-counting task). Students should understand that all three children are about the same age and at the same stage of cognitive development.

Development: DEVELOPMENT THEORISTS

Screen 1

This demonstration was written by Elaine Epstein, with fundamental ideas and structure contributed by Andrew Peck, The Pennsylvania State University

About: In this activity, the development theorists Freud, Erikson, Piaget, and Kohlberg are presented along with interactive tables that introduce their theories.

For additional information about any screen activity, click on the illuminated gray tab; use the last "Consider This…" activity screen to promote class discussion.

RELATED TOPICS: The developing person, continuity and stages, Freud and psychosexual stages, Erikson and psychosocial development, Piaget and cognitive development, Kohlberg and development of moral reasoning.

Note: This activity can be use in conjunction with the ActivePsych activity "Life-Span Timeline."

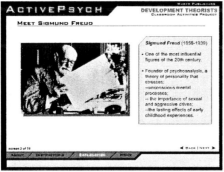

Screen 2

Explanation: Point out that Freud studied medicine and became a physiological researcher. Partly because of a research dispute (over the medical potential of cocaine!) and partly due to anti-Semitism in his home city of Vienna, Austria, Freud, who was Jewish, gave up research and opened a private practice as a neurologist, which led to his development of psychoanalytic theory.

Also point out that underlying Freud's psychoanalytic perspective was his belief that the mind is mostly hidden, like an iceberg. The conscious floats above the surface, while the much larger unconscious lies below. (NOTE: Screen 3 presents and discusses the iceberg model.)

Further point out that Freud was a prolific writer. Many consider his most important work to be *The Interpretation of Dreams* (1900). A popular book, *The Psychopathology of Everyday Life* (1904), focused on the influence of the unconscious on daily life (including Freudian slips—that is, inadvertent slips of the tongue). His 1930 book, *Civilization and its Discontents*, focused on humanity's destructive tendencies—interestingly, World War II began in that same decade.

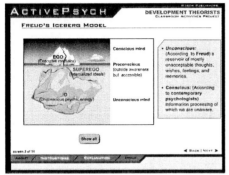

Screen 3

Instructions: For additional information about the id, ego, and superego, roll your mouse over the labels on the illustration. Click "Show All" if you would like to view all the descriptions.

Explanation: Make sure students note that the id is totally unconscious, while the ego and superego operate both consciously and unconsciously.

Remind students that Sigmund Freud (1856–1939) developed a theory of personality that stresses the influence of the unconscious, the importance of sexual and aggressive instincts, and lasting effects of very early childhood experience on personality.

Point out that Freud believed people repress, or block from consciousness, unacceptable passions and thoughts—however, repressed thoughts and feelings influence the work we do, the beliefs we hold, our everyday habits, and any troubling symptoms we may have.

Further point out that, according to Freud, personality arises from our efforts to resolve conflicts between our aggressive, pleasure-seeking biological impulses and social restraints. Through our personalities (and interaction among the *id*, *ego*, and *superego*) we attempt to satisfactorily resolve conflicts without also promoting guilt or punishment.

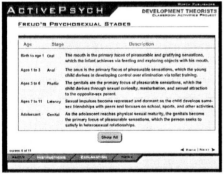

Screen 4

Instructions: In order, read each stage and age, and then have students speculate about what they think the focus of that psychosexual stage is, according to what they know of Freud's focus.

Roll your mouse over any text under the heading "Age" or "Stage" and the corresponding description will appear. Click "Show all" if you want to view the entire chart with all of the descriptions.

Explanation: For each stage, Freud believed an unresolved developmental conflict, *fixation*, exists. If frustrated, the child is left with feelings of unmet needs for his/her stage. If overindulged the child can feel reluctant to move on to the next stage.

Point out that Freud believed the most critical conflict occurred in the phallic stage. In this stage the child experiences the *Oedipal complex*. (Oedipus is a character from Greek mythology who, without knowing their true identities, killed his father and married his mother.) This conflict includes a child's possessiveness of the opposite-sex parent and competitiveness with the same-sex parent (i.e., a female child might proclaim, "I'll marry Daddy!" or a male child might say, "Don't kiss my Mommy, Daddy!")

Freud believed a boy would ultimately resolve this conflict when he realizes he cannot compete with his father and, instead, begins to identify with him (by imitating and internalizing his father's values and attitudes).

Whereas, Freud believed a girl would ultimately identify with her mother and, when she developed a superego (telling right from wrong), would endorse a taboo against incest. Freud also believed girls felt deprived because they do not have a penis (Freud termed this *penis envy*). This is one of Freud's most severely criticized ideas.

Screen 5

Explanation: Tell students that Erikson's Eight Psychosocial stages are: Trust vs. Mistrust, Autonomy vs. Shame and Doubt, Initiative vs. Guilt, Industry vs. Inferiority, Identity vs. Role Confusion, Intimacy vs. Isolation, Generativity vs. Stagnation, and Integrity vs. Despair. Then, explain that when talking about *identity* in relationship to Erikson, psychologists are referring to the values, beliefs, and ideas that guide the individual's behavior. (Note that Erikson's stages will be discussed further on the next screen.)

Students may be interested to know that Erikson, a Jew, was born in Germany and was living in Vienna when the Nazis invaded. He and his wife fled to the U.S. prior to World War II. His studies of Harvard students, Boston children at play, and Native American cultures led him to stress cultural diversity, social change, and psychological crises throughout the life span (Berger, 2006).

Screen 6

Instructions: In order, read each "Identity Stage" and set of "Issues," and then have students speculate about what they think the focus of that psychosocial stage is, according to what they know of Erikson's focus.

Roll your mouse over any text under the heading "Identity Stage" or "Issues" and the corresponding task description will appear. Click "Show all" if you want to view the entire chart with all of the task descriptions.

Explanation: Point out that adolescence is a time when the type of conflict Erikson discusses in personality development is particularly crucial.

The major conflict of adolescence, "identity vs. role confusion," was the focus of Erikson's 1968 book, *Identity: Youth and Crisis*.

Screen 7

Explanation: Point out that Piaget, who lived in Switzerland and France, observed his own three children as he developed his theory of cognitive development.

He believed the stages of cognitive development were biologically programmed for the respective ages he identified; in various cultures these stages unfolded at the same time and in a similar manner.

Also point out the following terms used by Piaget:
— *schema:* a concept or framework that organizes and interprets information

— *assimilation:* interpreting one's new experience in terms of one's existing schemas

— *accommodation:* adapting one's current understandings—or schemas—to incorporate new information

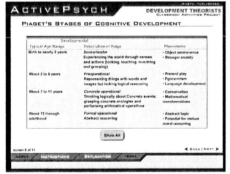

Screen 8

Instructions: In order, read each "Typical Age Range" and "Description of Stage" and then have students speculate what they think are the phenomena that exemplify that cognitive stage, according to what they know of Piaget's focus.

Roll your mouse over any text under the heading "Typical Age Range" or "Description of Stage" and the corresponding "Phenomena" will appear. Click "Show all" if you want to view the entire chart with all of the "Phenomena" displayed.

Explanation: Point out that even though Piaget believed the order of stages to be universal, he realized that heredity and environment could influence the rate at which any particular child progressed through the stages of development (Fishcer & Hencke, 1996).

Also point out that Piaget believed it is important that the child's environment provide many opportunities to learn through both guided and free exploration.

RELATED THEORIST: Lev Vygotsky (1896–1934) of Russia was born in the same year as Piaget. Vygotsky's theories focused on how cognitive development takes place within a social and cultural context.

Vygotsky agreed with Piaget that children could reach a particular cognitive level through their own efforts. However, Vygotsy argued that children are able to attain a higher level of cognitive development through the support and instruction they receive from others.

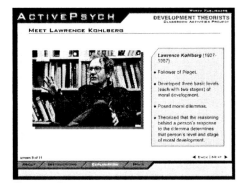

Screen 9

Explanation: Point out that Kohlberg's most popular dilemma is known as the Heinz dilemma (shown below).

The Heinz dilemma: Heinz is a poor man whose wife is dying. A local pharmacist has the only cure, a drug sold for thousands of dollars—far more than Heinz can pay and 10 times what the drug costs to make. Heinz went to everyone he knew to borrow the money, but he could only get together about half of what it cost. He told the druggist that his wife was dying and asked him to sell it cheaper or let him pay later. But the druggist said no. The husband got desperate and broke into the man's store to steal the drug for his wife. Should the husband have done that? Why? (Kohlberg, 1963)

You might have students respond to this dilemma as they would have in their childhood and as they do now (they should explain their reasoning). The chart on the next screen will help students determine the level and/or stage of moral development for themselves at these different ages.

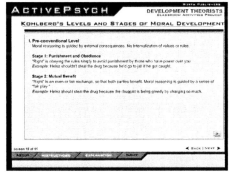

Screen 10

Instructions: Use the forward and back arrows to move between table screens. Read each "Level" and "Stage." Encourage students to share other examples they can think of for each stage.

Note that the summary of the Heinz dilemma was first presented on the explanation tab for the previous screen (screen 9).

Explanation: Help students distinguish the three levels of *pre-conventional*, *conventional*, and *post-conventional* reasoning and the two stages that relate to each.

Point out that children under the age of 10 reflect *pre-conventional* moral reasoning based on self-interest—they avoid punishment and maximize personal gain. From late childhood through adolescence and adulthood, people usually respond with *conventional* moral reasoning. That is, they emphasize social roles, rules, and obligations.

Kohlberg once thought that all people advance to *post-conventional* moral reasoning. In some longitudinal studies, subjects never reached stage 6—the stage in which people choose ethical principles and apply them universally (Colby & others, 1983).

Kohlberg came to believe that most adults are dominated by conventional moral reasoning, which reflects the importance of social roles and rules (Colby & Kohlberg, 1984).

Screen 11

Instructions: Click "Play" to watch a video of an interview with Jared. In this video, Jared discusses his thoughts on faith and religion, right versus wrong, his relationships with his friends and family, his sense of self in terms of his age, his experiences, and his beliefs.

Explanation: If these connections to stages of development don't come up in discussion, point out the following:

Freud: Jared is in the genital stage of Freud's psychosexual stages (due to his age).

Piaget: Jared is in the stage of formal operations in terms of Piaget's stages of cognitive development (due to his ability to consider situations and problems in life by using logic and abstract thinking).

Erikson: Jared is experiencing Erikson's psychosocial crisis of identity vs. role confusion (due to his pondering the questions of who he is and where he might be headed in life).

Kohlberg: Jared is likely to be at the conventional level/stage 3 (Interpersonal expectations) of Kohlberg's levels and stages of moral development (due to his focus on thoughts of conforming to a social norm, plus being a good and honest person).

Development: LIFE-SPAN TIMELINE

Screen 1

This demonstration was written by Andrew Peck, The Pennsylvania State University

About: This activity presents stages in the human life span with the significant events, or milestones, from each stage, presented as illustrations on a timeline or "wheel of time."

For additional information about any screen activity, click on the illuminated gray tab; use the last "Consider This…" activity screen to promote class discussion.

RELATED TOPICS: The developing person, continuity and stages

NOTE: This activity can be use in conjunction with the *ActivePsych* activity "Development Theorists."

Screen 2

Remember, this activity can be used in conjunction with the *ActivePsych* activity "Development Theorists."

Instructions: Roll your mouse over each segment of the wheel to see which segments represent 0–3 and 3–6 years.

To view a full-size photograph that illustrates just one developmental milestone for each age group (0–3 and 3–6 years), click that segment of the wheel. Click the "Back" button to return the photograph to its original position on the wheel.

To see all the photographs at once, click "Show all." Click "Hide All" to send the photographs back to their original positions on the wheel. Click "Play Slide Show" to view a slide show of all the photographs in chronological order.

Explanation: Invite volunteers to share other milestones they have experienced themselves (or observed in others) to add to the milestones presented in the slide shows for ages 0–6. Help students link the milestones with biosocial, cognitive, and psychosocial development.

Encourage students to point out influences related to gender, cultural, or social influences in the milestone images in the slide show, as well as the ones they name.

If students have previously studied development theorists (i.e., Freud, Erikson, Skinner, Piaget, Vygotsky, Kohlberg, etc.) and/or perspectives (i.e., psychoanalytic, behavorial, cognitive, sociocultural, etc.), help them link their ideas stimulated by the milestone illustrations with one of the theorists or perspectives they have studied.

Screen 3

Instructions: Roll your mouse over each segment of the wheel to see which segments represent 6–12 and 12–18 years.

To view a full-size photograph that illustrates just one developmental milestone for each age group (6–12 and 12–18 years), click that segment of the wheel. Click the "Back" button to return the photograph to its original position on the wheel.

To see all the photographs at once, click "Show all." Click "Hide All" to send the photographs back to their original positions on the wheel. Click "Play Slide Show" to view a slide show of all the photographs in chronological order.

Explanation: Invite volunteers to share other milestones they have experienced themselves or observed in others. Help them link those milestones with biosocial, cognitive, and psychosocial development.

Encourage students who have previously studied development theorists (i.e., Freud, Erikson, Skinner, Piaget, Vygotsky, Kohlberg, etc.) and/or perspectives (i.e., psychoanalytic, behavorial, cognitive, sociocultural, etc.) to link their ideas about the milestone illustrations with one of the theorists or perspectives they have studied.

You might pose the following questions for discussion:

–   What are some pressures adolescents experience related to their future career paths and social roles?

–   Does media have a greater influence on development of adolescents than other groups?

–   Do adolescents define themselves differently personally and socially? If so, how does this dichotomy confuse an adolescent's notion of who she is and where she's going in life?

Screen 4

Instructions: Roll your mouse over each segment of the wheel to see which segments represent early, middle, and late adulthood.

To view a full-size photograph that illustrates just one developmental milestone for each age group (early, middle, and late adulthood), click that segment of the wheel. Click the "Back" button to return the photograph to its original position.

To see all the photographs at once, click "Show all." Click "Hide All" to send the photographs back to their original positions on the wheel. Click "Play Slide Show" to view a slide show of all the photographs in chronological order.

Explanation: Invite volunteers to share other milestones for early, middle, or late adulthood. Help students link those milestones with biosocial, cognitive, and psychosocial development or with particular development theorists or perspectives they may have previously studied.

Have students discuss some problems that affect younger adults, including eating disorders (especially anorexia and bulimia), infertility, finding satisfactory relationships (including marriage), and starting a career.

Point out that many in middle adulthood end up in what is now called the *sandwich generation*—that is, adults who care for their own children while also caring for older family members.

Finally, explain that late adulthood is often considered in three phases: *young old* (generally those under 75, well integrated into the lives of families and their communities), *old-old* (generally those over 75, often suffering from physical, mental, or social deficits), and *oldest-old* (generally, those over 85, often dependent on others and requiring supportive services, such as nursing homes or hospital stays).

Screen 5

Explanation: You might ask students if old age is perceived differently than in the past. For example, "How do you determine when old age begins—and how is that determination the same or different than in the past?" Point out that how quickly people age depends in part of their health habits; the more active people remain, the more energy and vitality they retain.

You might also have students consider the influence of sexism or ageism. Point out that research indicates that negative stereotypes about aging do damage only if an older person identifies with them (Levy, 2003).

Sensation and Perception: COLOR SENSATION

Screen 1

This demonstration was written by Thomas E. Ludwig, Hope College

About: This activity includes interactive demonstrations on several aspects of color vision, including the color spectrum, the effect of colored filters, the relationship between wavelength and hue, and the difference between mixing colored lights (additive mixtures) and colored pigments (subtractive mixtures).

For additional information about any screen activity, click on the illuminated gray tab; use the last "Consider This..." activity screen to promote class discussion.

RELATED TOPICS: Sensation, vision, color vision.

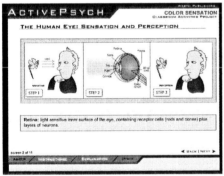

Screen 2

Instructions: Click each "Step" button to see:

- **Step 1** the overall process of sensation, as the light rays bounce off the object and enter the eye, where they trigger neural impulses that are passed to the brain.
- **Step 2** a close-up view of the way light rays are focused by the lens to project an upside-down image on the retina.
- **Step 3** how the person perceives the object.

Explanation: Point out that, the *pupil* is a small, adjustable opening through which light enters the eye.

The *iris* is a colored muscle that adjusts light intake by dilating and contracting the pupil in response to light intensity and, even, to inner emotions—for instance, amorous feelings can cause the pupils to dilate.

Explain that light rays travel in straight lines. So, rays from the top of the flower strike the bottom of the retina, and those from the left side of the flower strike the right side of the retina. The flower's retinal image is thus upside down and reversed.

The layers of neurons in the retina receive signals from the rods and cones and begin the processing of visual information.

Point out that the retina's *rods* are more sensitive to light than its *cones*, which are color sensitive. Some nocturnal creatures are color blind, having only rods that allow them to navigate in the dark. Cones will be discussed in greater detail later in this activity.

Screen 3

Explanation: Explain to students that most humans can distinguish more than seven million different color shades. The shades vary along three dimensions of color sensation: *hue*, *brightness*, and *saturation*.

Hue is what we perceive as color. This dimension of color is determined by the wavelength of light—or the distance from the peak of one light wave to the peak of the next. Point out that hue is measured in nanometers, and a nanometer is a billionth of a meter long.

Brightness is related to the intensity of the light—or the amount of light energy as indicated by the amplitude (height) of the light wave. What we perceive as an increase or decrease in brightness is determined by the relative increase or decrease in the energy of the light as it enters our eyes.

Saturation is the depth or richness of a color—like the difference between red and pink. It is related to the waveform (shape or complexity) of the light wave.

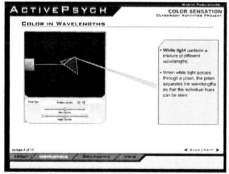

Screen 4

Instructions: Click "Light source" on the prism tool box. Then, click and hold your cursor on the prism and drag it into the beam of light. (NOTE: for the purposes of this experiment, this prism is made of glass.)

Using student suggestions, move the sliders to change the size and shape of the prism.

To rotate the prism, move your cursor over the prism until you see the red dot. As you click the red dot and drag your cursor, the prism will rotate. You can use the clockwise/ counterclockwise buttons to rotate the prism in small increments.

Students will observe the effect of the prism on the beam of light.

Note that the beam of light extends *beyond* the border of the prism tool box so that students can see the full spectrum of color.

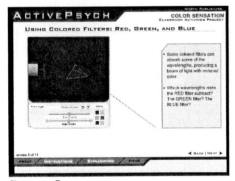

Screen 5

Explanation: Help students understand that a RED filter subtracts short and medium wavelengths, leaving only long wavelengths (which appear red).

A BLUE filter subtracts medium and long wavelengths, leaving only short wavelengths (which appear blue).

A GREEN filter subtracts short and long wavelengths, leaving only medium wavelengths (which appear green).

Instructions: Click "Light source" on the prism tool box. Then, click and hold your cursor on the prism and drag it into the beam of light.

Rotate the prism into a position that will show the full color spectrum, so that the individual wavelengths can be seen.

To rotate the prism, move your cursor over the prism until you see the red dot. As you click the red dot and drag your cursor, the prism will rotate. You can use the clockwise/counterclockwise buttons to rotate the prism in small increments.

To select the filter with which you would like to experiment, click on the RED, GREEN, or BLUE filter button located at the lower-right corner of the prism tool.

Finally, drag the colored filter into the beam of light and observe the effect on the color spectrum emitted through the prism.

Note that the beam of light extends *beyond* the border of the prism tool box so that students can see the full spectrum of color.

Screen 6

Explanation: Help students see and understand that CYAN subtracts only the long wavelengths, MAGENTA subtracts only medium wavelengths, and YELLOW subtracts only short wavelengths.

Instructions: Click "Light source" on the prism tool box. Then, click and hold your cursor on the prism and drag it into the beam of light.

Rotate the prism into a position that will show the full color spectrum, so that the individual wavelengths can be seen.

To rotate the prism, move your cursor over the prism until you see the red dot. As you click the red dot and drag your cursor, the prism will rotate. You can use the clockwise/ counterclockwise buttons to rotate the prism in small increments.

To select the filter with which you would like to experiment, click on the CYAN, MAGENTA, or YELLOW filter button located at the lower-right corner of the prism tool.

Finally, drag the colored filter into the beam of light and observe the effect on the color spectrum emitted through the prism.

Note that the beam of light extends *beyond* the border of the prism tool box so that students can see the full spectrum of color.

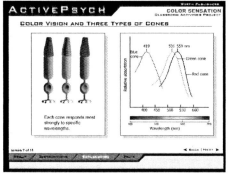

Screen 7

Explanation: Make sure students understand that color vision is possible because we have three types of cones, each tuned to best respond to a particular portion of the color spectrum. But, also remind students that the cones themselves are not colored; they simply respond differently to different wavelengths.

Point out the sensation of "blue" occurs when the short-wavelength cones respond more than the other two; the same is true for "green" and "red." But "yellow" occurs when the long-wavelength and medium-wavelength cones are responding at about the same level, while the short-wavelength cones are quiet.

Further point out that when all three types of cones are active, we sense "white;" when no cones respond, we sense "black."

RELATED THEORY: *Young-Helmholtz* or *trichromatic* theory says that the six or seven million cones within the human retina are divided into three types, and each type is tuned to a different wavelength of light.

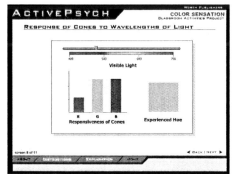

Screen 8

Instructions: Drag the slider slowly to the left or right to vary the wavelength of the light.

Observe the changes in the response level of the three types of cones, and notice how each pattern of cone response produces the sensation of a unique hue.

Explanation: As students respond to the experience of hue when cones respond to visible light, point out that the wavelength of visible light ranges from about 400 to 700 *nanometers*. (A *nanometer* is a billionth of a meter.)

Help students conclude that the color they see depends on the relative response of each type of cone to the various wavelengths.

Screen 9

Instructions: Click each of the lamps on and off individually to see each of the lights by themselves. Then, click two of the lamps on to see what happens when the lights are combined.

When you have tried all combinations of two lights, turn on all three lights. Pay special attention to what happens in the center area (it becomes white light).

Explanation: Point out that when you mix colored lights in an additive process, you add the wavelengths together in the light that enters the eye.

Make sure students see and understand that yellow is a combination of blue and green, magenta is a combination of red and blue, and cyan (light blue) is a combination of blue and green. When all these hues combine, they produce white light, which is a mixture that contains the entire spectrum of wavelengths.

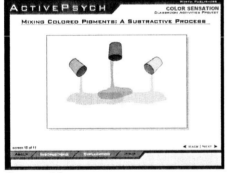

Screen 10

Instructions: Click each can to spill its paint onto the floor. Observe what happens as the paints, or pigments, mix.

Pay special attention to what happens in the center area (it becomes muddy gray pigment).

Explanation: Point out that the paints are pigments (substances that impart color). When you mix colored pigments or paints in a *subtractive process*, you subtract wavelengths from the light reflected into the eye from the pigments (because each pigment absorbs or captures a different group of pigments). If you mix enough pigments, all the wavelengths will be absorbed, thus providing no stimulation for the cones. (You will experience "dark gray" or "black.")

Make sure students see and understand that as you combine pigments, the mixture is darker (more wavelengths absorbed), and that the combination of all three paints produces a muddy gray rather than white.

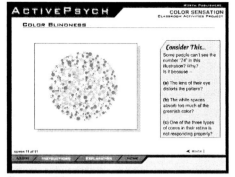

Screen 11

Instructions: Through a show of hands, let students make known which option they think is correct.

Explanation: The option 'C' is the correct response.

Point out that the most common type of color-deficient vision is called "red-green color blindness." Because the greenish dots are similar in brightness to the rest of the pattern, the number disappears when one cone type doesn't work properly.

More specifically, point out that red-green color blindness occurs mostly in males—the deficiency is a sex-linked genetic trait. People with this condition have a problem with either the long-wavelength or medium-wavelength cones, which makes it difficult to tell the difference between certain shades of red and green.

When a person with red-green color blindness looks at this illustration, he will see a random pattern of circles colored in various shades of red and brown. Whereas, a person with normal color vision will see the number 74, composed of circles colored in various shades of green.

Sensation and Perception: THE MCGURK EFFECT

Screen 1

This demonstration was written by Thomas E. Ludwig, Hope College

About: In this activity students consider how people's perception of sounds is influenced by what they see.

Screens 2 through 4 present examples of a person pronouncing several syllables with conflicting visual information. When the visual information does not match the auditory information, most people experience the McGurk effect, an auditory illusion that involves perceiving a syllable different from the one spoken.

For additional information about any screen activity, click on the illuminated gray tab; use the last "Consider This…" activity screens to promote class discussion.

RELATED TOPICS: Language, perception, sensory interaction, visual capture.

Screen 2

NOTE: If you have a large number of students, ask them write down what they hear. Ask for volunteers to describe what they heard.

Instructions: Click "Play" each time you want students to view the video clip. Follow the viewing instructions below.

1st Viewing: While the clip plays, ask students to call out what they hear.

2nd Viewing: Play the clip again and see if there is consensus about the syllable that is heard.

3rd Viewing: Tell students to close their eyes. Play the clip again and ask what syllable they hear.

4th Viewing: Tell students to open their eyes. Play the clip once again and ask for student reactions.

Explanation: Tell students that the video portion of this clip shows a person saying the syllable "fa," but the audio track is taken from a different clip of the same person saying the syllable "ba."

Point out that when listening with eyes closed, most students will hear "ba." But with eyes open, the visual information conflicts with the auditory information. Because the mouth movements associated with the syllable "fa" are very distinctive, the video usually wins. Most students listening with eyes open will hear "fa" (or perhaps "va").

Finally, point out that this is an example of *visual capture*; it shows the dominant role that vision has in our perception of the environment (video "fa" + audio "ba" = perception of "fa").

Screen 3

NOTE: If you have a large number of students, ask them to write down what they hear. Ask for volunteers to describe what they heard.

Instructions: Click "Play" each time you want students to view the video clip. Follow the viewing instructions below.

1st Viewing: While the clip plays, ask students to call out what they hear.

2nd Viewing: Play the clip again and see if there is consensus about the syllable that is heard.

3rd Viewing: Tell students to close their eyes. Play the clip again and ask what syllable they hear.

4th Viewing: Tell students to open their eyes. Play the clip once again and ask for student reactions.

Explanation: Tell students that the video portion of this clip shows a person saying the syllable "ga," but the audio track is taken from a different clip of the same person saying the syllable "ba."

Point out that when listening with eyes closed, most students will hear "ba." But with eyes open, the visual information conflicts with the auditory information. Because the mouth movements associated with the syllable "ga" are NOT very distinctive, the viewer's perceptual system has no clear solution to the problem; so, it selects a syllable that has some visual similarities to "ga" and some auditory similarities to "ba." Most students listening with eyes open will hear the syllable "da" (or perhaps "tha")—and those syllables do not appear in either the video or the audio!

Finally, point out that this finding was first reported by Henry McGurk in 1976; it has come to be called the "McGurk Effect" (video "ga" + audio "ba" = perception of "da").

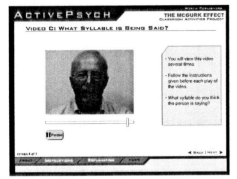

Screen 4

NOTE: If you have a large number of students, ask them write down what they hear. Ask for volunteers to describe what they heard.

Instructions: Click "Play" each time you want students to view the video clip. Follow the viewing instructions below.

1st Viewing: While the clip plays, ask students to call out what they hear.

2nd Viewing: Play the clip again and see if there is consensus about the three syllables that are heard.

3rd Viewing: Tell students to close their eyes. Play the clip again and ask what syllables they hear.

4th Viewing: Tell students to open their eyes. Play the clip once again and ask for student reactions.

You might want to try playing this clip with the audio turned off to see whether students can guess the three syllables actually used in the clip ("ma," "ga," "da").

Explanation: Tell students that the video portion of this clip shows a person saying the syllables "ma," "ga," "da;" but the audio track is taken from a different clip of the same person saying the syllable "ba" three times.

Point out that when listening with eyes closed, most students will hear "ba." But with eyes open, the visual information conflicts with the auditory information. Because the mouth movements associated with the syllable "ma" closely match those associated with "ba," most students will hear "ba" for the first syllable. Because the mouth movements of "ga" and "da" are not similar to "ba," most students will hear "da" and "tha" for the last two syllables.

Screen 5

Explanation: Point out that the auditory illusion of the McGurk Effect (named after the researcher who discovered it) may be based on a "degree of similarity" model in which networks in the brain rank the possible syllables in terms of the degree to which they match the visual information. The networks then do the same for the auditory information. Thus, the person "perceives" the syllable that has the highest ranking.

Further point out that although several different explanations have been proposed, Dominic Massaro, a leading researcher in the area, argues that this explanation has the strongest support (Massaro, 1999).

Screen 6

Instructions: Click "Play" to view a video in which the audio component lags behind the visual component, creating an effect similar to dubbing in movies.

Explanation: Point out that dubbed movies try to match the speech sounds to the position of the speaker's mouth, but often this is not possible. When the visual information does not correspond to the auditory information, it confuses the brain. Viewers find it difficult to understand the words, and the extra effort required to watch a dubbed movie makes viewers tired and unhappy. Viewers would have an easier time understanding the conversation if they closed their eyes—but then they would miss the action!

Students may be interested to know that, in the video clip on this screen, the audio was delayed by one second to produce the "dubbing" effect.

Screen 7

Instructions: Click "Play" to view a video in which the audio track has been removed.

Ask students to raise their hands if they were able to understand what the speaker was saying by "reading" the movements of the mouth and lips.

Explanation: Point out that reading lips demonstrates that some (but not all) of the important information about speech sounds is signalled by the position of the mouth and lips.

The fact that experienced lip-readers can understand 80–90% of a conversation from vision alone helps explain the power of the McGurk Effect. Our brain can't ignore the visual information, even if it conflicts with the auditory information.

Students may be interested to know that the student in the video clip on this screen is saying, "Read my lips." The first instance is spoken at a normal speed; the second instance is in a slower, more exaggerated manner.

Sensation and Perception: THE PONZO ILLUSION

Screen 1

This demonstration was written by Thomas Ludwig, Hope College

About: With this classic visual Ponzo Illusion, the perceived relative size of two objects is distorted by depth cues in the surrounding environment.

This activity consists of two phases with four trials in each.

Using student feedback, you will adjust the height of the yellow bar to match the height of the red bar. (In phase two, the correct height is indicated after each trial.)

At the completion of the four trials within each phase, you'll view graphs about the results.

For additional information about any activity screen, click on the illuminated gray tabs; use the last "Consider This..." activity screen to promote class discussion.

RELATED TOPICS: perception, perceptual illusions, depth perception, monocular clues.

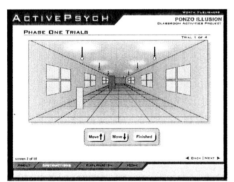

Screen 2

Instructions: Using the "Move" buttons, adjust the yellow bar so that it is the exact height of the red bar.

Ask students to call out "up" or "down" to estimate the length of the yellow bar.

Wait until students have agreed on a final length estimate.

Once students have come to agreement, press "Finished" to move to the next trial.

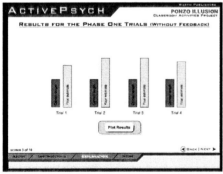

Screen 3

Explanation: The first bar in a pair shows the actual length of the red bar in each of the four trials.

The second bar in a pair is your estimate.

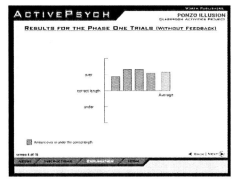

Screen 4

Explanation: The gray bars show your length estimates for each of the four trials, and the blue bar shows your average. (Since most people overestimate the length of the yellow bar, the average is usually over.)

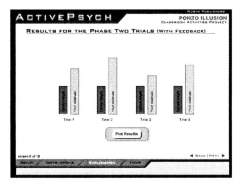

Screen 5

Instructions: Using the "Move" buttons, adjust the yellow bar so that it is the exact height of the red bar.

Ask students to call out "up" or "down" to estimate the length of the yellow bar.

Wait until students have agreed on a final length estimate.

Once students have come to agreement, press "Finished" to see the correct length. Then, press "Move to Next Trial" to move to the next trial.

In Phase Two, feedback will be provided after each trial.

If you have estimated the correct length, you will move immediately to the next trial without receiving feedback.

Screen 6

Explanation: The first bar shows the actual length of the red bar in each of the four trials.

The second bar in a pair is your estimate.

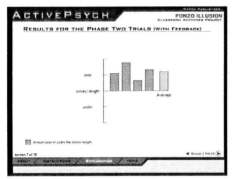

Screen 7

Explanation: The gray bars show your length estimates for each of the four trials, and the blue bar shows your average. (Since most people overestimate the length of the yellow bar, the average is usually over.)

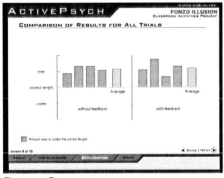

Screen 8

Explanation: The results of all the trials in both phases typically show that viewers overestimate the length of the yellow bar. But, in the trials with immediate feedback, the average error is lower.

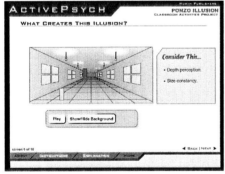

Screen 9

Instructions: Click "Play" to view the animation. For a view without depth cues, click "Show/hide background." (Note that you might want to hide the background before you play the animation for the first time.) To return the lines to their original position, click "Reset."

Explanation: Converging lines (linear perspective) and gradually-changing texture (texture gradient) give the impression that the red bar is more distant than the yellow bar.

The depth cues in the illustration create a strong impression that the yellow bar is closer to the viewer than the red bar.

Through size constancy, the brain corrects the perceived size of an object to adjust for its apparent distance. Therefore, we tend to overestimate the height of the red bar and then compensate by overestimating the length of the yellow bar.

The two bars are exactly the same height and cast identically sized images on the retina. BUT, experience suggests that a more distant object can create an image that appears the same size as the nearer object only if it is actually larger.

Eliminating the background illustration usually destroys the illusion. To demonstrate, click "Show/hide background."

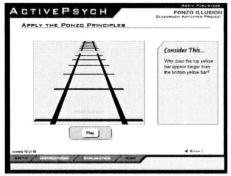

Screen 10

Instructions: Give students a chance to respond to the question. After students have responded, click "Play" to view the animation.

After a few seconds, the yellow bars will move back to their original position. Click "Play" to view the animation again. To return the lines to their original position, click "Reset."

Explanation: The same principles apply to the previous example and this new situation:

Here, the converging lines formed by rails, together with the texture gradient formed by the horizontal railroad ties, create the impression that the top yellow bar is farther off in the distance, while the bottom yellow bar is closer to the viewer.

To maintain size constancy, the brain corrects the apparent size of the two bars, perceptually expanding the top bar and shrinking the bottom bar.

As before, eliminating the background illustration usually destroys the illusion.

Sensation and Perception: SOME VISUAL ILLUSIONS

Screen 1

This demonstration was written by Elaine Epstein. The animations were given by permission.

About: In this activity, you will view some visual illusions and learn more about the principles that create the illusions.

For additional information about any activity screen, click on the illuminated gray tab; use the last "Consider This…" activity screen to promote class discussion.

The source material for this activity was written by Michael Bach. For more information on any of the illusions presented, visit his Web site, "61 Optical Illusions & Visual Phenomena," at: http://www.michaelbach.de/ot

NOTE: Some of the illusions in this activity need to launch in a new browser window. You do not need a live connection to view the illusions, but you may receive a prompt asking you to adjust your security settings for the Macromedia Flash Player.

If you receive this prompt, you will likely be directed to the "Macromedia Flash Player Settings Manager" on the Macromedia Web site. Once you've selected the option to "Always allow," relaunch the illusion from within the ActivePsych shell and it should display properly.

RELATED TOPICS: Sensation, perception; perceptual illusions; perceptual organization; distance, depth or motion perception; perceptual constancy; color; perceptual interpretation, Gestalt

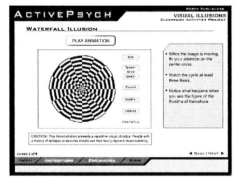

Screen 2

Instructions: To launch the illusion, click "Play Animation." (Note, the illusion will launch in a new window. If you are asked to adjust your security settings, select "Always allow.")

To begin the animation, press "Start." When students have watched the animation AT LEAST three times, press "Stop."

Then, have students cover one eye and observe the illusion through the other eye. Repeat the procedure for students in order for them to change the eye they are looking through.

Experiment with the buttons for increasing or decreasing "Speed." Have students note any changes in how they perceive the Buddha.

To change the direction of the bars and, therefore, the way the Buddha is seen, press the button that toggles between "Expand" and "Contract." To reset to the original settings, click "Defaults."

Explanation: After students describe what they see and speculate about their experience, point out that when you stare at movement in one direction, even for a short time, stationary objects or scenes seen afterward seem to move in the opposite direction.

A researcher, George Mather, reported that the ancient Greeks had noted this phenomenon, called *motion aftereffect*. The first modern report of *motion aftereffect* occurred in 1834 by Robert Addams, who observed the effect at a waterfall in Foyers, Scotland (Mather, Verstraten, & Anstis, 1998).

Further point out that, according to Mathers and other researchers, *motion aftereffect* is explained by adaptation in visual neurons that respond selectively to moving contours in the image. When the image of motion is not present, cells that had been observing one direction produce roughly equal response in the opposite direction (Mather, Verstraten, & Anstis, 1998).

Source: Illusion provided courtesy of Michael Bach, http://www.michaelbach.de/ot/index.html

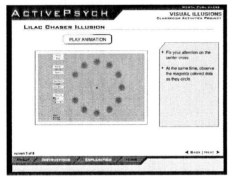

Screen 3

Instructions: To launch the illusion, click "Play Animation." (Note, the illusion will launch in a new window. If you are asked to adjust your security settings, select "Always allow.")

To begin the animation, press "Start."

As students watch the animation, you can change the animation's speed using the "Speed" buttons. Have students note any change in the illusion's effect.

After students have observed the effects of changing the animation's speed, use the "Saturation" buttons to change the depth of the color in the dots.

Set the color saturation to 20 percent or less. As students stare at the center of the screen, the magenta dots should disappear, leaving a single rotating green dot.

In addition, you can change either the dot color or the background color. Have students discuss how altering the color of the dots and background changes the illusion's effect. To reset to the original settings, click "Defaults."

Explanation: After students describe what they see and speculate about their experience, point out that when the magenta dots turn to green, students are experiencing an afterimage of the original color's complement.

Further point out that the illusion (created by Jeremy Hinton) is explained by a "negative retinal afterimage." When one hue stays in the same retinal position for a few seconds, the afterimage builds up as that retinal location adapts to the hue. When looking at a neutral background, the complementary color is seen.

The retinal afterimage usually fades away rapidly (under normal conditions, after a few seconds). In this illusion, though, the afterimage seems to rotate as a new image is uncovered as each previous afterimage fades.

Source: Illusion provided courtesy of Jeremy Hinton.

Screen 4

Instructions: To launch the illusion, click "Play Animation." (Note, the illusion will launch in a new window. If you are asked to adjust your security settings, select "Always allow.")

Students should watch as the tiles move left and right in alternating rows. When the tiles are not vertically aligned, the horizontal lines between the tiles appear to slope alternately upward and downward. This gives the impression that the tiles are wedge-shaped.

As students watch the illusion, start and stop the movement of the tiles (using the "±" button), making sure to stop the movement when the tiles are vertically aligned. Have students compare how the tiles look when they're aligned versus how they look when they're not aligned and in motion.

Students should observe that, when the tiles are vertically aligned or arranged in a checker board pattern, the lines are parallel and the tiles are all square of the same size.

Explanation: After students describe what they see and speculate about the sensation they are experiencing, point out that this illusion is made by possible because of simple image processing in the retina along with more complex processing in the visual cortex of the brain.

Point out that the perception students experience in this illusion occurs because some neurons spark response (excitatory connections) while other neurons thwart response (inhibitory connections). These excitatory and inhibitory neurons balance one another, allowing our visual system to quickly detect features, such as bright and dark contrasts.

Further point out that the converging slopes—with one end of tiles seemingly wide, while the other narrow—is due to processing that occurs in the back of the brain (primary visual cortex), which contains excitatory and inhibitory neurons that detect the orientation of the lines (Ranpura, 2006).

Source: Illusion provided courtesy of Michael Bach, http://www.michaelbach.de/ot/index.html

Screen 5

Source: Illusion provided courtesy of Richard Gregory
http://www.richardgregory.org

Instructions: This screen opens with the animation already playing. To stop and start the animation, press "Pause" or "Play." Students should watch the face mask as it rotates and discuss how the face looks and changes. (Note that the hollow, or negative, version of the face immediately switches back to a positive image.)

Explanation: After students describe what they see, explain that in this illusion the viewer cannot "hold" the "hollow" or negative version of a face, and the mask appears to immediately switch back to a positive view. The positive and negative versions of the mask differ only in the position of the light source.

Further point out that a person's past experiences of human faces influences how they perceive the mask. A face is such a strongly recognizable stimulus that your brain perceives the mask as a positive, rather than negative, image.

Finally, point out that by concentrating on the rod below the mask, the viewer may be able to "hold" onto the negative view, at least a bit longer.

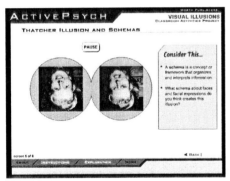

Screen 6

Source: Original illusion was created by Peter Thompson. Animated illusion courtesy of Michael Bach.

Instructions: This screen opens with the animation already playing. To stop and start the animation, press "Pause" or "Play." Students should observe how Margaret Thatcher's face changes when it is in an upright orientation.

Explanation: After students describe what they see (the faces look similar when they are upside down; viewed right-side up, the face on the left looks "normal" and "happy," while the face on the right looks distorted by features that have been inverted), point out that people best understand, or decode, facial expression when viewed in the same orientation the faces are seen in most of the time.

Compared to the first three illusions presented in this activity, this illusion is more about perception than sensation. Mostly, this illusion supports the idea of *Gestalt*—that is, the whole is perceived to be more than the sum of its parts; we automatically process the whole, effortlessly, and it takes time and effort to focus on specific component parts.

You might also want to point out that the photographs are of Margaret Thatcher, Prime Minister of Great Britain from 1979 to 1990 (for whom this illusion was named).

Consciousness: EEG AND THE STAGES OF SLEEP

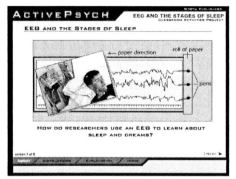

Screen 1

This demonstration was written by Thomas E. Ludwig, Hope College

About: This activity explores stages of sleep through EEG recordings of a research subject as he sleeps.

After students learn about the EEG, the sleep stages, and brain waves emitted during those stages, they will step into a simulated sleep research lab where the electrical brain activity of a sleep research subject is being recorded.

For additional information about any activity screen, click on the illuminated gray tab; use the last "Consider This…" activity screens to promote class discussion.

RELATED TOPICS: Consciousness, biological rhythms, sleep and dreams

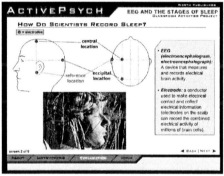

Screen 2

Explanation: Point out these facts: The electroencephalograph was invented by Hans Berger of Germany in the 1920s, but it wasn't until the 1950s that scientists began the kind of EEG recording of sleep that is explored in this activity.

Electrodes placed on a subject's scalp allow the EEG to pick up and record electrical signals from the brain—signals that result when millions of neurons within the brain fire simultaneously.

Explain that EEG researchers use a minimum of two electrodes placed on the scalp at "target" locations. The activity from those electrodes is compared with information from a reference electrode (usually placed on or behind the ear). Many researchers use 16 or 32 scalp electrodes to obtain a more complete profile of brain activity.

Make sure students understand that the EEG shows brain activity from moment to moment, but it can't know what the subject is thinking.

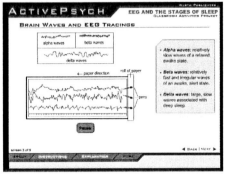

Screen 3

Instructions: Click "Play" to view an animation of EEG tracings showing brain waves during sleep.

To stop the animation, click "Pause." You can also click "Next" to move to the next screen.

Explanation: Point out that the electrical signals that are recorded from the electrodes, after processing and amplification, drive a pen that traces a path on a continuously moving roll of paper.

The paper, which moves at a constant speed, has evenly spaced markings so that the activity recorded on the tracing can be matched to other observations of the sleeping person. (Most researchers also save the EEG information in computer format.)

If researchers look at this tracing, they find a pattern: slower waves are associated with greater relaxation. Brain activity gradually slows as the person drifts to sleep, then gets steadily slower and more regular as the person moves into deeper and deeper sleep.

Help students distinguish *alpha* and *beta* waves as indicators of states of alertness and *delta* waves as indicators of sleep stages.

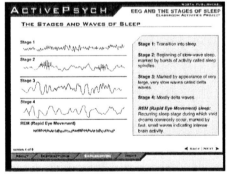

Screen 4

Explanation: Begin by telling students that in the 1950s, graduate student Eugene Aserinsky discovered an EEG pattern that he and the professor who presided over his lab, Nathaniel Kleitman, called REM (short for "rapid eye movement"). This was a milestone in sleep research (Morrison, 2003).

Make sure that students understand the different sleep stages shown in the illustration. To extend their understanding, you can point out that the pace (fast or slow) of the waves is called *frequency* and the depth (high or low) of waves is called *amplitude*.

Explain that, in a typical sleep pattern, a person usually reaches stage 4 within the first 45 minutes of sleep and stays there for only a short time before moving back through the stages in reverse order. A person will pass through all the sleep stages several times each night.

Further point out that, after the person passes back through Stage 2, EEG tracings will show REM sleep—fast and irregular waves, similar to the pattern of alert wakefulness. During REM sleep muscles are relaxed (except for minor twitches) but other body systems are active—hence the reason for another term that describes REM sleep: *paradoxical sleep.*

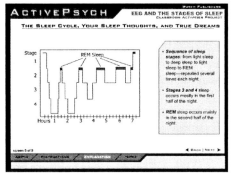

Screen 5

Explanation: Point out that most individuals who sleep six to nine hours per night have three to five periods of REM sleep— experiencing several dreams per night. Dreams are usually forgotten by morning unless you are awakened during the dream or within about three minutes after REM period ends.

Also point out that when sleep subjects are awakened during slow-wave sleep (Stages 2, 3, or 4) about half the time they report no mental activity. But in 50 to 60 percent of cases, subjects experience *sleep thoughts*—thoughts about an issue or event from the previous day, not as vivid or action-packed as a dream.

Further point out that, when awakened during REM sleep, subjects almost always report experiencing an engaging, realistic, or even bizarre sequence of events, called a true dream. In these, subjects report not just *thinking*, but actually *performing* actions that are accompanied by vivid sensory experiences.

Tell students that this helps to explain why REM sleep is sometimes called *paradoxical sleep*—the mind is active but the muscles are relaxed (except for minor twitches).

Screen 6

Instructions: Explain to students that the EEG records the subject's brain waves while he sleeps. The EEG tracings show researchers which stage of sleep the subject is experiencing.

If you want to review the stages of sleep, click "Review Sleep Stages" to see the chart from screen 4.

Click "Hide Stages" to close the chart.

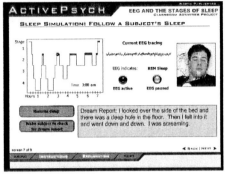

Screen 7

<u>Instructions:</u> This sleep simulation shows a subject's sleep cycle in 15 minute increments across an entire "night." Tell students that the subject is relaxed and drowsy and the electrodes are in place. You will wake the subject several times during the "night" to check whether or not he is dreaming.

Click "Begin Session" to start the simulation. On the graph, students can follow the red dot to watch as the subject passes through each stage of sleep (time of night is indicated in the lower right corner of the box). In addition, students can follow the subject's moment-to-moment brain activity by watching the EEG tracing.

Click "Wake subject to check for dream report" to pause the simulation. At this point, the subject will describe what he was dreaming about (in the "Dream Report" box). To put the subject back to sleep, click "Resume sleep."

You should wake the subject several times during the "night" and tell students to notice how the reports differ with each sleep stage. When you come to the end of sleep cycle, click "Begin Session" to start again.

<u>Explanation:</u> Help students connect the various sleep waves and stages. When the subject is first truly asleep, *spindles*—marked bursts of activity—appear in the EEG tracing. When completely asleep, large and slow *delta waves* appear. During REM sleep, small, frequent waves indicate intense brain activity.

Remind students that *sleep thoughts*—thoughts related to conscious concerns—occur for up to 60 percent of people awakened during slow-wave sleep (stages 2, 3, and 4) and that, during REM sleep, people report *true dreams* (engaging, realistic, often strange, sequences of events in which they are *acting*, not *thinking*).

Finally, remind students that during REM sleep (and for about 10 minutes after) the body's voluntary muscles become paralyzed (and some feel this odd sensation upon awakening). REM sleep is also known as *paradoxical* sleep (internal arousal during external calm).

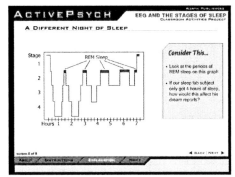

Screen 8

Explanation: Remind students that, during a typical night of six hours or more of sleep, people move from light sleep to deep sleep to light sleep to REM sleep (with approximately three to five periods of REM sleep).

Help students interpret the graph by comparing the two halves of the subject's sleep: The first half shows more time in stages 3 and 4; the second half shows more periods of REM sleep, when vivid dreaming occurs. Therefore, with fewer hours, fewer vivid dreams would probably be reported.

Further point out that after a person reaches stage 4 (usually 45 minutes into the sleep cycle) the first REM period occurs after approximately 90 minutes. The first dream is not as long as dreams in later REM periods, which may last up to an hour.

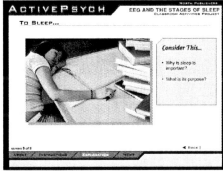

Screen 9

Explanation: Point out to students that this sleep simulation showed that the sleep subject's brain never turned off. The subject's brain was always active while he slept, emitting waves that the EEG could record.

Explain to students that brain activity is reduced by about 10 percent during sleep. Though research into why we sleep is not conclusive, it seems to indicate that this dip in activity may have the following advantages: (1) it reduces energy expenditures so that the body can restore itself, repairing tissue and growing (until the growth process is complete in adulthood); and (2) it allows the brain to organize and consolidate memories of the day's events without distraction.

On the other hand, tell students that the brain's synaptic connections seem to degenerate if not used on a regular basis. So, the brain alternates periods deep sleep with those of intense brain activity (REM sleep and dreams).

Consciousness: ALCOHOL PROGRESSION THROUGH THE BRAIN

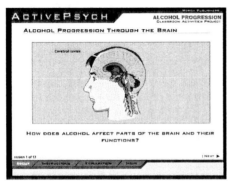

Screen 1

This demonstration was written by Karsten Look, Columbus State Community College

About: This demonstration helps students locate and understand certain brain parts and their functions. (Note: to begin this activity, you can roll your mouse over the various brain structures shown on this screen. As you move your mouse, the names of the structures will be displayed. Let students know that these are the areas of the brain that will be discussed in this activity.)

Some screens juxtapose animations of alcohol's progress in the brain with behaviors that result when that brain part is under alcohol's influence.

Students have the opportunity to speculate about (and then have confirmed through animations) behaviors based on the relationship between alcohol consumption and brain part functions.

For additional information about any activity screen, click on the illuminated gray tabs; use the last "Consider This…" screen to promote class discussion.

RELATED TOPICS: Neuroscience and behavior, localization of the brain, psychoactive drugs and behavior, binge drinking.

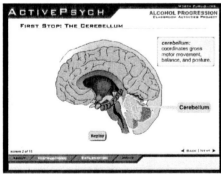

Screen 2

Instructions: Have your students watch an animation that highlights the cerebellum and describes its function.

If you would like to view the animation again, click "Replay."

Explanation: Point out that one of the first noticeable effects from alcohol ingestion and digestion takes place in the cerebellum. Alcohol can inhibit certain functions of the cerebellum.

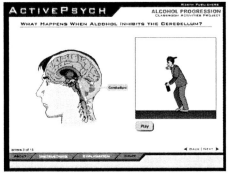

Screen 3

Instructions: Invite students to speculate about, or even act out, a person's possible behavior as alcohol reaches the cerebellum and inhibits it.

Click "Play" to view a person whose cerebellum has been affected by the ingestion of alcohol. If you would like to replay the animation, click "Play" again.

Explanation: Point out that when the cerebellum is inhibited, it becomes difficult to walk and track with your eyes (among other things).

Many tests for drunkenness actually test the functioning of the cerebellum. Police use a field sobriety test—walking (in a straight line, heel-to-toe), touching a fingertip to the nose while the head is tipped back and eyes are closed, standing on one foot, reciting all or part of the alphabet.

Point out that it takes only 30 seconds for ingested alcohol to reach the brain. It takes about an hour to metabolize one drink (1 ounce of liquor, 4 ounces of wine, 12 ounces of beer). Factors that affect blood levels of alcohol are body weight, gender, food consumption, and rate of alcohol consumption. (The interactive body. Retrieved September 14, 2005, from http://www.collegedrinkingprevention.gov/collegestudents

In the U.S., legal limits of alcohol are determined by Blood Alcohol Content (BAC). Someone with a BAC of 0.08 (i.e. 80 mg of alcohol in 100 ml of blood) is over the legal limit for driving.

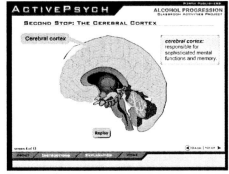

Screen 4

Instructions: Have your students watch an animation that highlights the cerebral cortex and describes its function. If you would like to view the animation again, click "Replay."

Explanation: Point out that when alcohol progresses to the cerebral cortex, tasks involving higher learning and memory are affected. Alcohol can inhibit areas of the cerebral cortex.

Additionally, point out that the cerebral cortex is involved in the regulation of emotional responses. Inhibition of the cerebral cortex can lead to excessive emotional outpourings.

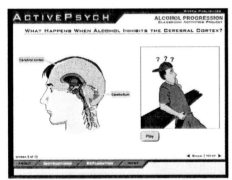

Screen 5

Instructions: Invite students to speculate about, or even act out, a person's possible behavior as alcohol reaches the cerebral cortex and begins to inhibit it.

Click "Play" to view a person whose cerebral cortex has been affected by the ingestion of alcohol. If you would like to replay the animation, click "Play" again.

Explanation: Point out that when the cerebral cortex is inhibited, memory, problem-solving, and other mental functions become impaired.

Also, inhibitions tend to diminish (because the area that helps us plan our actions is also located at the front of the brain).

Bring up this statement by a researcher: "when people have been drinking, the restraining forces of reason may weaken and yield under the pressure of their desires." (Murphy et. al., 1998)

You might point out another interesting finding: intoxicated people have an increased tendency to leave extravagant tips in restaurants (Lynn, 1988).

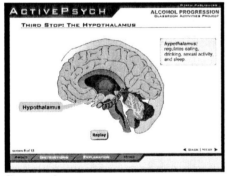

Screen 6

Instructions: Have your students watch an animation that highlights the hypothalamus and describes its function. If you would like to view the animation again, click "Replay."

Explanation: Point out that the hypothalamus helps to regulate a variety of behaviors related to bodily maintenance. For example, the hypothalamus influences hunger, thirst, body temperature, and sexual behavior—and thinking about sex can stimulate the hypothalamus to secrete hormones that in turn prepare the body for sexual activity.

Also point out that the hypothalamus contains "pleasure centers," which can produce a pleasurable sensation when stimulated. Students may be interested to know that when experimenters rigged a lever which rats could push to stimulate their hypothalamic pleasure centers, the rats often did so at a feverish pace (over 100 times per minute) until they dropped from exhaustion (Olds, 1958).

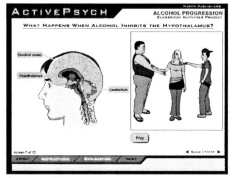

Screen 7

Instructions: Invite students to speculate about, or even act out, a person's possible behavior as alcohol reaches the hypothalamus and inhibits it.

Click "Play" to view a person whose hypothalamus has been affected by alcohol ingestion and digestion. If you would like to replay the animation, click "Play" again.

Explanation: Point out that inhibition of the hypothalamus may cause a person to seek more extreme forms of satisfaction to trigger their pleasure centers.

Help students follow the progress of alcohol on brain parts by reminding them that while the hypothalamus influences sexual drive, the previously affected brain part, the cerebral cortex, is responsible for sophisticated mental function—including decisions or judgments.

RELATED FACT: Some scientists believe that addictive disorders, including alcoholism and drug abuse, may stem from a reward deficiency syndrome—that is, a genetic deficiency in the pleasure centers that leads people to crave whatever may provide that missing pleasure (Blum & others, 1996).

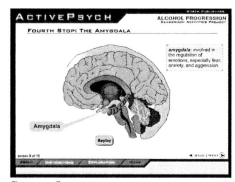

Screen 8

Instructions: Have your students watch an animation that highlights the amygdala and describes its function. If you would like to view the animation again, click "Replay."

Explanation: Point out that the amygdala is involved in the experiences of fear, anxiety, and aggression.

Explain to students that the amygdala influences, but does not control, our feelings of aggression and fear. It also plays a role in our conscious awareness of the positive and negative consequences of our actions.

With normal functioning, the amygdala can bypass the cerebral cortex (LeDoux & Armony, 1999), allowing the body to have an immediate emotional response to a stimulus in less time than it would take the cerebral cortex to rationally process it (for example, when someone reacts to a dark room immediately with fear before considering why the room is dark or what the room really contains).

In addition, the amygdala appears to play a key role in sexual motivation and its inhibition is associated with increased sexual behavior.

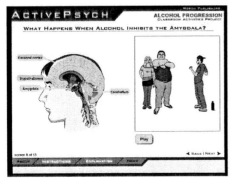

Screen 9

<u>Instructions:</u> Invite students to speculate about, or even act out, a person's possible behavior as alcohol reaches the amygdala and inhibits it.

Click "Play" to view a person whose amygdala has been affected by the ingestion of alcohol. If you would like to replay the animation, click "Play" again.

<u>Explanation:</u> When a person's amygdala is inhibited from excessive alcohol consumption, the person may become less anxious and fearful. This inhibition may explain feelings of calmness and the abatement of stress, anger, and anxiety that are associated with drinking. However, inhibition of the amygdala may also provoke people to fearlessly approach situations where a little fear or anxiety might serve them well—often with unpleasant consequences.

An interesting finding about the amygdala: When researchers surgically lesioned the part of an aggressive monkey's brain that contains the amygdala, the monkey acted mellow even when poked, prodded, or pinched. It also showed symptoms of hypersexual behavior (Klüver, 1939).

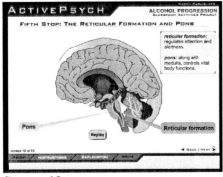

Screen 10

<u>Instructions:</u> Have your students watch an animation that highlights the reticular formation and pons and describes their functions. If you would like to view the animation again, click "Replay."

<u>Explanation:</u> Point out that when these brain structures stop functioning normally, an intoxicated person passes out.

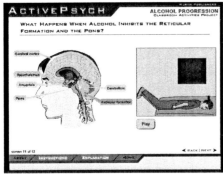

Screen 11

<u>Instructions:</u> Invite students to speculate about, or even act out, a person's possible behavior as alcohol reaches these brain structures and hampers them from functioning properly.

Click "Play" to view a person whose reticular formation and pons have been affected by the ingestion of alcohol. If you would like to replay the animation, click "Play" again.

<u>Explanation:</u> Tell students that, unfortunately, the results can be fatal if you pass out and your brain gives out the signal to vomit. (NOTE: Students will learn the reason for this on the last "Consider This…" screen of this activity.)

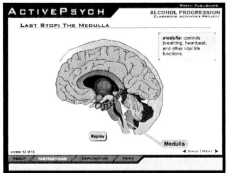

Screen 12

Instructions: Have your students watch an animation that highlights the medulla and describes its function. If you would like to view the animation again, click "Replay."

Once they have watched the animation, invite students to consider what happens when the medulla becomes inhibited because of alcohol consumption. (NOTE: Correct responses will be confirmed during discussion prompted by material on the next screen.)

Screen 13

Explanation: Point out that when people drink a lot of alcohol very fast, the control centers of the medulla can become inhibited, causing death. With slower alcohol consumption over a period of time, people usually pass out before the medulla becomes inhibited.

Additionally, when people die after passing out and vomiting, it is usually because they are unable to clear their face (because they are unconscious); they breathe the vomit into their lungs and die from asphyxiation.

Point out that the legendary rock musician Jimi Hendrix, pictured above, died from asphyxiation after he passed out and was unable to clear vomit from his mouth. Also point out that this reaction resulted from the combination of alcohol and barbiturates. Students should be aware that, since different drugs affect the brain in different ways, the effects of alcohol may be dangerously amplified by the use of other drugs.

RELATED FINDINGS: Of 119 colleges in a national survey, close to 50 percent of males and 40 percent of females engaged in binge drinking—that is, four or more drinks for women and five or more drinks for men in an hour. (Wechsler & others, 2002).

Aggressive behavior, sexual assault, accidents, and property damage are related to binge drinking (Hingson et. al., 2002; Wechsler et. al., 2002). Challenge students to relate those behaviors to the progression of alcohol through the brain.

Learning and Memory: THE STROOP EFFECT

Screen 1

This demonstration was written by Jennifer O. Peluso, Florida Atlantic University

About: This activity is based on findings from the original 1935 thesis by John Ridley Stroop.

Stroop tasks demonstrate how interference affects making choices and influences a person's ability to control what he or she pays attention to.

Either a class volunteer or small groups of three students each will perform the three Stroop asks in this activity.

For additional information about any activity screen, click on the illuminated gray tabs; use the "Consider This…" activity screens to promote class discussion.

RELATED TOPICS: Memory, automatic processing, retrieval, context effects, recognition, priming.

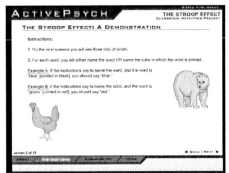

Screen 2

Instructions: The Stroop task lists (each accompanied by instructions) appear on screens 4 though 6.

Divide the class into groups of three students each: speaker, time keeper, and answer recorder. Each group will perform all three Stroop tasks. [NOTE: If you have an large number of students, you may want to have three volunteers perform the demonstration for the rest of the class.]

You will provide each group of students with a response sheet on which to record results from all three Stroop task. (Note that the printable response sheet is available on screen 3.)

Screen 3 provides further instructions on roles for group members.

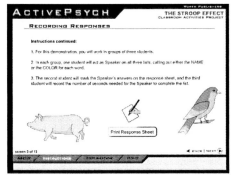

Screen 3

Instructions: Make sure that each group has a response sheet. (Click "Print Response Sheet." Once you have opened the PDF response sheet file, you can print and distribute copies to each group.)

A stop clock will appear along with the tasks on screens 4 through 6.

When you say "Go," you will start the clock, the task list will appear on screen, and speakers can begin their task.

Speakers should work from top to bottom of each list and as quickly as possible. (REMINDER: The same group speaker should perform all three tasks.)

Recorders should mark correct answers on the response sheet and, afterward, record the number of errors a speaker made.

Time keepers should watch the clock to track the seconds it takes their speaker to complete a task. (Time is also recorded on the response sheet.)

Screen 4

Instructions: For this task, speakers are asked to name the printed word, such as "red" or "blue" for the item in each row.

Remind student speakers to work from the top to the bottom of the list and to begin as soon as the list appears.

When you say "Go" (and click "Start"), the clock will begin to record the task time, the list will appear on screen, and speakers can begin their task.

Click "Stop" when a class speaker or all group speakers have finished. The list will remain on screen. Allow time for students to check the speakers' answers against the list items. Then move to the next task on screen 5.

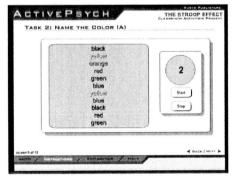

Screen 5

Instructions: For this task, speakers are asked to name the color in which the item on each row is printed. For instance, if the word "red" were colored blue, the answer would be "blue."

Remind speakers to work from the top to the bottom of the list and to begin as soon as the list appears. If the speakers make errors and correct themselves, recorders should write the final answer on the response sheet.

When you say "Go!" (and click "Start"), the clock will begin to record the task time, the list will appear on screen, and then speakers can begin their task.

Ask groups to indicate when they have completed the task. Click "Stop" when all group speakers have finished. The list will remain on screen. Allow time for students to check the speakers' answers against the list items. Then move to the last task on screen 6.

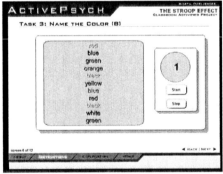

Screen 6

Instructions: For this task, speakers are asked to name the color in which the item on each row is printed. For instance, if the word "red" were colored blue, the answer would be "blue."

Remind student speakers to work from the top to the bottom of the list and to begin as soon as the list appears.

When you say "Go" (and click "Start"), the clock will begin to record the task time, the list will appear on screen, and speakers can begin their task.

Click "Stop" when a class speaker or all group speakers have finished. The list will remain on screen. Allow time for students to check the speakers' answers against the list items.

The next screen presents a definition and discussion of the Stroop effect in relationship to the tasks they have just completed.

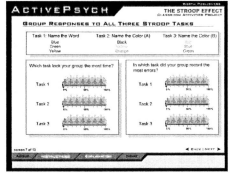

Screen 7

Instructions: Ask the groups to compare the time needed to complete each of the three lists, and then record the class responses by using the sliders on this screen.

Ask the groups to compare the number of errors made on each of the three lists, and then record the class responses by using the sliders on this screen.

Then, encourage the groups to try to analyze the types of errors that the speaker made.

Explanation:

In most cases, groups will find that the length of time and number of errors increased from Task 1 through Task 3 because of the increased incidence of potential interference presented in each of the three task lists. (Task 1 presented no interference; Task 2 presented facilitation with little or no interference; Task 3—with colors not matching the words named—presented interference.)

NOTE: Reasons for individual task results (no interference, facilitation, interference) are presented and discussed on screens 9 through 11, following a presentation of the definitions for *Stroop effect* and *interference theory* on screen 8.

Screen 8

Explanation: Point out that most adults are inclined to first respond to one particular feature of an item: the *meaning* of a printed word.

Furthermore, if people are inclined to automatically respond to a particular item feature (say, *meaning* of a word), the response to that feature interferes when attempting to identify another item feature (say, *color* of a printed word).

Reinforce what students may have already guessed from their group test experiences: people can't help but respond to certain features automatically.

NOTE: Task results and reasons for those results are presented and discussed on screens 9 through 11.

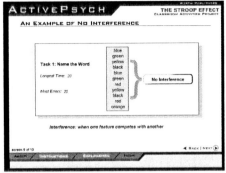

Screen 9

Instructions: Ask students the relationship between "No interference" and their results from Task 1.

When you click "No interference," the expected reason for the results in Task 1 is displayed.

Note that the class results recorded on Screen 7 are displayed beside "Longest Time" and "Most Errors."

Explanation: Tell students that in the Task 1 list speakers were asked to identify a feature (name of word) about items that probably seemed automatic to them—that is, the *meaning* of printed words.

The task was probably easy to do; reading was automatic so speakers were probably very fast on this list; speakers probably made no or very few errors.

OPTIONAL: You might want to present the term *automatic processing*, which means: "unconscious encoding (processing of information into the memory system) of incidental information, such as space, time, and frequency of well-learned information, such as word meanings."

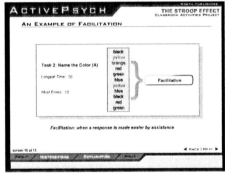

Screen 10

Instructions: Ask students the relationship between "Facilitation" and their results from Task 2.

When you click "Facilitation," the expected reason for the results in Task 2 is displayed.

Note that the class results recorded on Screen 7 are displayed beside "Longest Time" and "Most Errors."

Explanation: Remind students that in the Task 1 list only one feature changed from row to row—the printed word.

Point out that in the Task 2 list both words *and* colors appear, but the words themselves were the names of the colors in which the words were printed. Although the words themselves are processed more automatically than the color in which they are printed, both features provide the same information.

In this case, the relationship between the two features of each item facilitated, or allowed, a speaker to make the identification that was requested (name the color).

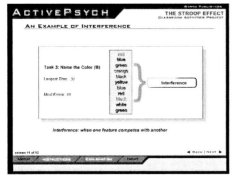

Screen 11

Instructions: Ask students the relationship between "Interference" and their results from Task 3.

When you click "Interference," the most expected reason for the results in Task 3 is displayed.

Note that the class results recorded on Screen 7 are displayed beside "Longest Time" and "Most Errors."

Explanation: Tell students that in the Task 3 list group speakers were asked to identify a feature (name of color) of items that probably did not seem as automatic to them as the requested identifications of features on lists for Task 1 and Task 2.

The feature that seemed automatic to speakers (meaning of words) probably interfered and made the task (naming the color) more difficult.

The Task 3 list was probably not as easy as the lists for Tasks 1 and Task 2; speakers were probably slower on the Task 3 list; speakers also probably made more errors.

OPTIONAL: For students who learned about *automatic processing* in the class discussion on screen 9, point out that automatic processing of information into the memory system created interference when speakers were asked to respond to color rather than word meaning.

Screen 12

Explanation: Point out that reading is a task most adults do automatically (after years of practice). Children do not read automatically—they may just be learning to read or may not even know the words used as items in a Stroop task.

Adults, though, may have more difficulty identifying colors because that is not a skill they use more often or more automatically than reading words for meaning.

Interestingly, on the other hand, children are often asked to identify or label by color. That may affect how automatically they can name colors of items in Stroop tasks.

Screen 13

Explanation: Explain to students that in this Stroop task the friend should be asked to name the feature of the words and items, rather than the words and items themselves.

Further explain that the challenge for the friend would be to name the features and to ignore the more automatic response, which would be to name the printed word.

For example, naming the animal would be easy in the case of the chicken, but difficult in the other cases, because the nearby word interferes with the process and would be read automatically.

Learning and Memory: LEVELS OF PROCESSING

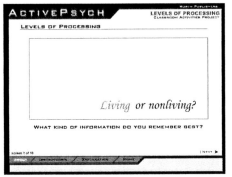

Screen 1

This demonstration was written by Antoinette R. Miller, Clayton State University

About: Using the recall demonstration in this activity, students will determine whether visual, auditory, or semantic encoding of words results in better memory retention.

In each of three recall tasks, a list of 10 words is presented to the class. Students are given a question (visually-oriented, acoustically-oriented, semantically-oriented) and then asked to view the list. After students complete a recall task for each list, the results will be graphed and compared.

Recall tasks are presented on screens 3 through 5. On screen 6, you will gather information about student responses. Screens 7 and 8 offer an analysis and discussion of the results.

For additional information about any activity screen, click on the illuminated gray tab; use the last "Consider This…" activity screens to promote class discussion.

RELATED TOPICS: Memory, information processing, encoding, retrieval, levels of processing.

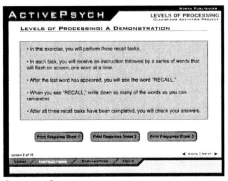

Screen 2

Instructions: Provide students with a response sheet for each of the three recall tasks presented in this exercise. To print the response sheet, click "Print Response Sheet" (1, 2, or 3). Once you have opened the PDF response sheet files, you can print and distribute copies to your students.

To begin each task, you will: hand out the appropriate response sheet; verbally give students a task instruction; and click "Begin" to start the display of words.

Important: Tell students they should NOT look at any response sheet before they begin the task; they should HIDE the sheets before they begin the second and third tasks (so that they are not used as retrieval cues); and they CANNOT take notes while the words are flashing.

After you click "Begin," 10 words will flash on screen one at a time (for two seconds each). The last word displayed in each task is "RECALL."

When students see the word "RECALL," they should write as many of the flashed words as they remember on the response sheet. "RECALL" will remain on screen for 90 seconds (until it changes to the word "STOP"). When "STOP" is displayed, the recall task ends. Students should stop writing and hide their response sheets before you move on to recall tasks 2 and 3.

Screen 3

Instructions: Provide students with the response sheet for the first recall task. Tell students they should NOT look at the response sheet and they CANNOT take notes while the words are flashing.

BEFORE you click "Begin Task 1," tell students the following: ***Ten words will flash on screen, one word every two seconds. Your task is to note whether or not the word contains the letter "e."*** Then, click "Begin Task 1."

After the tenth word has flashed on screen, the word "RECALL" will remain on screen for 90 seconds. While "RECALL" is displayed, students should pull out the provided response sheet, write down as many words as they remember, and answer the response sheet question (a reiteration of your original instruction).

After 90 seconds, "RECALL" will change to "STOP." Students should stop writing and put away their response sheets (so that they are not used as retrieval cues).

When students have completed Task 1, click "Next" to go to Task 2.

Screen 4

Instructions: Provide students with the response sheet for the second recall task. Tell students they should NOT look at the response sheet and they CANNOT take notes while the words are flashing.

BEFORE you click "Begin Task 2," tell students the following: ***Ten words will flash on screen, one word every two seconds. Your task is to note how many syllables are in each word.*** Then, click "Begin Task 2."

After the tenth word has flashed on screen, the word "RECALL" will remain on screen for 90 seconds. While "RECALL" is displayed, students should pull out the provided response sheet, write down as many words as they remember, and answer the response sheet question (a reiteration of your original instruction).

After 90 seconds, "RECALL" will change to "STOP." Students should stop writing and put away their response sheets (so that they are not used as retrieval cues).

When students have completed Task 2, click "Next" to go to Task 3.

Screen 5

Instructions: Provide students with the response sheet for the third recall task. Tell students they should NOT look at the response sheet and they CANNOT take notes while the words are flashing.

BEFORE you click "Begin Task 3," tell students the following: ***Ten words will flash on screen, one word every two seconds. Your task is to note whether the word represents a LIVING or NONLIVING thing.*** Then, click "Begin Task 3."

After the tenth word has flashed on screen, the word "RECALL" will remain on screen for 90 seconds. While "RECALL" is displayed, students should pull out the provided response sheet, write down as many words as they remember, and answer the response sheet question (a reiteration of your original instruction).

After 90 seconds, "RECALL" will change to "STOP." Students should stop writing.

At this point, students can pull out their response sheets from tasks 1 and 2. When you move to the next screen, students will check their answers and you will record the class results.

Screen 6

Instructions: Have students check the words they recalled against the full word lists from each of the three recall tasks. Make sure students enter the total number of words they correctly recalled at the bottom of each sheet. That number will indicate the percentage of words they recalled in each task—for example, if they correctly recalled 3 words they recalled 30 percent of the list.

When students have finished checking their Task 1 results, click the "Go To…" button to check their results for Tasks 2 and 3. When they have finished checking their results against all three word lists, click "Record Class Results."

Ask students to raise their hands if they recalled a higher percentage of Task 1 words (that is, if they recalled more words on Task 1 than they did in either Tasks 2 or 3). Then, using the sliders, record the percentage of students who raise their hands. Repeat this procedure for Tasks 2 and 3.

The class percentage results will be displayed on screen 8 so that you can contrast your students results with the results from similar research on levels of processing in memory recall by Fergus Craik and Endel Tulving.

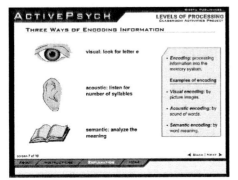

Screen 7

Explanation: Make sure students connect the Task 1 instruction to *visual encoding* (the *appearance* of the words; words with the letter "e"), the Task 2 instruction to *acoustic encoding* (the *sound* of the words; number of syllables), and the Task 3 instruction to *semantic encoding* (the *meaning* of the words; living vs. nonliving).

Point out that rhymes and jingles in advertising use acoustic encoding to help with memory retention. Most people remember a rhyming phrase better than a non-rhyming sentence with the same basic meaning. For instance, "no pain, no gain" is more easily remembered than "If you don't feel discomfort, you most likely will not become stronger."

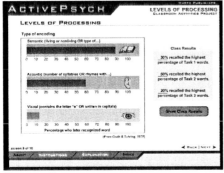

Screen 8

Instructions: Have students speculate which type of encoding produced word recall in the largest number of people in the Craik and Tulving recall study.

To view the study results, click each icon on the graph (the *eye*, *ear*, or *book*). The percentage of people who later recognized words from the Craik and Tulving recall study will be displayed on the graph. Notice the higher percentage produced with each style of encoding.

When students have finished discussing the Craik and Tulving results, click "Show Class Results" to display the class recall percentages recorded on screen 6. Invite students to compare their results with those from the study. Did more students remember a higher percentage of words using visual encoding? Acoustic encoding? Semantic encoding?

Explanation: As students look at the results from the Craik and Tulving (1975) recall study, explain that these researchers found that processing a word deeply (by its meaning) produces better recognition of it at a later time than does shallow processing (by attending to a word's appearance or sound).

Students may be interested to know that Craik and Tulving performed their experiment on students, in a study similar to the one in which your own class has just participated. For the words on their list, they asked the following questions: "Is the word in capital letters" (note that less than 15 percent of the students remembered the words); "Does the word rhyme with *train*?" (just under 60 percent of the students remembered the words); and "Would the word fit in this sentence: "The girl put the _____ on the table " (just under 90 percent of the students remembered the words).

Screen 9

Explanation: Explain that, essentially, any method that requires a person to pay attention to the meaning of the word constitutes semantic processing of information.

You might help students by listing some ways of processing information semantically. For example students might:

– restate new information in their own words to make sure it is understood.

– relate new information to material they already know (seeking connections that make the information meaningful).

– find their own examples of the new information, especially from personal experiences.

– decide if the information would fit into a particular sentence (i.e. "Can you buy _____ at the grocery store?" "Is _____ bigger than a loaf of bread?").

– create fictional stories about the concepts.

– try teaching the information to someone else.

Screen 10

Explanation: Remind students that any method that requires students to think about the *meaning* of a concept is processing at the semantic level, and those methods would be more beneficial than straight rote memorization.

For instance, students might use any of the methods of semantic encoding presented on the previous screen (screen 9).

Learning and Memory: SERIAL POSITION EFFECT

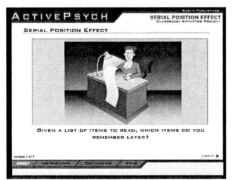

Screen 1

This demonstration was written by Antoinette R. Miller, Clayton State University

About: In this activity, students participate in an exercise that demonstrates the serial position effect—that is, our tendency to recall best the last and first items from a list.

Students are shown 20 words, one at a time; afterward, they are asked to list the words they remember. Results of student recall are then presented in a bar graph that the class can analyze in relationship to the serial position effect.

For additional information about any activity screen, click on the illuminated gray tab; use the last "Consider This…" activity screens to promote class discussion.

RELATED TOPICS: Memory, information processing, encoding, retrieval.

Screen 2

Instructions: You will provide students with a response sheet on which to record the words they remember. To print the response sheet, click "Print Handout." Once you have opened the PDF handout file, you can print copies for your students.

Tell students they CANNOT take notes as the words in the list flash on the next screen.

Further, tell students that the last word on demonstration screen 3, "RECALL," is NOT part of the list. It is a cue for students to begin writing down as many of the words as they can remember on their response sheet.

The word "RECALL" will appear on screen for two minutes. After two minutes has passed, a message will tell students, "Get ready to check your responses." With that message, the next activity screen will automatically appear.

Screen 3

Instructions: To begin displaying the list of 20 words, click "Show Word List."

After all 20 words have been displayed, students will see the word "RECALL."

"RECALL" will appear on screen for two minutes. During this time, students should write down the words they remember from the list.

Once you see the message "Get ready to check your responses" you can move to the next screen.

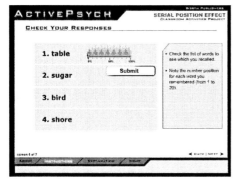

Screen 4

Explanation: A chart that shows words students recalled is presented on the next screen.

Before you move to that screen, you might have students speculate about the words remembered from the list. Can they draw any conclusions about which words were remembered, and why?

Instructions: Explain to students that they should check their lists of recalled words against the word list as it is displayed on screen. The original word list will be displayed four words at a time.

Tell students that they should make note of the number position (from 1 to 20) of each word they recalled from the list. This information will be useful when students view the results of this demonstration on the next screen (screen 5).

When students are ready to begin checking their lists, click "First Four Words" to show the first four words from the list.

For each word, note the percentage of students who remembered the word correctly and move the slider to indicate that percentage.

After recording the information, click "Next Four Words" to continue checking the student responses. Once you've checked all 20 words, move to the next screen to see the class results.

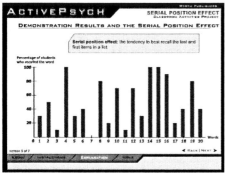

Screen 5

Explanation: Point out that serial means "arranged in a series; by rank or row." The serial position effect relates to the first and last positions in just about any kind of list of items, numbers, or concepts—including concepts and terms as they are positioned and presented in an introduction to psychology textbook!

RELATED TERMS: Remembering the first few items is called the *primacy effect*, and remembering the last few items is called the *recency effect.*

The serial position effect occurs through a combination of the primacy and the recency effects.

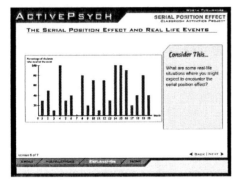

Screen 6

Explanation: Help students brainstorm situations by making a few suggestions, such as meeting people at a party, remembering phone numbers, directions, and memorizing lines in a play or speech.

So, the last few names someone learns at a party may be remembered in the short term since they are the most recently learned (the *recency effect*).

But, if you rehearse the names of everyone you meet at the party, you will have rehearsed the first names more often than the names learned at the party's middle or end. In that case, the first names are remembered best (the *primacy effect*).

Note that, when there is a delay in time between viewing the list and recalling the items, the primacy effect remains but the recency effect has less potency the longer the delay.

RELATED CONCEPTS: Rehearsal is the conscious repetition of information, either to maintain it in consciousness or to encode it—that is, process information into the memory system.

Screen 7

Explanation: Help students apply the concept of serial position effect to their need to rehearse parts of a list equally—from vocabulary in language courses to equations in math classes to dates of important events in history to principles and concepts in any course of study, including psychology!

Automatic processing is the unconscious encoding of incidental information and well-learned information—like the meanings of words used often.

On the other hand, some items and concepts require greater effort or *effortful processing*—that is, encoding the items into memory requires attention and conscious effort.

RELATED CONCEPTS: In addition to rehearing items and concepts in all positions from a list, suggest that some items students learn by studying might be processed into memory automatically.

Thinking, Language, and Intelligence: THE AVAILABILITY HEURISTIC

Screen 1

This demonstration was written by Martin Bolt, Calvin College

About: This activity demonstrates the *availability heuristic*: Estimating the likelihood of events based on how readily they come to mind.

Students will make judgments between two possibilities about various categories—from populations of refugees and threatened mammal species to caloric content of snacks.

Student judgments will be recorded on screen and later discussed along with related facts.

For additional information about any activity screen, click on the illuminated gray tabs; use the last "Consider This…" activity screens to promote class discussion.

RELATED TOPICS: heuristics, organizing concepts, decisions and judgments, thinking.

Screen 2

NOTE: A discussion of the availability heuristic is presented on Screen 5.

Class choices are presented, along with the correct answers, on Screen 6.

Instructions: Click the button next to a pair of countries, and those countries will be highlighted on the world map.

For each of the 3 pairs of countries, ask the class which country has the larger refugee population. Once you have brought the class to consensus, click the country label that indicates the class choice. (The star shows that their choice has been recorded.)

Explanation: Use this information about refugee populations to tell students whether their choices were correct or incorrect. (Note that the information should NOT be used to help students make their choices.)

- Kenya: 233,700 /Sweden: 142,200
- Germany: 903,000 / United States: 485,200
- India: 168,900 / China: 297,300

SOURCE: UNHCR, 2002 as quoted in *Economist* (2005). *Pocket World in Figures*, 2005 Edition. London: Profile Books, p. 25.

Screen 3

NOTE: A discussion of the availability heuristic is presented on Screen 5.

Class choices are presented, along with the correct answers, on Screen 6.

Instructions: Click the button next to a pair of countries, and those countries will be highlighted on the world map.

For each of the 3 pairs of countries, ask the class which country has more mammal species under threat. Once you have brought the class to consensus, click the country label that indicates the class choice. (The star shows that their choice has been recorded.)

Explanation: Use this information about mammal species under threat to tell students whether their choices were correct or incorrect. (Note that the information should NOT be used to help students make their choices.)

- United States: 37 / Indonesia: 147
- Australia: 63 / Japan: 37
- Russia: 45 / Brazil: 81

SOURCE: Economist (2005). *Pocket World in Figures*, 2005 Edition. London: Profile Books, p. 106.

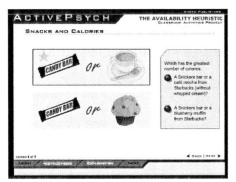

Screen 4

NOTE: A discussion of the availability heuristic is presented on Screen 5.

Class choices are presented, along with the correct answers, on Screen 6.

Instructions: In the gray box, you can click the button to highlight the picture of that pair of snacks.

For each of pair of snacks, ask the class which has the greatest number of calories. Once you have brought the class to consensus, click the picture that indicates the class choice. (The star shows that their choice has been recorded.)

Explanation: Use this information about beverages, food, and candy bars to tell students whether their choices were correct or incorrect. (Note that the information should NOT be used to help students make their choices.)

- 16 oz café mocha from Starbucks (without whipped cream): 300 calories
- regular size Snickers bar: 266 calories
- blueberry muffin from Starbucks: 380 calories

SOURCES: Nutritional information for Starbucks beverages and fresh foods. Retrieved July 21, 2005 from http://www.starbucks.com/retail/nutrition_info.asp

McDonald's USA nutritional facts for popular menu items. Retrieved July 21, 2005 from http://www.nutritiondata.com/facts-001-02s047p.html

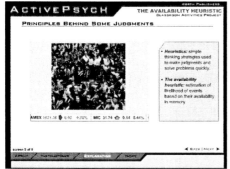

Screen 5

Explanation: Point out that people often employ a general rule of thumb to reduce the number of possible situations, and the time it takes to make decisions, and this strategy may produce errors.

Also point out that with the availability heuristic, available memory may be available because it's vivid. Instances that readily come to mind may be presumed as common even if, factually, they are not.

To extend discussion, have students point out ways in which the availability heuristic confuses statistical facts with common knowledge—for example, in sports: "Do the best statistics belong to the most well-known players?" or in the stock market: "Do the daily largest profits come from companies whose names people are familiar with?" (Colet, 1999).

Screen 6

Explanation: The results are based on your students' choices along with the correct answers from questions posed on screens 2, 3, and 4 about refugee populations, species of mammals under threat, and the calorie content of snacks.

Most people use a rule of thumb in which they estimate the likelihood of events (or circumstances) based on how readily the events come to mind (or are "available in memory")—and that is the availability heuristic.

In each of the judgments made on the previous screens, the more "available" or vividly remembered alternative is most often chosen even when it is factually incorrect.

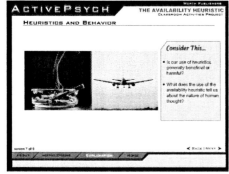

Screen 7

Explanation: Share with students this example of making a decision without the use of heuristics: If you didn't have a memory of using an index to find something in a source, you might start reading every word of a book, beginning with page 1, to find the mention of "Einstein" on page 540.

Individual decisions based on the availability heuristic may be grossly misguided. For instance, many feared flying after the September 11th attacks of 2001. But 266 more Americans died in car accidents that year than in the four plane flights from that day. (Gigenerenzer, 2004)

Human nature might make us easily turn to, and depend on, vivid memory when making quick judgments. However, facts must be taken into account in order to make sound judgments and accurate decisions.

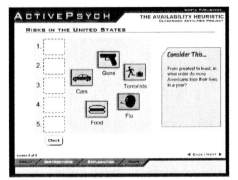

Screen 8

Instructions: Ask students to call out which item has the greatest risk for Americans. As students respond, drag the item to its suggested position on the list (from 1 to 5).

When you have dragged all five items into position, click "Check." Items in the correct position will remain in place. Incorrectly placed items will bounce back to their original position. Continue with the exercise until all five items are correctly placed.

Correct order of risk: 1. cars; 2. flu; 3. guns; 4. food; 5. terrorism.

Explanation: Point out that during his presidency, George W. Bush spoke about risks to Americans from WMDs (Weapons of Mass Destruction)—and that 500,000 lives could be lost in such an event.

In counterpoint, years do not go by without American deaths from car accidents, flu (along with pneumonia, a related disease), gun use, or food-borne illnesses.

Enhance class discussion by telling students that Ivo Daalder (an ex-national security officer and author) said of U.S. foreign policy focused mainly on threats from WMD: "There are worse threats out there. Climate change. H.I.V./AIDS."

Enhance discussion further with Norman Minetta (the U.S. Transportation Secretary in 2004), who said about comparing deaths from plane and car accidents: "If we had 115 people die a day in aviation crashes, we wouldn't have a plane in the sky." (Kristof, 2004)

Screen 9

Explanation: As an example, you might want to point out a big story from the 1990s about Jessica McClure, a little girl from Texas who fell into a well and was rescued three days later.

The U.S. Vice President at that time compared Jessica's struggle with statistics about children worldwide: During a similar three-day period, over 100,000 children worldwide died of preventable starvation, diarrhea, and disease (Gore, 1992).

You might want to challenge students to think of a more recent media story that captivated the attention of many viewers or listeners while omitting facts that point out a broader picture about a similar situation.

Thinking, Language, and Intelligence: THE CONFIRMATION BIAS

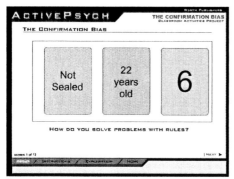

Screen 1

This demonstration was written by Jennifer O. Peluso, Florida Atlantic University

About: This activity demonstrates how people use the confirmation bias to solve problems, often incompletely if not incorrectly.

Students will be asked to play three versions of a game. Each version involves making choices about a set of four cards, with each set related to a rule. Class choices for solving the problems will be discussed in light of the confirmation bias.

For additional information about any activity screen, click on the illuminated gray tab; use the last "Consider This…" activity screens to promote class discussion.

RELATED TOPICS: Thinking, problem-solving, obstacles to problem-solving.

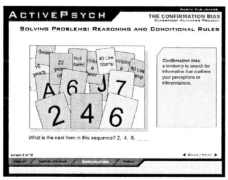

Screen 2

Explanation: After students have had a chance to consider the *confirmation bias* (a tendency to search for information that confirms your perceptions or interpretations), describe a 1960 experiment by Peter Wason: British university students were presented with the sequence "2-4-6" and asked to guess the rule by which the series was chosen. (Wason's rule was "any three ascending numbers.")

Explain that, before submitting their answers, his students were allowed to generate new sets of numbers. Each time, Wason told them whether their sets conformed to his rule. When his students had done enough testing to be sure they knew the rule, they shouted it out. Wason found that they seldom guessed the correct rule—but that they had *convinced* themselves of the accuracy of the wrong rule.

Point out that Wason found his students first formed a wrong idea (for example, "counting by twos") and then searched only for evidence which would confirm their idea was correct. Wason concluded that once people have the wrong idea, they often will not change their minds (Wason 1960).

Tell students they will better understand the errors made by the British students after they play the next three games, which demonstrate the influence of the confirmation bias.

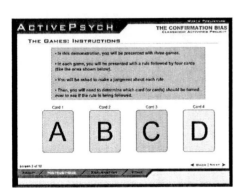

Screen 3

Instructions: Make sure that students understand the game instructions presented on this screen.

In each of the three games, you will record the percentage of students who believe a card should be turned over to determine if the rule is being followed.

So: In each game, you will go through all four cards—one at a time—asking students if that card should be turned over to determine if the rule is being followed.

Then, using the slider below the card, record the percentage of students who believe that card should be turned over.

Student choices and the correct answers will be presented and discussed on the screens that follow the games.

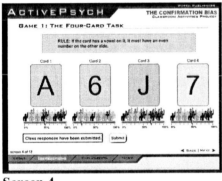

Screen 4

Instructions: Ask, "Which of the four cards needs to be turned over to determine if this rule is being followed. Remember, you can choose more than one."

Once students have had time to consider their decisions, go through each card, one at a time, asking students if they think that card should be turned over.

Have students raise their hands to indicate whether they think that card should be turned over. Then, adjust the slider beneath the card to indicate the percentage of students who raised their hands.

Click "Submit" and move to the next game only after all four cards have been assessed.

NOTE: Student choices for this game, along with correct answers, are presented and discussed on screen 7.

Screen 5

Instructions: Ask, "Which of the four cards needs to be turned over to determine if this rule is being followed. Remember, you can choose more than one."

Once students have had time to consider their decisions, go through each card, one at a time, asking students if they think that card should be turned over.

Have students raise their hands to indicate whether they think that card should be turned over. Then, adjust the slider beneath the card to indicate the percentage of students who raised their hands.

Click "Submit" and move to the next game only after all four cards have been assessed.

NOTE: Student choices for this game, along with correct answers, are presented and discussed on screen 8.

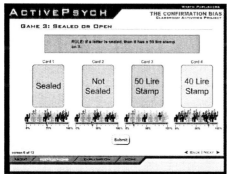

Screen 6

Instructions: If you think it's necessary, you can let students know that the lire is no longer the Italian national currency. As part of the European Union, Italy now uses the euro and a typical stamp costs € 0.65 or € 0.70.

Then ask, "Which of the four cards needs to be turned over to determine if this rule is being followed. Remember, you can choose more than one."

Once students have had time to consider their decisions, go through each card, one at a time, asking students if they think that card should be turned over.

Have students raise their hands to indicate whether they think that card should be turned over. Then, adjust the slider beneath the card to indicate the percentage of students who raised their hands.

Click "Submit" and move to the next screen only after all four cards have been assessed.

NOTE: Student choices for this game, along with correct answers, are presented and discussed on screen 9.

Screen 7

Instructions: Click each card, and the percentage of students who chose that card will appear under "Student Responses."

After reviewing student choices for all four cards, lead students in a discussion of why they made their choices.

Once students have finished discussing their choices, click "Show Answers" to view the correct answer—that is, the cards that actually need to be turned over to determine if the rule is being followed.

The percentage of students who chose each card will remain displayed under "Student Responses" so that you can contrast their choices with the correct answers.

To remove the student response percentages and answers, click "Reset Responses."

Explanation: Point out that just like the British students who thought the rule "counting by twos" explained the series "2-4-6," we tend to seek out information that confirms a rule or expectation and stop there once we find this evidence. We tend NOT to continue on to try to find any *disconfirming* information against the rule or expectation.

In this example, most students will correctly determine that card A needs to be turned over. But this is not enough, to know if the rule is being followed. We also need to find a case that *disconfirms* the rule is being followed. So, we must also turn over card 7. If there is a consonant on the other side, it follows the rule; if there is a vowel, we find evidence that does not fit the rule. Turning over card 6 is not informative, since the rule doesn't say that vowels are the only thing that can appear on the back of an even number. Card J is also not useful, since the rule does not say anything about consonants.

Let students know that this game involved an *abstract* rather than *concrete* rule (if vowel, then even number). The rule is arbitrary—not based in any facts with which students might be familiar. With very abstract problems, the confirmation bias tends to be quite influential.

Finally, tell students that in Wason's original research, only 4 percent of the participants chose the correct response, which was to turn over both cards A and 7.

Screen 8

Instructions: Click each card, and the percentage of students who chose that card will appear under "Student Responses."

After reviewing student choices for all four cards, lead students in a discussion of why they made their choices.

Once students have finished discussing their choices, click "Show Answers" to view the correct answer—that is, the cards that actually need to be turned over to determine if the rule is being followed.

The percentage of students who chose each card will remain displayed under "Student Responses" so that you can contrast their choices with the correct answers.

To remove the student response percentages and answers, click "Reset Responses."

Explanation: Tell students that when we are presented with a more concrete problem (like the one presented here and on the next screen), whether we experience the confirmation bias as we reason through the problem depends on our familiarity with the subject or objects in the game.

Explain that this game is identical in structure to "The Four-Card Task" presented on screen 4. To test that the rule is being followed, you need to turn over both "drinking a beer" (confirming evidence) and "16 years old" (disconfirming evidence). Further explain that a problem about beer and age is concrete as well as familiar, especially for college students. In this case, students most likely find it easier to correctly decide to check for *disconfirming* evidence as much as for *confirming* evidence.

In 1982, Griggs and Cox presented games similar to the ones shown on screens 4 and 5. In their studies, they found that the "The Four-Card Task" was not solved correctly by any of their participants, but the rule about drinking was tested properly by a significant number of participants even though its underlying structure is the same. No participants selected incorrect responses to turn over "22 years old" or "drinking a soda" and almost 75% of the participants correctly selected to turn over BOTH "drinking a beer" and "16 years old."

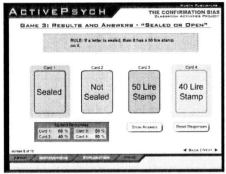

Screen 9

Instructions: Click each card, and the percentage of students who chose that card will appear under "Student Responses."

After reviewing student choices for all four cards, lead students in a discussion of why they made their choices.

Once students have finished discussing their choices, click "Show Answers" to view the correct answer—that is, the cards that actually need to be turned over to determine if the rule is being followed.

The percentage of students who chose each card will remain displayed under "Student Responses" so that you can contrast their choices with the correct answers.

To remove the student response percentages and answers, click "Reset Responses."

Explanation: Explain that this game has the same structure as those presented on screens 4 and 5. To test the rule, you need to turn over both *"Sealed"* (confirming evidence) and "40 Lire Stamp" (disconfirming evidence). There is nothing to be learned by turning over "50 Lire Stamp" as the rule is simply about what must be on the flip side of a sealed envelope. It does not say anything about what must be on the flip side of an envelope with a 50 lire stamp on the front. Students should remember to take the rule very literally and not make inferences beyond what is stated.

In 1972, Johnson-Laird, Legrenzi, and Legrenzi presented similar games to Italian participants. Their participants performed much better on "Sealed or Open" than on "The Four-Card Task." Interestingly, when the same problem was given to British and American participants, they did not perform well at all. Why? It seems the Italian postage system is fairly complicated and the Italian participants were used to this sort of stamp rule. British and American participants, accustomed to simpler postal systems, were not familiar with the rationale behind the rule, so they did not correctly (or completely) test it. This suggests that the concreteness of the rule is not the only important element. *Familiarity* with the rule is also vital in human reasoning.

Explain that, like "Beer or Soda," "Sealed or Open" presents a concrete problem. But unlike the "Beer or Soda," many students won't have the same familiarity with foreign postage. If you are working with a problem that is concrete, but with which you are not familiar, you will most likely still experience the *confirmation bias*.

Screen 10

Explanation: Explain that this screen makes reference to a controversial study on the biasing power of diagnostic labels. In 1973, David Rosenhan and seven others went to mental hospital admissions offices complaining of "hearing voices." Apart from this complaint, and giving false names and occupations, they answered questions truthfully. All eight were diagnosed mentally ill. Each stayed in the hospital for an average of 19 days. Though none exhibited other symptoms during their hospital stays, clinicians analyzed their life histories and were able to "discover" the causes of their disorders based on the gathered histories as well as the patients' everyday actions.

Encourage students to speculate how the confirmation bias may have caused the clinicians to misdiagnose the researchers—pointing out that "labels" can create preconceptions that guide or bias perceptions or interpretations.

RELATED STUDY: People rated a job applicant seen in a videotape interview. One group was told the applicant was ordinary; another group was told the applicant was a psychiatric or cancer patient. The latter group saw the applicant as "different from most people" (Langer and colleages, 1974, 1980).

Screen 11

Explanation: Point out that critical thinking and skepticism in science are aimed at evaluating the possibility of alternative explanations for hypotheses or for apparent observation. For example, although we may believe that Variable A is related to Variable B (perhaps in a *specific* way), we should ask, "What else might possibly underlie this relationship?" or "Is there a Variable C that creates the A-B relationship we observe?"

Also point out that evidence testing and "falsifiability" are the general rule in science. If we only look for evidence supporting a particular hypothesis, we may never determine (1) if there are alternative explanations or better explanations, or (2) if the hypothesis is, in fact, generally false.

Finally, point out that assertions or hypotheses that are not "testable" (i.e., falsifiable) are not scientific—they cannot be considered or evaluated using the tools of science.

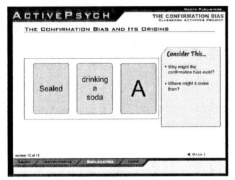

Screen 12

Explanation: Point out that, according the *selective human processing bias*, humans prefer to (and tend to) think about positive information rather than negative information (Evans, 1989; Klayman & Ha, 1987); humans may also be motivated to focus on gains or benefits without being exposed to uncertainty and risks (Lewicka, 1998). Thus, humans may have a biologically-based preference for being right without exposing themselves to the risk of being wrong.

Also point out that, according to *error avoidance* or *cognitive "conservatism,"* individuals may seek to avoid what they perceive to be the costly consequences of (mis)judging a hypothesis to be false—allowing knowledge to persist even in the face of what may appear to be initial evidence to the contrary or evidence of falsehood (Nickerson, 1998).

Finally, have students consider what the course of science might have been if, for example, every new theory and its associated hypotheses was thrown out when the first bit of evidence to the contrary was introduced!

Thinking, Language, and Intelligence:
LANGUAGE DEVELOPMENT IN INFANTS AND TODDLERS

Screen 1

This demonstration was written by Stavros Valenti, Hofstra University, and Amy Obegi, Grossmont College

About: In this activity you will use video clips to show milestones in language development for children from birth through age six.

Students will become familiar with language development in children exposed to a language other than English, or to multiple languages, as well as in children who attend child care centers.

For additional information about any screen activity, click on the illuminated gray tab; use the last "Consider This…" activity screens to promote class discussion.

RELATED TOPICS: The developing person, infancy and childhood, language development.

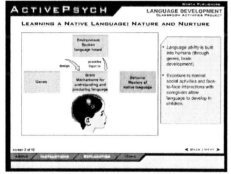

Screen 2

Instructions: Click "Play" to view an animation of the relationship between genes and environment and their influence on language development.

Explanation: Point out that, in terms of brain development, hearing the sounds of a language is something the brain is expecting in order to develop normally (what is known as *experience-expectant*).

The particular language a child is exposed to varies worldwide. Thus, the specific sounds the brain will hear are environmentally determined (what is known as *experience-dependant*).

You can also point out that there are about 6,000 human languages spoken around the world. However, half of these languages are spoken by fewer than 10,000 people and the top 20 languages are spoken by nearly half of the world's population (Gibbs, 2002).

Finally, students might be curious to know that by the time the average secondary school student graduates, he or she knows some 80,000 words (Miller & Gildea, 1987). That would average out to nearly 5,000 words each year after the age of one—or 13 words per day.

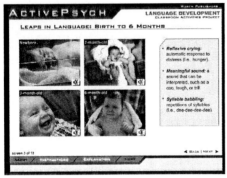

Screen 3

Instructions: Click the sound icon on any of the four displayed images to hear an audio example of the sound a child of that age would make.

To replay any of the audio tracks, click the icons again.

Explanation: Point out that in addition to milestones in speech, children and their caregivers communicate through *primary interobjectivity* (sharing of emotion, where each partner focuses on the emotional expression of the other) and *secondary interobjectivity* (sharing of awareness of objects in the environment by an infant and caregiver).

Because the brain doesn't know what language a child will be exposed to, the infant is ready to hear and produce any phoneme. Explain to students that a *phoneme* is the smallest unit of sound in a language that can signal a change in word meaning (like "bat" versus "cat").

Further point out that the sounds a child hears trigger synaptic connections in the brain, making later recognition and sound production possible. Any phoneme a child is not exposed to will not trigger such synaptic connections, and over time the ability to hear and produce those sounds will be lost.

If the goal is for a child to learn more than one language, it is recommended the child be exposed to both languages at an early age (Gerken, 1993).

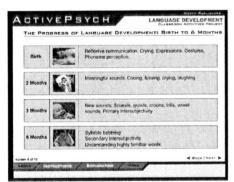

Screen 4

Instructions: To view a video of language milestones for each age represented in the chart, click any of the images shown on screen. Once the video has loaded, click the Play button to start the video.

When you are through watching any of the videos, click "Reset Page" to get back to the original chart.

Explanation: Point out that *synchrony*, or the "coordinated, rapid, and smooth exchange of responses between a caregiver and infant," is an important component of respectful language interactions. It helps adults become attuned to the child, and provides practice for the turn-taking of language.

Talking with infants is important, but it is recommended to bathe children in language rather than drown them in it. With this consideration in mind, you may want to pose the following question: "What are some ways adults can facilitate language development in children?" To answer the question, discuss some theories of language acquisition with your students.

One theory contends that caregivers must *teach* language, reinforcing an infant's vocal expression by using words to describe objects and experiences in the infant's life.

Another relies on an inborn "language acquisition device," meaning that, in a normal environment with the usual exposure to language, a child will talk.

A third theory stresses *social interaction*, implying that infants will learn in a socially supportive context.

A hybrid of all three models is believed by some to best explain language acquisition.

Screen 5

Instructions: Click the sound icon on any of the four displayed images to hear an audio example of the sound a child of that age would make.

To replay any of the audio tracks, click the icons again.

Explanation: Point out that many mistakenly believe a child's first words are her first attempt to communicate. Nonverbal communication (including face/body language, gestures and hand symbols) all play a large role in communication. If caregivers use hand gestures of baby signs with language, children have been found to have an average of 20 signs for words that they aren't yet able to communicate verbally (Goodwyn, Acredolo, & Brown, 2000).

Also point out that comprehension of language precedes the ability to speak. At 12 months, a child can understand many more words than the one or two she can speak.

Finally, point out that children's first words are typically nouns and proper names. This makes sense considering that in the *sensimotor* stage of cognitive development (according to Piaget) children rely heavily on concrete, meaningful, hands-on experiences.

You might have students speculate reasons for this finding: While families are the first and most important teachers of their children, it has been found that when attending high-quality child care settings children develop larger vocabularies (Todd, 2001).

Screen 6

Instructions: Click "Play" to view a video of two examples that show how a social interaction can result in children experiencing new words.

Explanation: Point out that social context affects language development, especially in the boy who learns the word *modi* for "shell."

The average child knows about 500 words at age 2 and more than 10,000 at age 6. One scholar points out that 2- to 6-year-olds learn 10 words a day (Clark, 1995).

Explain that when children *underextend (undergeneralize)*, they make assumptions about word meanings, but sometimes these "good guesses" are wrong. For example, a child might insist that an ant is NOT an insect because the child does not yet appreciate that insect is a word for a large category of objects that contains things like ants.

When children *overextend (overgeneralize)*, they apply a word to objects that are similar (i.e., the word *pig* might be applied to a picture of a *dog* or a *zebra* applied to a picture of a *horse*).

Screen 7

Instructions: Click 'Play" to view a video of a child using language and employing grammatical morphemes.

Explanation: By age three, a child's grammar is quite impressive. Children typically use the correct *syntax* (the rules for the ordering of words in a language) to create phrases or sentences.

Since syntax varies across languages (For example: English puts the adjective before the noun, while Spanish puts it after), it is recommended that adults don't intermix languages within the same sentence (e.g., speaking "Spanglish"). This way the child has practice hearing and understanding the proper grammar structure of each language.

Point out that although grammar is improving, children are still prone to errors, particularly with *overregularization*—that is, when children overapply a rule, such as adding -ed to all past tense words. (e.g., "We eated," instead of "We ate"; "We goed," instead of 'We went.")

Also point out that it is not considered necessary to "correct" children explicitly when they make a grammar error (i.e. "You said that wrong, you should say it this way…").

Screen 8

Instructions: Click "Play" to view a video of some children employing private speech and other children engaged in collective monologues.

Explanation: *Private speech* is an important way children practice language, order their thoughts, and problem-solve. Many of us still engage in this practice. Most often it becomes an internal dialogue, but sometimes we continue to talk to ourselves out loud about what it is we are doing!

While peers do engage in meaningful dialogue or conversations with each other, the fact that children tend to be egocentric in the preschool years means that they are more prone to collective monologues.

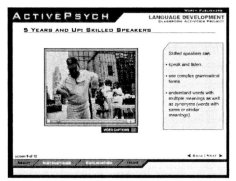

Screen 9

Instructions: Click "Play" to view a video of children using their language skills to tell jokes.

Explanation: Remind students that for children to become skilled communicators, they need frequent exposure to language-rich environments. In addition to verbal communication strategies, other strategies that promote language are the use of literacy props (i.e., puppets, dramatic play items, books), as well as the integration of art activities, poetry, songs, storytelling, and adequate time for play into a child's daily life. (Stegelin, 2005).

Also point out how television-viewing impacts language development. Research has shown that children ages 2–5 who view time-regulated amounts of high-quality, age-appropriate television programming have increased comprehension, receptive vocabulary, expressive language, letter-sound knowledge, and knowledge of narrative and storytelling (Close, 2004).

However, viewing of programming aimed at a general or adult audience is correlated with poor language development in preschoolers, specifically lower vocabulary and poorer expressive language (Close, 2004).

Screen 10

Explanation: Point out that synapses in the brain adjust to whatever pronunciation a child hears.

When children express themselves, they may transpose syllables, drop consonants, convert difficult sounds, and make other pronunciation errors. BUT, they hear distinctions—for instance, psychologist Kathleen Berger relates that when her young daughter said *yeyo yayipop* and her husband then repeated the mispronunciation, the daughter said to her father, "Daddy, sometimes you talk funny." (Berger, 2006)

Further point out that research shows that very young children can master vocabulary and grammar of more than one language (Bates, et al., 2001; Mayberry & Nicoladis, 2000). The years before age six may also be the best years to learn native pronunciation.

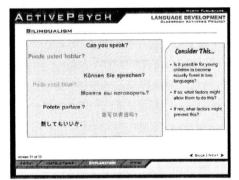

Screen 11

Explanation: Point out the term *balanced bilingualism* refers to someone equally fluent in two languages, not favoring one or the other. Developmental research shows that balanced bilingualism is possible (Romaine, 1999).

Explain that the ability to achieve equal fluency in two languages is influenced by a number of factors including the parents' abilities in one or more languages, the parents' actual use of language with the child, the languages spoken by other family members (siblings, grandparents, etc.), and the language the child uses in the community (Rosenberg, 1996).

Other factors that influence the achievement of balanced bilingualism are the stability of the languages in the child's environment, the relationship the child has with the person(s) speaking the language (closer relationship more likely to develop skills), and the attitude toward each language as expressed by parents, other family members, the school, the community, etc. (Rosenberg, 1996).

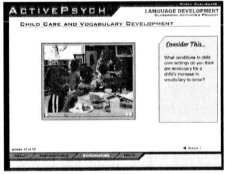

Screen 12

Explanation: The 2001 National Institute of Child Health and Human Development (NICHD) Child Care Study found that children who attended high-quality child care settings had better vocabularies.

The characteristics of these high-quality programs were:

1) well-educated staff
2) responsive and sensitive caregivers
3) low teacher-to-child ratios
4) stimulating environment.

Emotion and Motivation: ORIGINS OF EMPATHY

Screen 1

This demonstration was written by Thomas E. Ludwig, Hope College

About: Based on results of Albert Bandura's famous experiments on observational learning and more recent research by Giacomo Rizzolatti into the existence and function of mirror neurons in the brain, students consider how certain behaviors (like aggression or empathy) are learned.

Screens 4 through 6 present a simulation of the Rizzolatti experiment on mirror neurons in which the neural activity of a monkey is viewed on a monitor while the monkey engages in observation and/or action.

For additional information about any screen activity, click on the illuminated gray tab; use the last "Consider This…" activity screens to promote class discussion.

RELATED TOPICS: Social psychology, learning, learning by observation, the brain, neurons.

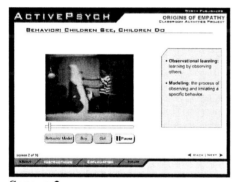

Screen 2

First, click "Behavior Model" to view the adult who modeled behavior (using the Bobo doll as a subject) for the children in the experimental group.

Next, click "Boy" to view how a boy in the experimental group behaved with the Bobo doll after viewing the model's behavior.

Finally, click "Girl" to view how a girl in the experimental group behaved with the Bobo doll after viewing the model's behavior.

Instructions: On this screen students will observe three short videos from the original experiment on observational learning by Albert Bandura. You should show the video clips one at a time, in order.

Explanation: Point out that the boy and girl in the videos were part of the "experimental group," meaning that they watched the model before spending time with the Bobo doll; whereas, children in the "control group" (not seen in the videos) didn't watch the model before spending time with Bobo.

Further point out that in the original experiment, when left alone in a room with the Bobo doll, the control group children displayed less aggressive behavior. They mainly limited themselves to punching Bobo with a fist.

Contrast this behavior with the behavior of the children in the experimental group. They displayed highly aggressive actions in direct imitation of the model (who performed five specific actions with Bobo, punching it, kicking it, throwing it in the air, hitting it with a hammer, and sitting astride it).

Finally, explain that Bandura's experiment showed that children learn from *modeling*. They learn to act aggressively (and specifically) just by observing another person's behavior. Note that they learn by observing *prosocial* (kind or helpful) *behavior* as well as *antisocial behavior*.

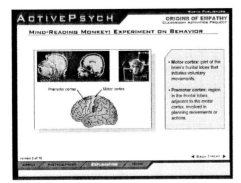

Screen 3

Explanation: Point out that in Italy in the 1990s, researchers at the University of Parma (led by neuroscientist Giacomo Rizzolatti) demonstrated that cells in the premotor cortex of a monkey brain "fire" both when the monkey performs an action and when it watches that action performed by another monkey or human (Rizzolatti, 1996).

In the photo at upper right, a monkey is shown with an electrode inserted into his brain. The electrode was used to record the electrical activity of the cells in his brain.

Explain that, though monkey and human brains differ in size and shape, the individual brain structures are quite similar.

Screens 4 through 6 present a simulation of this experiment, followed by analysis of the experiment results.

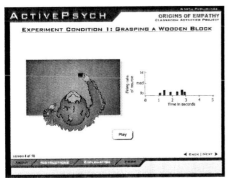

Screen 4

Instructions: Tell students that the monkey in this simulation is named Rizzo (after Giacomo Rizzolatti, the Italian neuroscientist who was a pioneer in this kind of research).

In experiment condition 1, Rizzo will be tested as he grasps a wooden block.

Click "Play" to watch Rizzo's brain activity as he grasps the wooden block located at the front of the table.

Have students monitor the activity of the firing neuron as displayed on the graph.

Explanation: Tell students that while anesthetized, an electrode was inserted into an area of Rizzo's premotor cortex called *F5* (shown in the illustration on the previous screen). The electrode has been tested to make sure it is successfully recording the activity of a single neuron that responds to certain hand movements.

After students view the animation, have them speculate about Rizzo's neural activity.

When they have finished speculating, point out that while Rizzo performed the action of grasping the wooden block the neuron fired a few times, but the overall activity was low.

Further help students understand that from the neural activity viewed on the graph, it seems as though this neuron might be specialized for some other activity.

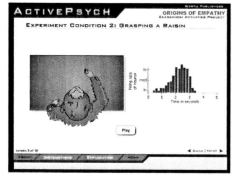

Screen 5

Instructions: Tell students that in experiment condition 2, Rizzo will be tested as he is presented with a raisin.

Explain that raisins happen to be one of Rizzo's favorite snacks.

Click "Play" to watch Rizzo's brain activity as he grasps the raisin presented to him.

Have students monitor the activity of the firing neuron as displayed on the graph.

Explanation: After students view the animation, have them speculate about Rizzo's neural activity.

When they have finished speculating, point out that while Rizzo performed the action of grasping the raisin the neuron fired more rapidly and continuously than when Rizzo grasped the wooden block.

Further help students understand that this pattern of neural activity, as viewed on the graph, suggests that this particular neuron is specialized for this particular type of hand movement.

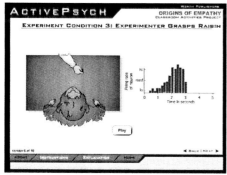

Screen 6

Instructions: Tell students that in experiment condition 3, Rizzo will be tested as he observes the experimenter grasp a raisin.

Remind students that raisins happen to be one of Rizzo's favorite snacks.

Click "Play" to watch Rizzo's brain activity as he observes the experimenter grasping the raisin.

Have students monitor the activity of the firing neuron as displayed on the graph.

Explanation: After students view the animation, have them speculate about Rizzo's neural activity.

When they have finished speculating, point out that while Rizzo observed the experimenter perform the action of grasping the raisin, the neuron got very excited. Note that the pattern of activity was very similar to the activity of the neuron when Rizzo was grasping the raisin himself.

Further point out that researchers believe that this neuron is actually helping Rizzo understand the experimenter's hand movement by relating it to his own hand movement.

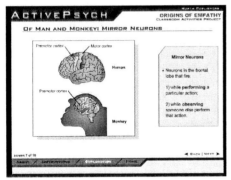

Screen 7

Explanation: Point out that experiments similar to the one in this simulation have demonstrated that each neuron in the F5 area of the monkey's premotor cortex is specialized for single types of motor actions (such as grasping with the hand).

The even more amazing phenomenon shown by these experiments is that each neuron responds *the same way* when a monkey watches another monkey (or human) perform the action! This observation has led researchers to call the class of neurons *mirror neurons*.

Also point out that research (using non-invasive EEG and brain scanning methods) with humans shows that a similar mirror neuron system exists in the human brain. In humans, though, mirror neurons are even more sophisticated than those in monkeys.

Finally, tell students that researcher Giacomo Rizzolatti has said that mirror neurons help us to understand the actions, intentions, and emotions of others. "Mirror neurons allow us to grasp the minds of others not through conceptual reasoning but through direct simulation. By *feeling*, not *thinking*."

Screen 8

First, click "Behavior Model" to view the adult who modeled behavior for the children in the experimental group, using the Bobo doll as a subject. (NOTE: This video was also shown on screen 2 of this activity.)

Next, click "Boy and Girl" to view how a boy and girl from the experimental group behave when left alone with the Bobo doll. (NOTE: in this video, the boy and girl have already observed the model with Bobo.)

Instructions: On this screen students will observe two short videos from the original experiment on observational learning by Albert Bandura. You should show the video clips one at a time, in order.

Explanation: Tell students that some researchers believe that the main function of mirror neurons is to promote observational learning. The discovery of mirror neurons provides a mechanism for explaining how this form of behavioral learning occurs, and why it happens so quickly.

When we observe another person performing an action, mirror neurons help our brain understand the action and "practice" the action without moving our muscles. This allows children to learn new actions (good and bad) by simply watching another person.

With this video of the boy and girl, Bandura demonstrated that exposure to an aggressive model has a general arousing effect on children, leading children to invent their own novel forms of violent behavior—actions that go beyond mere imitation.

Finally, point out that in the January 2006 issue of *Media Psychology* researchers reported that when children watched violent television programs, mirror neurons, as well as several brain regions involved in aggression, were activated, increasing the probability that the children would act violently.

Screen 9

Instructions: Click "Play" to show students an animation that shows what happens when a ball accidentally hits a girl as a boy looks on.

Explanation: Point out that neuroscientists like Christian Keysers and Bruno Wicker have expanded on the original Rizzolatti research.

Their research has shown that when we see another person experiencing a painful event, the pain areas in our own brains become active. We actually "feel" the other person's pain, and this helps create empathy and understanding of the other person's emotions. "People who rank high on a scale measuring empathy have particularly active mirror neurons systems" (Keysers, et. al., 2004).

Further point out that this type of brain activity has been shown in other emotions, such as happiness, anger, and fear.

Finally, let students know that Keysers has said that social emotions like guilt, shame, pride, embarrassment, disgust, and lust are based on a uniquely *human* mirror neuron system and that "humiliation appears to be mapped in the brain by the same mechanisms that encode real physical pain."

Screen 10

Explanation: Point out that the same basic emotions that adults express on their faces also show up on the faces of babies, even very young infants.

Further explain that young infants are also able to imitate adult facial expressions, such as sticking out a tongue. Mirror neurons allow this to happen by triggering facial expressions similar to the person being observed. These facial expressions help the infant understand the emotion of the other person.

Emotion and Motivation: FAT RATS: A SIMULATED EXPERIMENT

Screen 1

This demonstration was written by Thomas E. Ludwig, Hope College

About: In this activity students will simulate experimental conditions in which the rat hypothalamus was either damaged or stimulated.

In the simulation, electrodes are placed in either the lateral hypothalamus (LH) or ventromedial hypothalamus (VMH). The body weight and food consumption of the rats are monitored over a ninety-day period; the results are presented on graphs, and students are encouraged to draw conclusions based on their observations.

For additional information about any activity screen, click on the illuminated gray tab; use the last "Consider This…" activity screens to promote class discussion.

RELATED TOPICS: Neuroscience and behavior, the brain, research and experimentation, motivation, physiology of hunger.

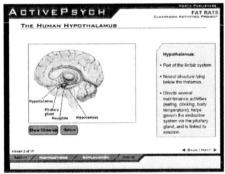

Screen 2

Instructions: Click "Show Close-up" to view a larger image of the hypothalamus. To return to the full illustration of the brain and limbic system, click "Return."

Explanation: Tell students that the limbic system is associated with emotions and drives (such as those for food and sex). This system includes the *hypothalamus*, which regulates thirst, hunger, and body temperature, and influences motivated (or reward) behavior; the *amygdala*, which is linked to fear and aggression; and the *hippocampus*, which is involved in memory.

Point out that the *pituitary gland* is part of the endocrine system—a set of glands that secrete hormones into the bloodstream. The hypothalamus helps to govern the endocrine system via the pituitary gland.

Explain that the hypothalamus as a "reward center" was discovered by a researcher who accidentally stimulated the hypothalamus of a rat and discovered that the rat, on its own, continuously sought to return to the location on a table top where it had been stimulated (Olds, 1975).

Finally, point out that the relationship between hunger and the hypothalamus cannot be studied ethically by manipulating the brains of living humans. Instead, information comes from studying people with damaged hypothalami or from studying rats.

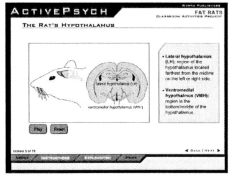

Screen 3

Instructions: Click "Play" to view an animation that zooms in for a closer look at the rat's lateral hypothalamus (LH) and ventromedial hypothalamus (VMH). Click "Reset" to return the animation to its original orientation.

Explanation: Point out that *ventromedial* comes from the words *medial*, which means "in the middle" and *ventro*, which means on the same side of the body as the stomach (as opposed to the back). The *ventromedial hypothalamus* (VMH) is the region located in the bottom/middle of the hypothalamus.

Lateral means on the side, the opposite of medial. The *lateral hypothalamus* (LH) is the region of the hypothalamus located farthest from the midline on the left or right side.

Explain that, in the following experiment, students will simulate the stimulation or destruction of the rat's hypothalumus (both the LH and the VMH). Students will witness the effect this experiment has on the rat's eating pattern.

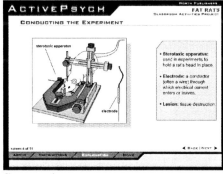

Screen 4

Explanation: Point out that experiments on the hypothalami of rats occurred mostly during the mid-twentieth century. In them, an electrode was carefully inserted into either the LH (lateral hypothalamus) or VMH (ventromedial hypothalamus) and would cause either stimulation to, or destruction of, the selected brain part. (Note that destruction causes a *lesion*.)

Explain to students that in this experiment they will use the "virtual" electrode to either stimulate or destroy the "virtual" rat's LH or VMH. Of course, no rats are harmed during this experiment!

With *stimulation*, a weak electric current travels through the electrode and stimulates, without destroying, a target, thus activating the behavior controlled by the target region. With *destruction*, a strong electric current travels through the electrode and causes damage to the target.

To ensure that the electrode is inserted into the correct portion of the rat's brain, its head is clamped into a device called a *sterotaxic apparatus*.

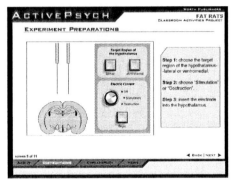

Screen 5

Instructions: Explain to your students that, on this screen, they will learn how to manipulate and place the electrodes. On the next screen (screen 5), the class will conduct the simulated experiment.

Click the "lateral" or "ventromedial" buttons to select the hypothalamus target region to which the electrode will be applied.

To choose an electric current that will run through the electrode, click the "Electric Current" dial once to select "Stimulation" or twice to select "Destruction." (Remember, *stimulation* produces a weak current; *destruction* a strong one.)

Once the target region and current have been set, click "Begin." The electrodes will move into position in the rat's brain.

Explain that, in the simulated experiment, the graphs will plot the rat's body weight and food consumption (both in grams) over a period of 90 days after the surgery. (Results of the simulated experiments will be shown and discussed on screens 7 through 9.)

When students understand how to conduct the experiment, click "Next" to move to the next screen.

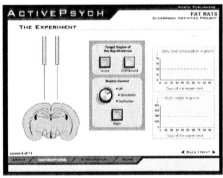

Screen 6

Instructions: As shown on the previous screen (screen 5), set the electrode target region (lateral or ventromedial hypothalamus) and the electric current (stimulation or destruction).

Click "Begin" to start the experiment. Allow time for students to study the graphs as they plot the food consumption and body weight of the rat over a 90-day period.

When the graphs are fully plotted, students should discuss the relationship between the hypothalamus and the rat's eating pattern.

When students are ready for the next simulation, select new electrode settings. There are four different electrode settings to apply: LH stimulation, LH destruction, VMH stimulation, and VMH destruction.

When all four simulations have been completed, press "Next" to move to the next screen. Screens 7 through 9 will discuss the experiment results.

Screen 7

<u>Explanation</u>: Compare and contrast the findings shown on this screen with the observations students made after each of the four simulations.

Point out that in the original laboratory research, the VMH-lesioned rat weighed more than three times that of her sister rat, who had not undergone any surgery.

Remind students that the hypothalamus acts as a sensor for such things as glucose—a form of sugar that circulates in the blood and provides the major source of energy for body tissues. Low levels of glucose make us feel hunger.

Further point out that since the original experiments were performed, researchers have discovered that damage to the LH and VMH have more than one effect—these effects include a change in the hormone level of insulin, sensory reactivity (the taste and attractiveness of food), glucose and lipid levels in the blood, and metabolic rate.

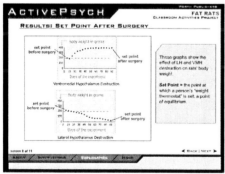

Screen 8

<u>Explanation</u>: One hunger theory proposes that manipulating the VMH or LH alters the body's *set point* (Keesey & Corbett, 1983). Set point is a biological predisposition to keep our body in equilibrium at a stable weight. Below the set point, hunger increases and energy expenditure decreases; above it, hunger decreases and energy expenditure increases.

In this simulation, the rat with VMH destruction ate itself far past the point of filling its stomach. Whereas, the rat with LH destruction never received the signal to be "hungry" and, consequently, didn't eat. Point out to students that, though this suggests a connection between the hypothalamus and eating behavior, there are problems with this conclusion.

Ask students if they noticed that the rat with VMH destruction did not keep on gaining weight indefinitely. Instead, it appeared to level off after about 40 days at a higher, but stable, weight. In the original experiments, rats with LH destruction reached a lower but stable weight level (if they were kept alive long enough to recover). This suggests that damage to the VMH or LH may merely readjust the set point for the system that maintains body weight, rather than destroying the rat's ability to feel hungry or to feel satisfied.

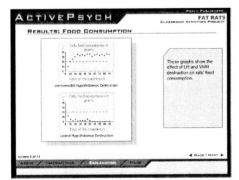

Screen 9

Explanation: Further, point out that other research has found similar disturbances in eating behavior can be produced by damage or stimulation to different regions of the rat's brain (not only the hypothalamus). This strongly suggests that the VMH and LH may be no more than links in a complicated chain of neural networks. Eating habits may change if any of the links are either stimulated or destroyed.

For example, hunger is also affected by body chemistry. When the blood sugar (glucose) level of a rat is low, the LH releases a hormone (*orexin*) that triggers hunger. Researchers found that rats given orexin became extremely hungry (Sakurai & others, 1998).

Researchers have learned that some people with tumors in the hypothalamus eat in excess, becoming overweight (Miller, 1995).

Screen 10

Explanation: Point out that recent research supports the idea that hunger is motivated by a concert of physiological mechanisms. These include the body's need to restore its (metabolically) depleted energy stores, as well as systems that induce people (and animals) to eat when food is available (unless the stomach signals that it is full).

Another finding shows that a substance called *cholecystokinin*, released from the wall of a distended stomach, sends a signal to the brain that the stomach is full—even if the stomach is full of nothing but water.

Humans also have psychological motivations for hunger, including learned associations having to do with times and places for eating. (It's noon; must be time for lunch. Can't watch a movie without popcorn.)

Screen 11

Explanation: Tell students that the feeling of being satiated is mostly related to digestive hormones released in the gut as a meal is being consumed. There are various hormones related to specific foods and their changing amounts as they are consumed.

Further point out that the hypothalamus monitors a protein hormone called *leptin*, produced by bloated fat cells. Increased levels of leptin in the brains of mice signal that eating should be curbed and activity increased (Halaas & others, 1995).

Finally, point out that in eating disorders, such as an *anorexia nervosa* and *bulimia nervosa*, in which people starve themselves, the psychological motivation for abnormal thinness overwhelms normal homeostatic pressures—that is, the tendency to maintain a balanced and constant internal state.

Emotion and Motivation: EXPERIENCING HUNGER

Screen 1

This demonstration was written by Thomas E. Ludwig, Hope College

About: In this activity some aspects of the physiology and psychology of hunger are explored. This exploration mainly focuses on people who do not suffer from eating disorders such as anorexia nervosa or bulimia nervosa.

Two screens (Screens 3 and 4) present animations about the absorption and fasting phases of food consumption.

For additional information about any screen activity, click on the illuminated gray tab; use the last "Consider This…" activity screens to promote class discussion.

RELATED TOPICS: motivation, health.

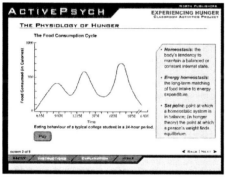

Screen 2

Instructions: Click "Play" to view the pattern of food consumption for a typical college student during a 24-hour period.

Explanation: First, tell students that the body's energy homeostasis or "energy balance" (energy intake versus expenditure) appears to be regulated by mechanisms so sensitive that a small imbalance could lead to a disproportionately large weight gain over time.

Then, ask: "How does the body maintain its energy balance to prevent such a substantial change in body weight?" Allow students to speculate, then explain that some researchers believe the body adjusts both energy (food) intake and energy expenditure in order to maintain a stable weight. Energy intake is regulated by modifying the hunger drive, and energy expenditure is regulated by modifying the body's metabolic rate.

Hunger researchers generally refer to the body's predisposition to maintain a particular weight level as the body's *set point*. If some component of our internal state falls below its set point, we are motivated to engage in behaviors that will bring that component back to its normal level (Keesey & Corbett, 1983).

Finally, explain that most people eat substantial amounts of food three or four times a day; the body then distributes the energy obtained during a meal and stores the excess energy for later use. The regular pattern of obtaining energy from food, storing the energy, and then retrieving and using the energy is called the *food consumption cycle* or *energy metabolism cycle*.

Screen 3

Instructions: Click "Play" to view the absorptive phase of food consumption. (Descriptions for each point in this phase will automatically appear during the animation.) If you would like to view the animation again, click "Replay."

Explanation: Provide students with this summary of the food absorption process: As we eat, components of our food (primarily carbohydrates) are converted to *glucose* in the stomach. The glucose passes through the intestines to the bloodstream for distribution throughout the body. The more we eat, the more glucose is transported through the bloodstream. The rising glucose level in the bloodstream causes the pancreas to release *insulin*.

Insulin does three things: It enables the cells to "burn" the glucose as fuel for energy, the liver and muscles to convert it to *glycogen* for storage, and adipose tissue to store the glucose as fat for later use. Glucose that is not stored is burned by the brain.

Point out that "hunger pangs" are related to sensory receptors in the stomach that detect when the stomach is stretched (from food consumption) or contracted (when food moves from the stomach into the intestines).

Screen 4

Instructions: Click "Play" to view the fasting phase of the food consumption. (Descriptions for each point in this phase will appear during the animation.) If you would like to view the animation again, click "Replay."

Explanation: Provide students with this summary of the fasting process: When all food has been absorbed into the digestive tract, the body enters the second phase, the *fasting phase*. The brain continues to burn unstored glucose, and so the level of glucose in the bloodstream drops. As a result, the pancreas reduces its secretion of insulin and begins releasing high levels of a hormone called *glucagon*. The body's cells are then no longer able to use glucose for energy; glycogen (from the liver and muscles) is converted back to glucose, which is used as brain fuel; and the adipose tissue (fat cells) releases *free fatty acids*, which are burned as fuel by the body cells. (Note that the graphs are based on Example 1: Eat breakfast at 7:00 a.m.)

Point out that the level of glucose in your blood is highest in the hour or two after you have eaten. At that point, you sense being full and have a low desire to eat—a state called *satiation*. When your blood glucose level drops below its set point (point of internal balance), you begin to feel hunger and motivation to eat until your glucose level returns to its normal range.

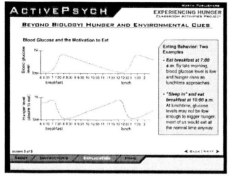

Screen 5

Explanation: Explain that the graphs show an inverse relationship between glucose and hunger—the lower the glucose level, the higher the hunger level. (Note that the graphs are based on Example 1: *Eat breakfast at 7:00 a.m.*)

Then, let students know that in "Eating Behavior" example 2, physiological factors would predict that our glucose levels would not have fallen low enough for us to experience hunger at lunchtime. But most people would probably eat lunch at their "normal" time, showing the power of expectations and time cues in influencing hunger and food consumption.

RELATED ISSUE: Pre-meal "Appetizers" Physiological theories would predict that people who have been snacking before a meal should already have high glucose levels before they sit down to eat, and thus should eat less than individuals who skipped the appetizers and went directly to the main meal. Yet research has shown that people who consume a substantial amount of calories in appetizers (up to half the amount of calories in a normal meal) generally eat a full meal—about the same amount of food as those who skipped the appetizers. It appears that psychological factors can override the normal glucose-level regulation of hunger.

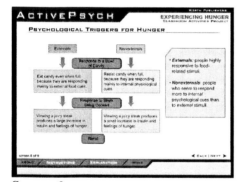

Screen 6

Instructions: Have students discuss the possible effects a bowl of candy or steak being cooked might have on externals versus nonexternals.

When students have completed their discussion, click either "Response to a Bowl of Candy" or "Response to Steak Being Cooked" to view the effect of those two stimuli on externals and nonexternals (based on studies by Judith Rodin).

Explanation: Point out that psychologist Judith Rodin conducted a series of studies that demonstrated that people differ in the degree to which their hunger is influenced by external stimuli. When she measured blood levels of insulin (the hormone that controls the body's use of glucose) in externals and nonexternals as they viewed steak being prepared, insulin levels rose higher in externals. Other studies have shown that just the *thought* of food can raise insulin in some externals.

Explain that researchers have found that people (especially externals) respond to the sight, smell, and sound of food—but not all foods trigger hunger. Hunger may be triggered by attractively presented food, food with a pleasant aroma, or food with a "normal" appearance. These findings suggest that another psychological factor in hunger is the positive *incentive* value of the available food.

Finally, remind students that different cultures gauge differently which foods are attractive, aromatic, and "normal" (hence with positive incentive value). For example, people in some areas of China prize fried grasshoppers, though they might not appeal to people in the U.S.

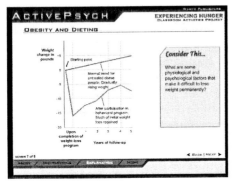

Screen 7

Explanation: Point out that in addition to genetic factors that predispose some people to weight gain, researchers have pinpointed other factors: consuming more calories each day (increased portion sizes, more snacking between meals); eating a higher proportion of fats and refined sugars, with a lower proportion of non-nutritive fiber; and burning fewer calories per day, mainly due to less walking or physical labor.

Point out that when people reduce their calorie intake through dieting, their bodies respond by slowing the metabolic rate, burning less calories per hour, and by signaling the brain to be on the lookout for food. This makes weight loss difficult, particularly for externals. This also helps explain why dieters quickly regain weight when the diet ends.

Further point out that, according to the Centers for Disease Control, 55 percent of Americans are classified as overweight and 30 percent are considered obese (weighing 20 percent or more than their "ideal" body weight). The physiological theories of hunger predict that overweight individuals should experience diminished hunger leading to reduced food intake, which would eventually allow their body fat to return to its original level. But that rarely happens; overweight individuals generally continue to gain weight and add body fat.

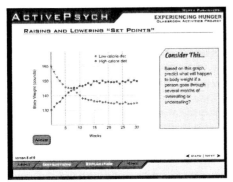

Screen 8

Instructions: Have students discuss the question shown on the screen. When they have completed their discussion, click "Answer."

Explanation: Help students understand what the graph shows: Body weight tends to fluctuate around a set point that will remain stable so long as no major pressures push that point up or down.

Point out that if you consistently overeat for several months, your body weight will drift upward, eventually stabilizing at a higher set point. Conversely, if you eat less for several months, your initial weight loss will soon taper off as your body metabolism slows down, causing your weight to stabilize at a lower set point.

Finally, remind students that the body's energy balance (energy homeostasis) is determined by food intake versus energy expenditure. This balance appears to be regulated by mechanisms so sensitive that a small imbalance could lead to a disproportionately large weight gain over time.

Screen 9

Explanation: Point out the following advice from researchers for those who want to lose weight:

— **Set realistic and moderate goals:** Large weight losses achieved quickly almost never last. You are more likely to achieve permanent weight loss if you go slowly, gradually reducing your food intake, aiming to lose 10 percent of your body weight in six months.

— **Boost your metabolism:** Eating less will cause some initial weight loss, but the loss will stop once your body's metabolic rate slows down. So in order to keep losing weight, you need to raise your metabolism by exercising.

— **Control the external stimuli:** Recognize that your brain and body will respond to food cues, so keep tempting food out of the house, avoid looking at food advertisements, and eat a full meal before grocery shopping.

Personality: LEARNED HELPLESSNESS

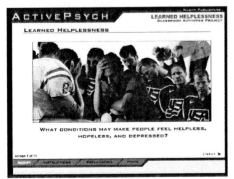

Screen 1

This demonstration was written by Thomas E. Ludwig, Hope College

About: In this activity, students learn about the social-cognitive perspective theory of learned helplessness and the relationships between personal control, learned helplessness, and depression.

Some activity screens present interactive simulations of animal experiments conducted by the psychologist Martin Seligman and their subsequent results, which led to the theory of learned helplessness.

For additional information about any screen activity, click on the illuminated gray tab; use the last "Consider This…" activity screen to promote class discussion.

RELATED TOPICS: Personality, the social-cognitive perspective, personal control, learning, classical conditioning, psychological disorders, depression.

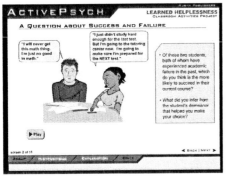

Screen 2

Instructions: Click "Play" to show animations of the two college students depicted on this screen.

After students have watched the animation, ask them to answer the questions shown on the screen.

Explanation: Ask the class to decide which student in the animation is most likely to succeed academically.

Initiate a class discussion about why the students made their choices and allow time for them to give their reasons for choosing one animation over the other.

Point out that students with negative attributional styles about themselves and their academic approach more often continue to receive bad grades as compared with students who adopt more positive attributional styles—the later are more likely to feel more hopeful and adopt an attitude that their good efforts, study habits, and discipline will make a positive difference (Noel & others, 1987; Peterson & Barrett, 1987). Mere wishing for success without acting to acquire success does not tend to motivate people to actually succeed and meet their wishful expectations (Oettingen & Mayer, 2002).

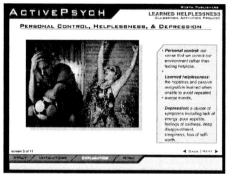

Screen 3

Explanation: Point out that personal control and learned helplessness are concepts linked to the *social-cognitive perspective*—the view that behavior is influenced by interactions between persons (and their thinking) and their social context.

Further point out that people may feel that chance or outside forces beyond their control determine their fate. This is called having an ***external locus of control***.

Alternately, people may feel that they control their own fate. This is called having an ***internal locus of control***.

Finally, explain that Martin Seligman, who developed the learned helplessness theory, noted the following, "A recipe for severe depression is pre-existing pessimism encountering failure" (1991).

Screen 4

Resources: For more information about the ethical issues involved in research with animals, your students can visit the American Psychological Association's Web site and read "Guidelines for Ethical Conduct in the Care and Use of Animals"

They can also reference the following text: **Baird, R. M., & Rosenbaum, S. E.** (1991). *Animal Experimentation: The Moral Issues*. Buffalo, NY: Prometheus Books.

Explanation: Point out that noted psychologist Martin Seligman and his colleague, Steven Maier, performed these animal experiments in the 1960s. What students experience in this presentation is a simplified version of some main points of the study.

Research History: The research that helped Martin Seligman develop the theory of learned helplessness began as research into finding out if classical conditioning responses would affect the process of operant conditioning in dogs.

Important Note About This Research: Before beginning this demonstration, you may want to discuss the ethical treatment of animals with your students. Since this study was originally conducted, it has become quite controversial. Your students may be concerned that the animals were treated cruelly in this experiment and may question whether the results justified the physical and psychological harm to the dogs. Explain to them that the painful electric shocks the dogs received in this experiment prompted the APA (American Psychological Association) to develop a set of ethical guidelines for the use of animals in research.

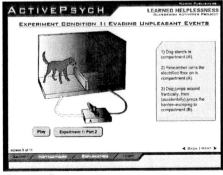

Screen 5

Instructions: Click "Play" to view an animation showing the first part of Experiment 1. Review with your students what happens in this part of the experiment (described in the textbox on screen).

Once your students understand that, after jumping around frantically, the dog accidentally jumps to the non-electrified floor of compartment (B), click "Experiment 1: Part 2" to view the next part of the experiment. Click "Play" to view the second animation. Again, review with your students what happens in this part of the experiment (described in the textbox on screen).

Explanation: Point out that in the first part of the experiment, the dog accidentally escape the shock from the electrified floor in compartment (A).

However, in the second part of the experiment, the dog *learns* to escape from the shock in compartment (B).

Explain that, in Seligman's original experiment, the dog continued to accidentally jump the barrier when the electrified floor was turned on. But, after a few trials, the dog experienced *escape learning*—that is, it learned to get away from the shock (Seligman & Maier, 1967).

In terms of learning theory, the dog received negative reinforcement for crossing the barrier whenever the electrified floor was turned on (ending the shock = reward).

Screen 6

Instructions: Click "Play" to view an animation showing the first part of Experiment 2. Review with your students what happens in this part of the experiment (described in the textbox on screen).

Once your students understand that, after jumping around frantically, the dog accidentally jumps to the non-electrified floor of compartment (B), click "Experiment 2: Part 2" to view the next part of the experiment. Click "Play" to view the second animation. Again, review with your students what happens in this part of the experiment (described in the textbox on screen).

Explanation: Allow time for students to explain what they think happened and why.

Then, point out that the dog's behavior after 50 trials is referred to as *avoidance learning*. That means the dog *learns* to anticipate the shock and to avoid it completely by responding to the warning signal.

Screen 7

Instructions: Review with your students what happens in part 3 of the Experiment (described in the textbox on screen). Once your students understand that the dog is harnessed and cannot jump to the non-electrified floor, click "Experiment 3" to view the next part of the experiment.

Click "Play" to view the animation. Again, review with your students what happens in this part of the experiment (described in the textbox on screen).

Explanation: Explain that Seligman came to the conclusion that the dogs in the harness had learned they could not escape or avoid the shocks. Instead, they learned they were helpless and that the shocks were uncontrollable.

Related Research: Students may be interested to learn that after these initial experiments by Seligman and Maier, further experiments demonstrated learned helplessness in other species, including primates, cats, rats, fish, and even cockroaches (LoLordo, 2001).

However, you should also point out that learned helplessness is not irreversible. In their experiments, Seligman and Maier found that if they forcibly dragged the dogs over the barrier while the shock was being administered, the dogs eventually overcame their passivity and began to jump the barrier on their own (LoLordo, 2001; Seligman, 1992). Let students know that they can overcome *academic* learned helplessness by establishing a sense of control over their schoolwork, being prepared for their assignments, and planning ahead (McKean, 1994).

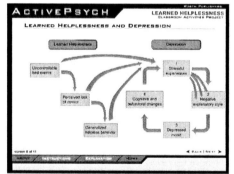

Screen 8

Instructions: First, click "Learned Helplessness" to view an animation that describes the flow of events related to that condition.

Next, click "depression" to view an animation that not only follows the flow of events related to that condition, but also to describes a relationship between depression and learned helplessness.

Explanation: Point out that Seligman proposed that depression is a learned reaction to stressful events that seem to be inescapable. People who have developed this sense of learned helplessness give up trying to improve their situation, even if they actually do have control over it.

Further point out that more recently, other researchers recognize that learned helplessness can be explained by perceived lack of control (the inescapable bad events) and by the attributions that people make to explain the events.

When people attribute the bad events to permanent, general aspects of their abilities or their environment, they may develop *hopelessness*—that is, a sense that the bad situation will never change, which is a risk factor for serious depression.

Finally, it is important to point out that, while it is true that this type of cognitive processing can lead to depression, it does not explain ALL depression.

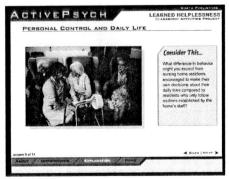

Screen 9

Explanation: Explain that, in a study by Judith Rodin and Ellen Langer, one group of nursing home residents (*the experimental group*) were encouraged to make small decisions about their daily routine (such as when and where to meet with guests).

The other group of residents (*the control group*) had daily decisions made for them by the experienced nursing home staff.

Point out that, unlike the residents in the control group, the experimental group residents displayed significant improvements in their behavior. They were more cooperative and sociable, they reported less depression and more satisfaction with life, and they had a hopeful feeling about the future.

Screen 10

Explanation: Point out that, although Seligman's theory does not explain depression completely, it does help us to understand why so many depressed individuals have feelings of helplessness and hopelessness.

For instance, victims of abuse have experienced repeated inescapable and stressful events and may have lost their sense of personal control over the events in their lives. These victims of abuse (like the dogs in the harnesses who later have the harnesses removed) may no longer attempt to escape the events that cause pain.

Further point out that prisoners often develop learned helplessness from their repeated and inescapable unpleasant experiences in prison. As a result, they become so hopeless that they stop working for parole.

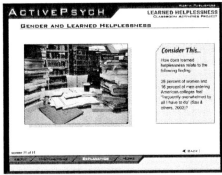

Screen 11

Explanation: Explain that, in the study noted in the question on screen, men reported spending more of their time in activities such as sports, watching TV, and partying—possibly avoiding activities that might make them feel overwhelmed.

In addition, point out that a woman might worry and act anxious (or depressed). Whereas, a man might, instead, drink, act out, become involved in work, or watch sports (Nolen-Hoeksema, 2001; Seligman, 1994).

Further point out that studies show women experience a doubled risk of depression—that is, they tend to think when trouble strikes; whereas men tend to act. In addition, women often have vivid recall for horrible as well as wonderful experiences; whereas men remember such experiences more vaguely (Seidletz & Diener, 1998).

Personality: FREUD DEMONSTRATION

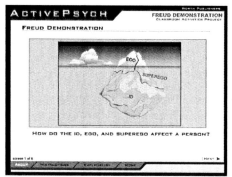

Screen 1

This demonstration was written by Karsten Look, Columbus State Community College

About: In this demonstration, students role-play the three aspects of personality, according to Freud's theory: the id, ego, and superego.

Working in groups of three, students role-play either the id, ego, or superego in a simulated daily real-life decision. The ego comes up with a situation about which he or she needs to make a decision every single day; the id and superego play the parts of lawyers, arguing the cases from their perspectives; the ego makes the final, realistic judgment.

For additional information about any activity screen, click on the illuminated gray tab; use the last "Consider This…" activity screens to promote class discussion.

RELATED TOPICS: Personality, the psychoanalytic perspective, the unconscious.

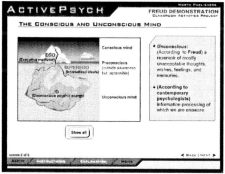

Screen 2

Instructions: For additional information about the id, ego, and superego, roll your mouse over the labels on the illustration. Click "Show All" to view all the descriptions.

Explanation: Make sure students note that the id is totally unconscious, while the ego and superego operate both consciously and unconsciously. (Illustration adapted from Freud, 1933, p. 111.)

Remind students that Sigmund Freud (1856–1939) developed a theory of personality that stresses the influence of the unconscious, the importance of sexual and aggressive instincts, and lasting effects of very early childhood experience on personality.

Point out that Freud believed people repress, or block from consciousness, unacceptable passions and thoughts—but repressed thoughts and feelings influence the work we do, the beliefs we hold, our everyday habits, and any troubling symptoms we may have.

Further point out that, according to Freud, personality arises from our efforts to resolve conflicts between our aggressive, pleasure-seeking biological impulses and social restraints. Through our personalities (and interaction among the *id, ego,* and *superego*) we attempt to satisfactorily resolve conflicts without also promoting guilt or punishment.

Screen 3

NOTE: The next screen provides instructions for students to perform their own Freud demonstration.

Instructions: Have the class brainstorm a common problem college students face—for instance: You just learned about a party that will begin at 8 PM, but you had earlier planned on studying for a math quiz you think your instructor might give your class the next morning. What do you decide to do?

Click on "ID" and read the words in the speech bubble. Then, ask students to answer the question "What should the person do" from the ID's perspective. Follow the same procedure when you click on "SUPEREGO" and, finally, "EGO."

Explanation: Suggest to students that they think of a newborn in relationship to the id. Operating on the *pleasure principle* the newborn cries out at the very moment it seeks satisfaction in terms of its needs. Also, an id-driven adult may be someone who lives only for the present (i.e., I'll go to the party and not study for tomorrow's test). Those without a future time perspective tend more often to use tobacco, alcohol, and drugs.

Suggest to students that they think of a young child who learns to wait his turn to go down a slide in relationship to the ego. That child operates on the *reality principle*—the ability to postpone gratification until the appropriate time. This role creates the executive role of the ego in mediating between the id and superego in everyday situations.

Point out that a child at around four or five years old begins to think in relationship to the superego. At that age (according to Freud), children can recognize the voice of conscience that considers not only the reality of a situation (ego) but the right and wrong behavior in that situation (superego).

Screen 4

NOTE: If you have a large number of students, you may want to have three volunteers perform the demonstration for the rest of the class.

Instructions: Click "Play" to view the roles students will play in their Freud Demonstration. In groups of three, have members assign the role of Judge Ego, the lawyer for Id, or the lawyer for Superego. Remind students that, as a group, they will role-play three aspects of personality in relationship to an everyday decision that is made.

Ask each group to come up with a situation that demands a judgment, which a person might face during a typical day. Have the lawyers for Id and Superego argue for their clients, based on Freud's theory of personality. Then have Judge Ego make a judgment, providing a brief explanation for his or her decision.

Invite volunteer groups (or your single demonstration group) to act out their demonstration, but without identifying the role each group member is playing. Make sure students watching the demonstration can identify the Id, Ego, and Superego and that they clearly understand the role each plays in decision making.

Screen 5

Explanation: Point out (as the animation on screen shows) that an ego in conflict often feels anxiety, as it fears being unable to resolve a battle between the demands of the id (immediate gratification, pleasure-seeking behavior) and the superego (the conscience that determines right from wrong).

Further point out that Freud proposed that the ego protects itself with *defense mechanisms*—that is, ways of reducing anxiety by unconsciously distorting reality. Some of these mechanisms are *repression* (banishing anxious thoughts from the conscious), *regression* (retreating to an earlier, childish mode of behavior), *reaction formation* (expressing feelings that are opposite of those that provoked the anxiety), *projection* (attributing anxious feelings to others), *rationalization* (self-justifying explanations in place of real, more-threatening, reasons for anxiety), *displacement* (redirecting anxiety toward an acceptable or less threatening object, outlet, or person), *denial* (not acknowledging existence of anxiety), and *undoing* (unconscious repentance in which someone atones for one action with another).

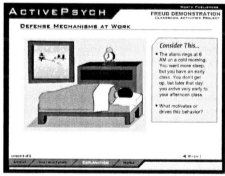

Screen 6

Explanation: Remind students that defense mechanisms, according to Freud, are ways of reducing anxiety by unconsciously distorting reality.

After students speculate and respond to the question, point out that one defense mechanism that Freud described, *undoing*, may explain the early arrival at classes after having made the decision to sleep beyond the alarm. *Undoing* is a form of repentance—perhaps the superego (the conscience considering if behavior is right or wrong) deemed that oversleeping was the wrong behavior. To make up for this lapse in behavior, you arrive earlier than necessary for an afternoon class, as if early arrival is a way of compensating for the morning's mistaken decision.

Disorders and Therapy: SOME MODELS OF THERAPY

Screen 1

This demonstration was written by Elaine Epstein, with contributions from Karsten Look, Columbus State Community College and Thomas E. Ludwig, Hope College

About: This activity offers an overview of the following therapies: psychodynamic, humanistic, behavior, cognitive, and biomedical. Note that these therapies may overlap or be used in combination (e.g., cognitive and behavior techniques are often combined; drug therapy can be used with any of the other therapies; patients can be treated one-on-one or in group sessions).

Videos, photos, and animations will help students better understand how a particular therapy or combination of therapies can help treat certain kinds of psychological disorders.

For additional information about any screen activity, click on the illuminated gray tab; use the last "Consider This…" activity screens to promote class discussion.

RELATED TOPICS: Psychological disorders, evaluating psychotherapies.

NOTE: This activity can be use in conjunction with the *ActivePsych* activity "Creative People and Psychological Disorders" and "Freud Demonstration."

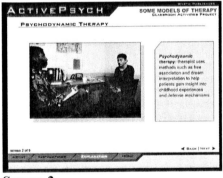

Screen 2

Explanation: Point out that psychodynamic therapy is based on the earlier method of (long-term) psychoanalysis developed by Sigmund Freud. In traditional psychoanalysis, the patient, lying on a couch, meets with the therapist several times a week, often for many years.

In modern psychodynamic therapy, patients may either lie down or sit upright in a chair meeting with the therapist face-to-face (depending on their mood or comfort level). Patients may also meet with the therapist less frequently (perhaps once a week, rather than several times a week) and for shorter periods (perhaps a few weeks to several months—though, in some cases, therapy may still continue for many years).

Also point out a variation on psychodynamic therapy, usually lasting three to four months, called *interpersonal psychotherapy*. This therapy seems to be effective in treating depressed patients (Weissman, 1999). Its goal is not personality change. Rather than focusing on undoing past hurts and offering interpretations, the therapist focuses on improving *current* relationships in a patient's life, as well as the patients' overall relationship skills, by gaining insight into the roots of their difficulties.

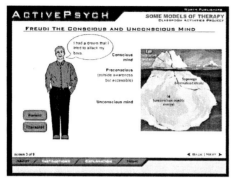

Screen 3

Instructions: First, click the "Patient" button to learn about the patient's problem and its relationship to the patient's mind.

Next, click the "Therapist" button to learn about the therapist's response to the patient's problem. Note that the response is intended to elicit information from the patient about his past experiences.

Explanation: Explain that, psychodynamic therapists are influenced by Freud. According to Freud, the *unconscious* is a reservoir of mostly unacceptable thoughts, wishes, feelings, and memories. According to contemporary psychologists, the unconscious refers to information processing of which we are unaware.

Make sure students note that the *id* is totally unconscious, while the *ego* and *superego* operate both consciously and unconsciously. (Illustration adapted from Freud, 1933, p. 111.)

Point out that Freud believed people repress, or block from consciousness, unacceptable passions and thoughts—but repressed thoughts and feelings influence the work we do, the beliefs we hold, our everyday habits, and any troubling symptoms we may have.

Further point out that, according to Freud, personality arises from our efforts to resolve conflicts between our aggressive, pleasure-seeking biological impulses and social restraints. Through our personalities (and the interaction between the *id*, *ego*, and *superego*), we attempt to satisfactorily resolve conflicts without also promoting guilt or punishment.

Screen 4

Instructions: Explain to students that you are going to embark on a session with a "computer therapist." To start, click "Begin Session." Then, invite a volunteer to create the "client" side of a conversation with the computer therapist. (Alternately, you can have the entire class collaborate to create the client.) Have the student(s) suggest client statements. "I think my mother hates me" is an example of a statement a client might make.

Type the first client statement into the "Type here" box, and press "Submit." Note that you should not press the "Enter" key or "Submit" button until you have typed your complete sentence (or phrase) because the therapist will respond each time you submit.

Continue the conversation one sentence at a time. The computer therapist will respond after each client statement you submit, reflecting back some of the client's feelings and probing for more details in an attempt to get him/her in touch with his/her feelings. The simulation will be more useful and interesting if client statements are sincere, with real-life problems and real feelings expressed.

Click "End session" to exit the computer therapist and see some final thoughts on the session.

Explanation: Point out that client-centered therapy is a humanistic therapy, developed by Carl Rogers (1902–1987). He (and other humanists) believed that most people already possess the resources for growth. When therapists genuinely express their true feelings, when they emphatically sense and reflect their clients' feelings, the clients may deepen their self-understanding and self acceptance (Hill & Nakayama, 2000).

Further point out that *active-listening* involves techniques of echoing, restating and seeking clarification of what a client expresses (verbally or nonverbally) and those who practice it acknowledge the expressed feelings. (Many school counselors use this technique).

Finally, to help therapists (and people in their own relationships) listen more actively, Carl Rogers suggested that the listener *paraphrase* (check understanding by summarizing the speaker's words), invite clarification (encourage the speaker to say more—for instance by asking "What is that an example of?"), and *reflect feelings* (mirror what he/she senses from the speaker—for instance, by saying "That sounds frustrating"). What seems to count most is the trust the patient places in the listener.

Screen 5

Instructions: Click "Play" to view an animation of a therapist using a behavior modification technique (aversive conditioning) to help a client change an unwanted behavior (nail-biting).

Explanation: Point out that *cognitive-behavior therapy* (CBT) combines the cognitive approach with behavior therapy to alter both the way people act (behavior therapy) and the way people think (cognitive therapy) by putting in place a more positive approach to everyday situations as well as new ways of thinking.

Point out that this animation illustrates *aversive conditioning*, which is one form of *counterconditioning* (a therapy that conditions new responses that take the place of unwanted behavior). This method associates an unpleasant state (such as nausea) with an unwanted behavior (such as nail-biting or alcohol abuse).

Point out that in *systematic desensitization* a pleasant and relaxed state is associated with gradually increasing anxiety-triggering stimuli to help a person overcome a phobia (such as public speaking or fear of riding elevators). Both aversive conditioning and systematic desensitization are forms of *classical conditioning*, which involves repeated pairing of neutral stimulus with a response-producing stimulus until the neutral stimulus elicits the same response.

Screen 6

Instructions: Click "Play" to view a video about a group therapy session in which a participant confronts his fear of riding in an elevator.

Note that in this video *group therapy* and *behavior therapy* are combined, illustrating a successful mixture of real-life exposure therapy and group support.

Explanation: Point out that, in addition to the time and money savings group sessions can provide for people, this kind of therapy also provides a social context, allowing people to discover that others have problems similar to theirs. In group therapy, patients can try out new ways of behaving with the possibility of receiving feedback that might allay feelings of anxiousness and self-consciousness.

Also point out the many self-help and support groups that have become popular (e.g., for the bereaved, addicted, divorced, or people seeking fellowship or growth). Studies show that more than 100 million Americans belong to small religious, interest, or self-help groups that meet regularly; nine out of ten report that group members "support each other emotionally" (Gallup, 1994).

Further point out that family therapy seeks to open up communication within families to help family members discover new ways of preventing or resolving conflicts (Hazelrigg & others, 1987; Shadish & others, 1993).

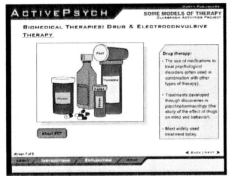

Screen 7

Instructions: To provide your students with information on electroconvulsive therapy (ECT), click "About ECT." This will bring up a description of ECT as well as a video showing electroconvulsive treatment.

Once the ECT material is shown on screen, click "Play" to view the video.

Explanation: Point out that today there are many categories of drugs used to treat psychological disorders—from antipsychotic drugs (e.g., Thorazine, Clozapine) to antianxiety drugs (e.g., Xanax, Valium) and antidepressent drugs (e.g., Prozac, Zoloft, Paxil). A simple salt, lithium, provides effective drug therapy for the mood swings in *bipolar* (manic-depressive) disorders.

Further point out that drugs for depression, like Prozac, treat an undersupply of the neurotransmitter *serotonin* in the brain. Serotonin affects mood, hunger, sleep, and arousal; the undersupply of this neurotransmitter is linked to depression. Prozac and some other antidepressant drugs treat the undersupply by raising serotonin levels.

Point out that *electroconvulsive therapy* (ECT) was introduced in 1938. Today it is limited as treatment for *severe* depression. After three sessions each week for two to four weeks, 80 percent or more of those receiving ECT improve markedly; they experience some memory loss during the treatment period without experiencing brain damage (Bergsholm & others, 1989; Coffey, 1993).

Screen 8

Instructions: Click "Play" to view the video of a person suffering from an anxiety disorder.

Name each kind of therapy, and lead students in a discussion of how each therapy might be used to treat the person shown. Might the therapies be combined? Is one therapy better than another?

The focus of each therapy model is presented on the "Explanation" tab for this screen. These points can help you guide the students in their discussion.

Explanation: With *psychodynamic therapy*, delving into the person's current behavior and past experiences while examining interpretations sheds light and provides patient with insight.

With *humanistic therapy*, acceptance and acknowledgement allow people to see life more clearly and hence take responsibility for their own growth.

With *behavior therapy*, the disorder is treated by having the person learn new ways to behave that eliminate the anxious behavior.

With *cognitive therapy*, the person learns to change self-defeating thinking and replace it with more positive thinking.

With *biomedical therapy*, drugs most likely are used as treatment. These drugs may remove feelings of anxiousness.

RELATED TOPICS: Explain the current controversy in psychology. Some science-oriented psychologists are working to extend the list of *evidence-based practice* with well-defined and validated therapies for various disorders. Other psychologists view therapy as more *art* than science, not something amenable to describing in a manual or testing in an experiment.

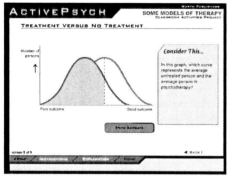

Screen 9

Instructions: After students have discussed the question, click "Show Answer" to show the correct response.

Explanation: Point out that the two normal distribution curves on the this graph represent data from 475 studies and show the improvement of both untreated people and psychotherapy clients. The outcome for the average therapy client surpassed that for 80 percent of the untreated people (Adapted from Smith and others, 1980).

Explain that psychotherapy is often less expensive than medical care for psychologically related complaints. When people seek *psychological* treatment, their search for *medical* treatment drops; one digest of 91 studies showed a drop of 16 percent (Chiles & others, 1999). In general, therapy is most effective when the problem is clear-cut (e.g., phobias or panic) (Singer, 1981; Westen & Morrison, 2001). In less focused problems (e.g., depression or anxiety), people might benefit in the short term but relapse later. Those with chronic schizophrenia or who wish to effect a full personality change are unlikely to benefit from psychotherapy alone (Zilbergeld, 1983).

Further point out that on certain matters of moral and cultural diversity, therapists may differ from one another and from their clients (Kelly, 1990). Value differences also can become significant when a therapist from one culture meets a client from another.

Disorders and Therapy: CREATIVE PEOPLE AND PSYCHOLOGICAL DISORDERS

Screen 1

This demonstration was written by Elaine Epstein and Karsten Look, Columbus State Community College

About: In this activity, students are presented with some of the creative people who have suffered from psychological disorders.

Screen 6 presents a video with John Nash, a mathematician and Nobel Laureate, who has suffered from schizophrenia and whose life is the subject of the Oscar-winning movie from 2001, *A Beautiful Mind.*

For additional information about any screen activity, click on the illuminated gray tab; use the last "Consider This..." activity screens to promote class discussion.

NOTE: This activity can be use in conjunction with the *ActivePsych* activities "Some Models of Therapy" and "Learned Helplessness."

Screen 2

Instructions: To learn how psychological disorders are viewed from a biopsychosocial perspective, click "Biological influences," "Psychological influences," and "Social-cultural influences."

When you click each item, you will see examples of the biological, psychological, and social-cultural influences that interact to produce specific psychological disorders.

To return the screen to its original position (with no influences shown), click "Reset."

Explanation: Point out that a biopsychosocial perspective recognizes that the mind and body are inseparable. For psychologists today, all behavior (whether it is considered normal or disordered) originates from an interaction of nature (genetic and physiological factors) and nurture (past and present experiences). All three factors (biological, social-cultural, and psychological issues) interact to produce a disorder.

Further explain that many disorders (e.g., depression, schizophrenia) occur in every culture (Brislin, 1993, Draguns, 1990). All humans share the same biological processes that support both healthy and unhealthy thinking, but different cultures have different social roles and different ways of coping with psychological stress. Thus, the likelihood of developing certain disorders varies across cultures.

Present these examples: In Japan, "Taijin-kyofusho" is a common social anxiety disorder that involves a readiness to blush, as well as a fear of eye contact. Reflecting the cultural emphasis of concern for others, people with this disorder fear that they will offend, insult, or embarrass other people. In Western culture, eating disorders (e.g., anorexia and bulimia nervosa) occur more frequently than in cultures from other parts of the world.

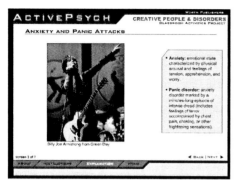

Screen 3

Explanation: Explain that Billie Joe Armstrong from the band Green Day has suffered from anxiety and panic attacks. Armstrong has said that he uses song writing as a coping mechanism, and his lyrics frequently talk about his experiences. In songs like "Basket Case" and "Bab's Uvula Who?" Armstrong talks about panic attacks, anxiety, and their physical effects.

Anxiety and panic disorders are described in the American Psychiatric Association's *Diagnostic and Statistical Manual of Mental Disorders* (DSM-IV-TR). It describes the disorders and lists them according to their prevalence (without explaining their causes). It mentions *neurotic disorders* (those that are stressful but still allow one to think rationally and function socially) and *psychotic disorders*, which are debilitating and marked by irrational behavior.

Point out that a panic attack (heart palpitations, shortness of breath, choking sensations, trembling, or dizziness) is a false alarm in the body. It is unpredictable and frightening, causing people to fear the fear itself. Smokers have a two- to fourfold risk of a first-time panic attack. (Breslau & Klein, 1999; Goodwin & Hamilton, 2002; Isensee & others, 2003).

Screen 4

Instructions: This screen opens with an excerpt from the poem "Elm" by Sylvia Plath.

To view another example showing a creative person who suffers from depression, click "Another Example" (James Hetfield of the rock band Metallica).

You can click "Return" to go back to the original example with Sylvia Plath.

Explanation: Explain that the text passage shown with the image of Sylvia Path (1932–1963) is from the poem "Elm" in her book *Ariel*. Tell students that Plath wrote the poems in *Ariel* in the last months of her life, before committing suicide. Her life was the subject of her novel *The Bell Jar*, which was made into a movie in 1979. In 2003, the actress Gwyneth Paltrow played Sylvia Plath in a biographical movie entitled *Sylvia*.

Click "Another Example" and explain that the person shown is James Hetfield from the band Metallica. Tell students that Hetfield went through individual therapy in a rehabilitation center, as well as group therapy with the other band members, to deal with psychological disorders that negatively affected everyone in the group. The 2003 film "Metallica: Some Kind of Monster" follows the band during the tense period in which they recorded their album *St. Anger* and sought the counsel of an on-call therapist.

Point out the following summary of facts that all depression theories need to address: many behavioral and cognitive changes accompany depression; it is widespread; women are twice as vulnerable to major depression, more so if they have been depressed before; most major depressive episodes self-terminate; and stressful events related to work, marriage, and close relationships often precede depression (Lewinsohn & colleagues, 1985, 1998).

Screen 5

Explanation: Point out that one of mania's maladaptive symptoms is grandiose optimism and self-esteem, which may lead to reckless behavior. When mania is strong, people need protection from their own poor judgment. In milder forms, however, the energy and free-flowing thinking of mania can fuel creativity.

Finally, point out that the risk of major depression and bipolar disorder increases if you have a depressed parent or sibling (Sullivan & others, 2000). The writer Ernest Hemingway (1891–1961) committed suicide, as did his father, brother, sister, and his granddaughter, the actress Margaux Hemingway. Margaux committed suicide in 1996, just one day shy of the anniversary of her famous grandfather's death.

Screen 6

Instructions: Click "Play" to view an interview with the mathematician and Nobel Laureate John Nash. The interview originally aired on the television program *60 Minutes* in March 2002.

OPTIONAL: As an extra credit assignment, you can ask students to do a film review of the movie *A Beautiful Mind*. As part of the assignment, duplicate and distribute the response sheet that accompanies this activity. (The response sheet presents questions that students may respond to in writing or in small discussion groups.)

To provide students with the handout, click "Print Handout." Once you have opened the PDF handout file, you can print copies for your students.

Explanation: Let students know that the 2001 Oscar-winning movie, *A Beautiful Mind*, was about the life of John Nash, including his struggle with schizophrenia. The video in this activity shows a 2002 interview with the real-life mathematician and Nobel Laureate John Nash. In the clip, the real Nash briefly discusses his thoughts about the movie and its casting.

Extend students' knowledge by explaining that some psychologists believe the disorganized thoughts of schizophrenics may result from a a breakdown in selective attention. People with this disorder may have difficulty clearing their working memory of distracting information and inhibiting irrelevant material (Schooler & others, 1997; Holden, 2003).

Further point out that schizophrenics may perceive things that are not there, or *hallucinations* (sensory experiences without sensory stimulation). Many of the hallucinations are auditory.

Finally, explain that researchers have studied brain abnormality and chemistry imbalances in relationship to schizophrenia. The nearly 1 in 100 odds of a person being diagnosed with schizophrenia becomes 1 in 10 among those who have an afflicted parent or sibling. Note that John Nash's son (who is also interviewed in the video) has also struggled with schizophrenia.

VIDEO SOURCE: "John Nash's Beautiful Mind," *60 Minutes*, 3/17/02 (CBS News)

Screen 7

<u>Explanation:</u> Let students know that these pictures were created by Louis Wain, a 20th-century artist. Wain was fascinated by cats and painted these pictures over a period of time during which he developed schizophrenia.

These pictures exemplify the effects of schizophrenia on the perceptions of a person suffering from the disorder. The disorder not only creates false sensory experiences of things that aren't there, it also distorts the person's thought processes, including the perception of things that actually *are* present. Occasionally, patients are frightened by common objects, misperceiving a coiled rope as a snake or branches of a tree as arms reaching toward them. The cats in these pictures show what schizophrenia can do to a person's *visual* perception.

Social Psychology: The Actor-Observer Difference in Attribution

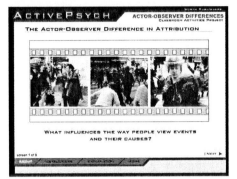

Screen 1

This demonstration was written by Martin Bolt, Calvin College

About: This activity explores the *actor-observer difference in attribution*: The tendency to explain our own behavior in terms of the situation and our tendency to explain another's behavior in terms of the person's disposition or personal qualities.

Students will respond to two questionnaires: (1) perceptions of the self; (2) perceptions of another (a former teacher). Students will anonymously indicate their responses on handouts. You will collect the handouts and record the results.

Results will be discussed in terms of the actor-observer difference in attribution, which is a *fundamental attribution error*.

For additional information about any activity screen, click on the illuminated gray tabs; use the last "Consider This..." activity screens to promote class discussion.

RELATED TOPICS: attribution theory, fundamental attribution error, blaming the victim.

Screen 2

Instructions: Provide students with handouts for the two questionnaires in this activity. (Click "Print Handout" on screens 2 and 3. Once you have opened the PDF handout file, you can print copies for your students.) Tell students the questionnaires should be answered independently.

For each pair of traits, students should choose the trait that is more characteristic of either themselves (for Perceptions of Self) or another (for Perceptions of a Former Teacher). If neither of the traits in a pair is more characteristic, students may choose "Depends on the situation."

Tell students they will have only 5 minutes to complete both questionnaires; therefore, they should use the first answer that comes to mind.

After students have completed the questionnaires, for each pair ask students to raise their hands ONLY if they indicated "Depends on the situation." Adjust the slider to show the approximate percentage of students who have raised their hands and click "Submit."

Responses for Perceptions of Self will be recorded on screen 2. Responses for Perceptions of a Former Teacher will be recorded on screen 3.

Screen 3

NOTE: The submitted responses for both questionnaires will be discussed on screen 4.

Screen 4

Explanation: Point out this simple example of how the actor-observer difference in attribution works: A person trips on a sidewalk that is not very well maintained. The person who tripped might first consider the cause of the trip to be the sidewalk's less-than-perfect condition. Someone observing from a distance might think, instead, that the person who tripped was quite clumsy.

You might also want to point out the attribution bias called *blaming the victim*—the tendency to blame an innocent victim of misfortune for having somehow caused the problem or for not having taken steps to avoid it. In hindsight it seems as if the victim should have been able to prevent or predict what was going to happen (Goldinger & others, 2003).

Remind students that the various attributions they make have a strong influence on their thoughts and feelings about other people.

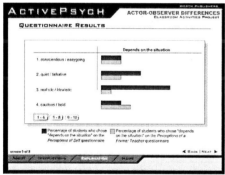

Screen 5

Explanation: You will most likely find that the majority of respondents indicate "depends on the situation" more often for themselves than they do for other people.

The discrepancy is due to the *actor-observer difference in attribution* (the tendency to explain our own behavior in terms of the situation and another's behavior in terms of that person's disposition or personal qualities).

Help students recall that the tendency to underestimate the situational influences on the behavior of others is called the *fundamental attribution error*.

Screen 6

VIDEO SOURCE: Footage from March 20, 2003 Antiwar Protest, San Francisco—Lisa Rein

Instructions: Click "Play" to view the video.

Have students work in small groups to formulate an explanation for the events on the video in terms of the actor-observer difference in attribution.

Explanation: To clarify this attribution discrepancy, you could present this real-life event: In 1979, the rock group The Who, whose performances often concluded with the band's violent destruction of their equipment, gave a concert at which a riot broke out. While a reporter from *Time* magazine (the observer) attributed the riot to the rock group's "violently destructive message," a concert-goer (the actor) wrote a letter to the magazine and attributed the riot to the "inhumane policy of festival seating at rock concerts." (Nisbett & others, 1973)

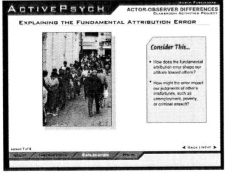

Screen 7

Explanation: Tell students that we tend to attribute causation to the focus of our attention. We have one focus for the cause of an event if we act and, often, a different focus for the cause of the same event when we observe it from the outside.

For instance: when we happen to be present at an event (for example, if we were waiting on the unemployment line shown in the photo on this screen) we usually view the cause of the event as being related to elements of the situation itself, rather than to our own personal qualities.

On the other hand: when we observe other people in an event (for example, if we were a foreign tourist passing by the unemployment line shown in the photo) we usually view the cause of the event as related to the people involved in it, as well as to their personal qualities. Note that when this photograph was taken the government of Argentina gave food subsidies to its unemployed citizens because of a serious, national recession. A foreign tourist may not be aware of another country's recession, nor of the seriousness of the situation, and so might attribute the unemployment as being the fault of the people on line.

Point out that the actor-observer difference in attribution often occurs in regard to behaviors that lead to negative outcomes.

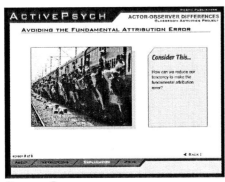

Screen 8

Explanation: To help students understand how one might make a fundamental attribution error, have them discuss possible causes for the crowded train shown in the photograph on this screen (as well as the behavior of the passengers). Then have students consider whether their initial analysis might be different if the person looking at the photograph personally knew any of the individuals on that crowded train.

Point out that the train scene is from Patna, a city in eastern India, in 2005. With a fast-rising population, the trains are often crowded and inadequate. An outsider may think that people in this region prefer to travel this way or, possibly, that these people didn't pay for tickets and, therefore, hopped onto the trains for a free ride. Whereas, someone from this region may be well aware of the inadequate transportation system.

Make sure students understand that the *fundamental attribution error* is the tendency to underestimate the situational influences on the behavior of others.

Point out that when we explain the behavior of people we already know, our familiarity with them allows us to become more aware of situational influences.

ActivePsych CD 1

Classroom Activities Projects: PowerPoint-Based Interactive Demonstrations

---

PowerPoint-Based Demonstrations: Usage Guide and Technical Information

In contrast to the highly interactive exercises offered in each Flash-based activity, the ActivePsych Classroom Activities Projects also offers 22 PowerPoint presentations designed with brevity in mind. Each PowerPoint activity focuses on a single question or group of related questions, and can be presented in only five to ten minutes. Students will learn to examine their own opinions on a variety of issues, including Research Methods: Illusory Correlations; Personality: Assessing Self Esteem; Neuroscience and Behavior: Name That Brain Damage; Learning and Memory: False Memory; Social Psychology: Snap Judgments; Emotion and Motivation: Intrinsic and Extrinsic Motivation; and Disorders and Therapy: Media, Pharmaceuticals, and Mental Illness.

Using the PowerPoint demonstrations

Each PowerPoint demonstration begins with an overview of the topic or question to be presented. In addition, many of the demonstrations are accompanied by printable handouts containing background information or survey questions.

After the overview, the activity moves on to a series of multiple-choice questions designed to promote class discussion. These questions work seamlessly with iClicker Classroom Response Systems. After the multiple-choice questions, each demonstration offers a summative statement about the material presented. Finally, the demonstration concludes with a critical-thinking "Consider This…" question, which can be used to prompt class discussion, a structured in-class debate, or for any number of homework assignments.

Using the iClicker Classroom Response System, students can enjoy seeing their responses presented in large, full color histograms almost immediately after they respond. They especially enjoy the instant and anonymous comparison with the rest of the class. If your classroom doesn't use an electronic response system, not to worry. The presentations will work just fine the old-fashioned way—by having students raise their hands or by collecting written responses.

Instructions on how to best present the demonstrations to your students in a classroom setting, as well as additional background information for each slide, are included in PowerPoint's "Notes" pane. The "Notes" pane is the area you see in "Normal" view in which you can type information to accompany any slide. If you want to bring the information to class, you can print these notes by selecting "Notes Pages" in the "Print" dialogue box.

ActivePsych PowerPoint demonstrations are a great way for students to apply their own experiences to an examination of the big issues in introductory psychology, and to see how their opinions and experiences match up to those of the other students in the class. These activities can help them feel that psychology is pertinent to the important things in their own lives, and can lead to some excellent discussions and debates.

Launching the PowerPoint-based demonstrations

You can launch any one of the ActivePsych Classroom Activities Projects (whether it's built in Flash or PowerPoint) from the **main menu**.

Click on any of the titles to launch the demonstration in a new window.

If the demonstration is accompanied by a handout, the handout name(s) will follow the demonstration title.

Click on the handout name and it, too, will launch in a new window.

If you would rather not launch the demonstrations or handouts from the ActivePsych interface, you will find the .ppt and .doc files at the root level of ActivePsych CD 1 in the **PPT** and **DOC** folders.

Please note that these PowerPoint demonstrations require **Microsoft PowerPoint** to run. Also, many activities are accompanied by handouts provided as separate **Microsoft Word** documents. Microsoft PowerPoint and Microsoft Word are NOT free software programs. If you do not have those programs installed on your computer, you will need to purchase a copy of each program to view the .doc or .ppt files provided in the collection of PowerPoint-based Classroom Activities Projects.

iClickers and ActivePsych

The 22 PowerPoint-based activities in the ActivePsych Classroom Activities Projects are designed to work with iClicker Classroom Response Systems, but can also be used with any comparable clicker technology. Using iClickers, you can immediately assess your students' understanding of a topic. iClickers can also help you identify the topics with which your students are struggling.

With opinion questions like the ones presented in the ActivePsych PowerPoint-based demonstrations, clickers record students' responses and offer a graphic representation of the distribution of those responses across the class as a whole. Using clickers encourages reading before lecture; students feel the course is a more personal experience and are often more inclined to pay attention and participate.

iClicker works on a radio frequency bandwidth for accurate, immediate results. It is exceptionally easy to install and use iClicker, with software available for both PC and Mac. For more information on using iClicker in your classroom, go to: http://www.iclicker.com. If you have any questions about iClicker, or want to set up a training session, contact zpage@bfwpub.com.

PowerPoint-Based Demonstrations: Descriptions and File Names

Introduction/History

Big Issues in Psychology   **File name = 01_BigIssues.ppt**

Description: This activity introduces some of the major issues addressed by psychologists and researchers. This activity may used as a course introduction. It also may accompany textbook reading that introduces the topic of contemporary psychology.

Related Topics: Behavioral genetics, evolutionary psychology, cultural influences, gender differences, reflections on nature and nurture.

Handouts: HO1_BigIssues.doc and HO2_BigIssues.doc (note that Handout 2 is used for scoring Handout 1). Before you begin this demonstration, duplicate and distribute both handouts to each student. On slide 2, students will be directed to use the handouts.

Research Methods

Illusory Correlations   **File name = 02_IllusCorrelation.ppt**

Description: This activity demonstrates illusory correlation—that is, the tendency to see a relationship where none exists. Ideas covered in this activity include stereotypes, confirmation bias, and superstitious beliefs. This activity helps illustrate these phenomena in the students' own lives and promotes discussion.

Related Topics: Correlation and causation, thinking critically.

Handouts: HO_IllCorrelation.doc (*The Findings*). Before you begin this demonstration, duplicate and distribute the handout that accompanies the activity to each student. On slide 2, students will be directed to use the handout.

Neuroscience and Behavior

Name That Brain Damage   **File name = 03_NameBrainDamage.ppt**

Description: Damage to certain areas of the brain can cause specific deficits in behavior. This activity links specific brain areas with their functions. You may wish to have students read their textbook chapter about the brain and behavior before presenting this activity. On slides 2–6, you will find illustrations of the various brain areas, labeled according to their general functions.

Related Topics: Neuroscience and behavior, the older brain, the cerebral cortex.

Handouts: This activity does not include handouts.

Consciousness

Lark or Owl?   **File name = 04_LarkOrOwl.ppt**

Description: With this activity students assess their tendency to be a "morning" or "evening" person. Our ancestors' body clocks were attuned to the rising and setting of the sun in a 24-hour day. But young adults today adapt to something closer to a 25-hour day, by staying up too late to get eight hours of sleep. With the help of the light bulb, our body clocks are nudged back.

Related Topics: Sleeping, dreaming, biological and circadian rhythms.

Handouts: HO_LarkOrOwl.doc (*Morning or Evening Person?*). Before you begin this demonstration, duplicate and distribute the handout that accompanies the activity to each student. On slide 2, students will be directed to use the handout.

Learning and Memory

False Memory   **File name = 05_FalseMemory.ppt**

Description: This activity demonstrates people's capacity to form a false memory. We do not recall exact copies of past events. Rather, we construct our memories. Memory can be assessed in different ways. This activity includes an experiment which allows students to experience memory construction first hand.

Related Topics: Memory construction, discerning true and false memories, recall.

Handouts: HO_FalseMemory.doc (*Recognizing the Words*). Before you begin this demonstration, duplicate the handout that accompanies the activity. Slide 2 offers suggestions on how and when to distribute the handout. On slide 19, students will be directed to complete the handout.

RUNNING THE ACTIVITY

– Please note that the "False Memory" activity includes a memory recall and recognition task. Because the word list is set to specific timings, you MUST view this PowerPoint file in "Slide Show" mode during your presentation.

– To do this, choose "View Show" under the "Slide Show" menu.

– You can advance each slide by clicking your mouse or hitting the "Enter" key on your keyboard. HOWEVER, once the word list appears, it will advance automatically.

– Once the word list is complete, you should go back to advancing each slide by clicking your mouse or hitting the "Enter" key on your keyboard.

Thinking, Language, and Intelligence

Multiple Intelligences   File name = 06_MultipleIntel.ppt

Description: This activity introduces the theory of multiple intelligences and presents questions that help students consider in what ways they are smart. Most people tend to think of intelligence only in terms of "school smarts" or academic ability. Researchers, however, define intelligence more broadly. The common theme in all the definitions is "the capacity to function effectively in one's environment."

Related Topics: Mental abilities, aptitude, individual differences.

Handouts: This activity does not include handouts.

Prototypes   File name = 07_Prototypes.ppt

Description: This activity introduces the idea of "prototype" and "stereotype" and demonstrates the power of gender schemas. This activity includes an experiment which will elucidate how students' own ideas about the world are affected by prototypes, stereotypes, and gender schemas.

Related Topics: Social psychology, prejudice and stereotypes, thinking, concepts and prototypes, perception and schemas.

Handouts: This activity does not include handouts.

Emotion and Motivation

Emotional Expressivity   File name = 08_ExEmotion.ppt

Description: This activity helps students assess outward displays of emotions by themselves and by other people. Some emotional facial expressions are universal—a smile, expressions for anger, and, to a lesser extent, fear and surprise. Findings indicate that expressions not only communicate emotion, they also amplify and regulate it.

Related Topics: Personality, Big Five personality traits.

Handouts: HO1_ExEmotion.doc (*Emotional Expressivity Scale*) and HO2_ExEmotion.doc (*Scoring the Emotional Expressivity Scale*). Before you begin this demonstration, duplicate and distribute both handouts to each student. On slide 2, students will be directed to use the handouts.

Emotion and Motivation *(cont.)*

Envy and Jealousy   File name = 09_Envy.ppt

Description: This activity helps students assess emotions of envy and jealousy in themselves and in other people. This activity uses the *DES (Dispositional Envy Scale)* to measure the students' levels of envy and discusses the relationship between envy, ill will, inferiority, depression, and self-reliance.

Related Topics: Social psychology, attitudes and actions.

Handouts: HO_Envy.doc *(DES / Dispositional Envy Scale)*. Before you begin this demonstration, duplicate and distribute the handout that accompanies this activity to each student.

Intrinsic and Extrinsic Motivation   File name = 10_Motivation.ppt

Description: What motivates your behavior? Those who are worried about their course grade or are eager for a reward are *extrinsically* motivated. Those who find the course material interesting, who learn in order to feel more competent, or who simply study for the joy of learning or to satisfy their curiosity are *intrinsically* motivated.

Related Topics: Learning, social thinking, behavior attribution.

Handouts: This activity does not include handouts.

Stress and Health

Your Stress Level   File name = 11_StressLevel.ppt

Description: This activity helps respondents assess their stress level and factors that lead to stress. When stress is short-lived or perceived as a challenge, stressors can have a positive effect. On the other hand, prolonged stress from severe child abuse puts children at later risk of chronic disease.

Related Topics: Psychological disorders, personality.

Handouts: HO_StressLevel.doc *(Susceptibility to Stress / SUS)*. Before you begin this demonstration, duplicate and distribute the handout that accompanies this activity to each student.

Stress and Health (cont.)

Managing Stress   File name = 12_StressManage.ppt

Description: This activity introduces students to stress management through attitude adjustment. It includes information about Rational Emotive Therapy (RET) as well as the A-B-C model of personality and how they can be used to change students' beliefs about stress and their ability to cope. You might want to use this activity after students have read about the stress response system, stress hormones, and the effects of chronic stress.

Related Topics: Stress and stressors, coping with stress, managing stress, therapy.

Handouts: HO1_StressManage.doc (*Stress Management*) and HO2_StressManage.doc (*Ten Trouble-Making Irrational Beliefs*). Duplicate each handout and distribute them to the class as directed on slide 4.

Coping with Health Problems   File name = 13_Health.ppt

Description: This activity helps students assess how they respond to health problems. That is, how our attitudes and behaviors affect our health and health maintenance. You may wish to use this activity as an introduction or accompanying exercise for textbook chapters on stress and health.

Related Topics: Personality, social-cognitive perspective and personal control.

Handouts: HO1_Health.doc (*Coping with Health Injuries and Problems Scale*) and HO2_Health.doc (*Scoring the Coping with Health Injuries and Problems Scale*). Before you begin this demonstration, duplicate and distribute both handouts to each student. On slide 2, students will be receive directions on how to complete and score the handout.

Personality

Assessing Self-Esteem   File name = 14_SelfEsteem.ppt

Description: This activity assesses respondents' level of self-worth. Once assessed, this activity goes on to discuss how life events affect self-esteem and how, in turn, self-esteem, affects student's lives.

Related Topics: Exploring the self, drives and incentives, cognition and emotion.

Handouts: HO1_SelfEsteem.doc and HO2_ SelfEsteem.doc (note that Handout 2 is used for scoring Handout 1, the *Self-Esteem Scale*). Duplicate the two handouts and distribute them to students as directed on slide 2.

Personality *(cont.)*

Profiling a Terrorist   File name = 15_Profiling.ppt

Description: This activity involves a classroom survey that develops a psychological profile of a terrorist. What motivates people to become involved in terrorism? Is it possible to develop a "profile" of a typical terrorist?

Related Topics: Theories of personality, social psychology, attribution.

Handouts: This activity does not include handouts.

Disorders and Therapy

Name That Disorder   File name = 16_NameDisorder.ppt

Description: This activity presents case studies in which individuals suffer from symptoms of psychological disorders. This activity consists of eight case studies; in each, an individual experiences symptoms of either panic disorder, obsessive-compulsive disorder (OCD), posttraumatic stress disorder (PTSD), bipolar disorder, paranoid schizophrenia, antisocial personality disorder, agoraphobia, or major depressive disorder.

Related Topics: Psychological disorders, psychotherapies.

Handouts: This activity does not include handouts.

Name That Therapy   File name = 17_NameTherapy.ppt

Description: This activity presents case studies for which you can identify the type of therapy employed. The activity consists of 10 case studies. Each case presents techniques of either psychoanalysis, humanistic therapy, behavior therapy, cognitive therapy, cognitive-behavior therapy, group and family therapy, or biomedical therapy.

Related Topics: Psychological disorders, psychotherapies.

Handouts: This activity does not include handouts.

Disorders and Therapy *(cont.)*

Media, Pharmaceuticals, and Mental Illness   File name = 18_MediaPharm.ppt

Description: This activity demonstrates how the media can influence the associations people make with mental illness and certain drug therapies. This activity addresses issues surrounding diagnosis of mental illness and the drug therapies which treat them, including which disorders merit drug therapies, should pharmaceutical companies advertise for drug therapies, and who should prescribe them.

Related Topics: Stress and health, psychological disorders, psychotherapies.

Handouts: HO_MediaPharm.doc (*Questionnaire: Adult ADD*). Before you begin this demonstration, duplicate the handout that accompanies this activity (a questionnaire entitled "Adult ADD"). Directions for distributing the handout are provided on slide 2.

Social Psychology

Snap Judgments   File name = 19_SnapJudgment.ppt

Description: This activity examines the role of snap judgments in people's everyday functioning. This activity presents two questions (slides 3 and 5) to help students determine how they use snap judgments in their everyday functioning. Along the way, they'll discover some surprising characteristics about these unconscious mental processes.

Related Topics: Social psychology, attitudes and actions, personality, perceptual set, context effects.

Handouts: This activity does not include handouts.

Belief in a Just World   File name = 20_JustWorld.ppt

Description: This demonstration offers ways to predict a variety of social attitudes and behaviors. This activity introduces the Just-World Phenomenon and uses the Just World Scale in order to foment thought and discussion about issues such as justice, prejudice, and the bystander effect.

Related Topics: Social psychology, social relations, prejudice.

Handouts: HO1_JustWorld.doc and HO2_JustWorld.doc (note that Handout 2 is used for scoring Handout 1, the *Just World Scale*). Before you begin this demonstration, duplicate and distribute both handouts to each student. On slide 2, students will be directed on how to complete and score the handout.

Social Psychology *(cont.)*

Trust   File name = 21_Trust.ppt

Description: This activity makes use of a questionnaire which helps respondents understand elements of trust, a key in loving relationships based on companionate love. This activity may help to introduce or enhance your textbook chapter on social psychology, especially after students read about the psychology of attraction.

Related Topics: Social psychology, the psychology of attraction, romantic love, emotions, expressed emotion.

Handouts: **HO1_Trust.doc** and **HO2_Trust.doc** (note that Handout 2 is used for scoring Handout 1, the *Trust Scale*). Before you begin this demonstration, duplicate and distribute both handouts to each student. On slide 2, students will be directed to complete and score the handouts.

The Ideal Romantic Partner   File name = 22_RomanticIdeal.ppt

Description: This activity is a classroom survey that measures characteristics of students' ideal romantic partner. Slides 3–6 present questions in the Ideal Romantic Partner Survey. In addition to the survey, you might have students write down a definition of romantic love or a description of their perfect soul mate.

Related Topics: Theories of emotion, adulthood, sexual motivation, attraction.

Handouts: This activity does not include handouts.

ActivePsych CD 2 and 3 / DVD 1 and 2 / VHS 1 and 2:

Digital Media Archive, Second Edition

*Edited by Joe Morrissey, State University of New York at Binghamton
(with the assistance of Ann Merriwether, State University of New York at Binghamton and
Meredith Woitach, University of Rochester)*

Video Descriptions and Segment Lengths

Neuroscience and Behavior
Neural Communication: Impulse Transmission Across the Synapse

Segment	Length:	File Name:
1	01:45 min	01_Neuro_Impulse.mpg

Source   Three-dimensional modeling by Animated Biomedical Productions:
www.medical-animations.com

Description

This segment is a computer generated image modeling the transmission of a nerve impulse across the synapse between two neurons. The electric impulse in this segment is represented by the green light. As the impulse, called an action potential, travels down the axon, it spurs the vesicles in the pre-synaptic ending to release neurotransmitters from the axon and into the synapse. These neurotransmitters are accepted by receptors on the post-synaptic end of the adjacent neuron, creating a new action potential and passing the impulse down the axon on to the next nerve cell.

Placement

This visual can be helpful in any of the neuroscience chapters, but is best applied to the initial coverage of the nervous system. When covering the nervous system from the cellular perspective a demonstration of the activity of the neuron is particularly helpful. Neuroscience material in general lends itself to diagrams and dynamic images such as this one.

Discussion Questions:

1. How do neurons—transmitting impulses—integrate to form thoughts and actions?

2. Given that sensory information must be transferred between neurons, what does this imply about areas of the body, such as the brain or the tongue, which have a high quantity and high density of neurons?

3. After viewing this segment, what might you predict will occur if the transmission of neurotransmitters across the synapse is blocked? What if it is facilitated?

Neuroscience and Behavior
Activity, Exercise, and the Brain

Segment	Length:	File Name:
2	05:01 min	02_Neuro_Exercise.mpg

Description

In the past, it was believed that human brain development remained relatively stable once we hit adulthood, with no further growth and only deterioration with age. Current research, in contrast, suggests that an enriching environment can both increase the number of nerve connections and extend the vascular system of the brain even during adulthood. In other words, brain growth and development continues throughout the human life span.

In this segment, Dr. Greenough explains current research being done with rats at the University of Illinois. Adult rats are either housed in a complex, changing environment with other rats or are isolated in a small cage. Rats experiencing the "enriched" environment show a more developed brain than those in the control condition.

In another experiment, rats are either trained on an obstacle course which evokes learning but requires little physical effort, or they run on a wheel, providing exercise but little learning. Both groups showed improvement, but in different areas, with mental exercise resulting in increased neural connections and physical exercise yielding an increase in the vascular supply.

Therefore, environment plays a key role in brain development throughout the life span. The results with rats reveal significant insight into human brain development, structure, and cognitive functioning.

Placement

This film segment can be used in a variety of contexts. First, it is germane to material that concerns the nature/nurture issue. The topic of intelligence is frequently brought up when discussing this matter. It is also relevant to the topic of learning. In a related fashion, it is an important part of coverage of neuroscience, especially the research on long-term potentiation. The changes that occur in the brain when we learn new information continue to be an important research topic in psychology.

Discussion Questions:

1. Why do we use the animal model in experiments like these?

2. What does the role of environment in these studies tell us about nature versus nurture as it applies to cognitive development?

3. What do these results tell us about the structure of cognitive functioning in the human brain? How does the brain change when we learn new information?

4. How might these findings be applied to serve the general population?

5. What does this say about humans raised in enriching versus unenriching environments?

Neuroscience and Behavior
Prenatal Brain Development: From Conception to Birth

Segment	Length:	File Name:
3	05:29 min	03_Neuro_PrenateBrain.mpg

Source   Three-dimensional modeling by Animated Biomedical Productions:
www.medical-animations.com

Description

This segment provides a descriptive animation of the process of prenatal brain development. The animation follows the developing nervous system of the fetus from conception to birth, showing the forebrain, midbrain, and hindbrain as they grow and specialize, and as the cerebral cortex expands. In weeks 28–40, the fetus' brain develops gyri and sulci: wrinkles and folds that allow a vast increase in the surface area of the cortex.

The brain continues to grow by forming new nerve cells, a process called neurogenesis. The oldest cells remain close to their place of origin and newer cells migrate continually outward, expanding the brain layer by layer. New nerve cells are guided to their final destination by glial cell fibers which form the underlying structure of the nervous system.

Upon reaching their destination, these new cells change form to match the characteristics and functions of that area of the brain and begin developing axons and dendrites, the structures needed to communicate with surrounding nerve cells. Because the creation of new synapses is rapid throughout the first year of life, it is often called exuberant synaptogenesis.

As the brain continues to develop through adolescence, some newly formed synapses are removed, a process called synaptic pruning. This is thought to create a more efficient brain and to tailor the cognitive processing of the brain to fit each individual's nervous system, in response to their learning and life experiences.

Placement

This segment is useful both for the topic of neuroscience and for developmental psychology. Texts that have a section of their coverage of the nervous system devoted to ontogenetic development will be particularly well accented by this film. Also, texts that have a portion of their coverage of developmental psychology devoted to physical development will also be complemented by this segment.

Discussion Questions:

1. The cerebral cortex is the largest area of the human brain and the last to develop. What might this say about the importance of this area in human life?

2. What is the purpose of synaptic pruning? Why might this be adaptive in human development?

3. What might the process of synaptic pruning imply about the nature versus nurture debate in cognitive development?

Development
Prenatal Animation: Fetal Development

Segment	Length:	File Name:
4	02:25 min	04_Dev_Prenatal.mpg

<u>Source</u> Three-dimensional modeling by Visible Productions: www.visiblep.com

Description

This segment shows a rapid-time animation of the cell division and development of a fetus from conception to birth. The sperm fertilizes the egg, which continues to develop through rapid mitotic cell division. The zygote attaches itself to the wall of the uterus and, as in the previous segment, we can see the neural tube forming first into what will become the central nervous system. Throughout the first trimester, the cells continue to specialize and we see rapid growth and development of the head. By the end of the third month, the heart and blood vessels, most of the internal organ systems, and the sex organs have developed. At this point, we can hear a faint heart beat and see spontaneous movement in the limbs.

Beyond the first trimester, bones begin to form and the lower parts of the body show rapid growth. As the cells continue to specialize, we can make out limbs and the sensory organs of the eyes, ears, mouth, and nose. During the second trimester, the fetus really begins to look like a human infant, with fully developed eyes, finger and toenails, and instinctive movements such as kicking.

Finally, in the final trimester, the cerebral cortex of the brain is developing most rapidly and the baby quickly gains weight. By the ninth month, the internal organs have begun to fully function, and the fetus positions itself for birth.

Placement

This segment would be well used in sections of the course that cover nature/nurture and developmental psychology. The ontogenetic development of the body is a rudiment of both of these topics. Other material covered in both of these areas depends upon an understanding of the progression of physical development.

Discussion Questions:

1. It has been shown that ontogeny does not recapitulate phylogeny, as was once believed. And yet, a human fetus looks very similar to the fetus of many other species, particularly at an early age. What about human prenatal development is unique? What is similar to that of other species? What do these similarities and differences suggest about humans versus nonhuman species?

2. A human infant is born essentially helpless, while other species bear more independent young. What are the evolutionary advantages and/or disadvantages of an extended childhood in human development?

3. Notice the sequence of development in the human embryo. What must be highly developed before the cerebral cortex can begin significant growth? When do the sensory organs develop?

Development
The Scale Errors

Segment	Length:	File Name:
5a	00:19 min	05a_Dev_ScaleA.mpg
5b	00:44 min	05b_Dev_ScaleB.mpg
5c	00:32 min	05c_Dev_ScaleC.mpg

<u>Source</u> Footage given by permission of Judy S. DeLoache, University of Virginia

Description

Taken from the DeLoache, Uttal, and Rosengren (2004) study, this segment includes three segments of young children between one and three years of age who make serious attempts to utilize miniature models in spite of the impossibility due to size. It is presumed that, for all three clips, the child was exposed to a full-scale model of the various stimuli and then later given the miniature model.

- In the first clip, an infant girl is given a toy model of a slide. When asked to play with the slide, she attempts to sit on it and "slide" down. She appears confused when she is obviously unsuccessful.

- In the second clip, a young boy is trying to fit himself into a small toy car. He continues to repeat that he wants to get "in" and attempts to force his foot into the door unsuccessfully.

- In the final clip, the male child prepares for "story time" by attempting to sit on a miniature sofa chair. When he falls off, he tries to get back on rather than sit on the floor.

Each of these children demonstrate what DeLoache, et al. (2004) refer to as a "scale error," a sign of immaturity in perceptual and inhibitory processes during normal child development. The authors propose that scale errors occur when perceptual information (the miniature size of the object) fails to inhibit the motor action (sliding down the slide, getting in the car, or sitting on the chair) associated with the normal sized versions of these objects.

Placement

This material is best used when covering the topic of cognitive development. Similar to Piaget's work, DeLoache has discovered a specific cognitive limitation that occurs during the early stages of human cognitive development. This inability sheds light on how our cognitive abilities take shape and why such gaps occur at certain ages.

Discussion Questions:

1. What do these findings suggest about the cognitive processing of visual information in this age group? What thought processes have the children developed when they no longer make these errors of scale?

2. What do the perceptual mistakes made by these children tell us about the way in which we learn and incorporate new information at a young age?

3. Deloache has also performed experiments exploring children's understanding of symbolic representation. She tested their ability to find a hidden object in a real room when shown where the object was hid, using a miniature scale model of the room. Do you predict that the children shown in the Scale Error segment would be successful in this task? Why or why not?

Development
The Strange Situation and Attachment

Segment	Length:	File Name:
6a	04:53 min	06a_Dev_AttachA.mpg
6b	04:17 min	06b_Dev_AttachB.mpg
6c	03:11 min	06c_Dev_AttachC.mpg

Description

This segment contains a series of video clips taken during Ainworth's Strange Situation experiments. Each participant is a parent and child who go through the same scenario. First, the mother is allowed to play with her child for three minutes in a room of toys. Then, a "stranger" (an experimenter whom the child has never met) enters the room and sits next to the mother for three minutes. The mother then leaves the room for three more minutes, allowing the stranger to interact with the child. For the next three minutes, the mother returns and the stranger leaves, followed by the mother again leaving the room for three minutes. This time, the child is left alone. When three minutes is up, it is the stranger that returns and attempts to comfort the child. Finally, the mother enters for a last time, the stranger leaves, and the mother attempts to re-interest the child in playing with the toys.

The child's reactions during these various "strange situations" have been organized by Dr. Mary Ainsworth into three attachment styles in Developmental Psychology: A child with Secure Attachment will feel comfortable exploring and playing even with strangers, as long as their mother is present. They will be visibly upset when the mother leaves and just as visibly relieved when the mother returns. This is the desired attachments style for developmentally healthy children. A child displaying an Anxious-Ambivalent Attachment is wary of strangers even when the mother is present, and is visibly upset when the mother leaves. When she returns, the child is often both resentful and relieved, resisting her attempts to re-instigate play, but wanting physical comfort. In contrast, a child displaying an Anxious-Avoidant Attachment style shows little difference between his or her reaction to the mother, the stranger, or being left alone. This child may ignore the mother completely and typically avoids much exploration regardless of whether or not she is present.

Example of Secure Attachment

The young boy in this clip is initially playing peacefully with his mother. When the stranger enters, he watches her enter, but shows little distress and with his mother's encouragement, continues playing comfortably. When the mother leaves, the child stops playing, but interacts with the stranger and visibly relaxes upon the mother's return. When left alone, the boy becomes very upset, crying and unable to be comforted by the stranger. However, when the mother returns, he is quickly comforted and responds well to her attempts to play.

Example of Anxious-Ambivalent Attachment

This clip begins with mother and child playing comfortably. When the stranger enters, the girl is wary and moves away. When her mother leaves, she warms up to the stranger slowly and ignores her mother upon her return. When left alone, the child becomes very upset and is unable to be comforted by the stranger. When the mother returns, the child is no longer crying and stays by her side, but does not quickly resume interaction with the mother.

Example of Anxious-Avoidant Attachment

In this clip, there is little interaction between the mother and her daughter even initially. Throughout each change in situation, there is little to no change in emotion. The child never becomes visibly upset, although she'll pause and assess her environment before continuing to play on her own. There is little change in reaction to the stranger but, when prompted, the child does show the stranger her doll. She explores very little throughout the session.

Placement

This segment is particularly helpful when discussing childhood development. The three clips can be used, along with research by Harlow, to supplement discussions of attachment. It might also be helpful in discussing the long-term effects of deficiencies in physical and/or psychological well-being during infancy and childhood. The clips are also useful when discussing research methods due to the fact that Ainsworth employed a two-way mirror to view the mother-child-stranger interactions. Thus this study is an example of one way to get around demand characteristics in psychological research.

Discussion Questions:

1. Why is attachment style an important aspect of our development?

2. What factors in the parent-child relationship lead to each attachment style? What advice would you give parents who want to know how to develop a secure attachment style with their children?

3. What effects might a nonsecure attachment style in childhood have on our psycho-social development later in life?

Development
Piaget's Conservation-of-Numbers Task

Segment	Length:	File Name:
7	01:47 min	07_Dev_Number.mpg

Description

This segment shows Piaget's classic conservation-of-numbers experiment with both a 4 ½-year-old and a 7-year-old child. Given two rows of six candies, evenly spaced, the child is told that one row belongs to the experimenter, and the other row of candy belongs to him or her. The child is then asked if each row contains the same number of candies. Both the 4 ½-year-old and the 7-year-old agree that yes, there are the same number of candies belonging to both.

Next, the experimenter moves the candies in the row belonging to the child farther apart from one another. There are still six candies in each row, but this time, when asked to compare the amounts in each row, the 4 ½-year-old believes that he now has more candy than the experimenter. He also shows confusion and irritation at the difficulty of such an analysis. The 7-year-old, however, easily knows that the number of candies in each row has not changed and can express this idea to the experimenter without difficulty.

The difference between the 4 ½-year-old and the 7-year-old child in this segment is their stage of development. The 4 ½-year-old has an intuitive understanding of "more" and "less," but no conception of "conservation"—that the number of candies remains unchanged despite a change in their configuration. This inability is typical of Piaget's preoperational stage of development. The 7-year-old, on the other hand, has likely advanced to the next stage of development, that of concrete operations.

Placement

This is a video segment that complements coverage of Piaget's theory of cognitive development. Conservation is a crucial task in his framework and it marks the progression from *preoperational* to *concrete operational* thinking. Piaget believed the ability to conserve was crucially tied to several cognitive abilities which are important in our understanding of mathematics.

Discussion Questions:

1. What cues did the 4 ½-year-old use to determine the difference between "more," "less," and "same"? What cues were used by the 7-year-old? What differed about the two thought processes?

2. Piaget has chosen a widely-supported stage theory to explain children's cognitive development. What does it mean to label a child as being in a particular *stage* of development? Do you think that children develop in stages? Why or why not?

3. Imagine that you are an educator. Given this research, what would be the focus of your mathematics curriculum for a kindergarten classroom? How might that focus change if you were suddenly asked to teach mathematics to second-graders?

Development
Piaget's Conservation-of-Liquid Task

Segment	Length:	File Name:
8a	01:19 min	08a_Dev_LiquidA.mpg
8b	00:54 min	08b_Dev_LiquidB.mpg

Description

Similar to the previous segment, this study illustrates another difference between the cognitive abilities of a child in the preoperational versus the concrete stages of development in Piaget's theory. In order to pass the conservation-of-liquid task, a child must not be fooled by irrelevant changes in the appearance of a stimulus while the amount remains unchanged.

In part A of this segment, an experimenter pours an equal amount of liquid into two identical cups in front of a 5-year-old child. The child correctly notes that both cups contain the same amount of liquid, even when the cups are moved around the table. Then, the experimenter pours the liquid from one cup into a shorter, wider bowl, again in front of the child. This time, when asked if the containers both held the same amount of liquid, the 5-year-old mistakenly answers that the bowl holds less liquid. When asked why this is so, the child answers that the larger container will contain more liquid.

In part B, a 7-year-old child is given the same task. Because the child is capable of concrete thinking, however, he is not fooled by the shape of the container. The 7-year-old is able to correctly determine that the amount of liquid is conserved despite a change in the shape of the container holding it, and can understandably express this idea to the experimenter.

Similar to the last segment, this is another illustration of the difference between children at the preoperational versus the concrete operational stages of Piaget's theory of cognitive development. The 5-year-old in part A is utilizing a schema, that the taller container must hold more, and thus fails the task. In contrast, the 7-year-old is capable of conservation, realizing that the amount of water remains the same regardless of container.

Placement
Just as the last segment, this segment is an important addition to lectures on cognitive development, showing another type of conservation task. This time liquid contained in different vessels is used instead of a number of solid items arranged differently. Piaget linked both of these tasks under the same cognitive heading of conservation.

Discussion Questions:

1. Why is research like that of Piaget, meant to increase our understanding of children's cognitive development, important? How do we utilize this knowledge in the real world?

2. How does the schema utilized by the 5-year-old differ from that of the 7-year-old?

3. How is the conservation task illustrated in this segment different from that shown in the last segment? How are they related?

Development
Moral Development: The Heinz Dilemma

Segment	Length:	File Name:
9a	00:28 min	09a_Dev_MoralA.mpg
9b	00:52 min	09b_Dev_MoralB.mpg
9c	01:47 min	09c_Dev_MoralC.mpg
9d	02:40 min	09d_Dev_MoralD.mpg
9e	01:51 min	09e_Dev_MoralE.mpg
9f	03:13 min	09f_Dev_MoralF.mpg
9g	00:59 min	09g_Dev_MoralG.mpg
9h	01:28 min	09h_Dev_MoralH.mpg

Description

The Heinz Dilemma experiment led to Lawrence Kohlberg's stages of moral development. Participants are read a scenario in which a man's wife is dying of a rare disease that can only be cured by a special, very expensive medicine produced by a pharmacist. The man cannot afford the medicine, but offers to pay the pharmacist a significant down payment and to continue to repay him over time. The pharmacist refuses to sell the drug, so the man breaks into the pharmacy and steals the drug as a last-ditch effort to save his wife.

- Clips A, B, and G, all interviews with young girls, demonstrate reactions to the Heinz Dilemma typical of children at the pre-conventional level of moral reasoning. Consisting of stages one and two, pre-conventional thinking judges the morality of an action based on the consequences, particularly to oneself. An action is morally wrong if the person will be punished. All three interviewees state that stealing is wrong no matter what the conditions. The young girl in Clip H even gives jail time as the reason why the man made the wrong decision to steal the drug for his wife.

- Clips C, D, F, and H are representative of the responses typical in the conventional level of moral reasoning. In stages three and four, right and wrong are based on social roles and society's laws. The interviewees in these clips judge the morality of the man's decision to steal based primarily on his good intentions. They all agree that he made the right decision, a decision they likely would have made themselves. However, none of the adolescents in these clips claim his stealing the drug is morally right. "Stealing is stealing," says the young man in Clip D. In Clips F and H, the interviewees agree that stealing is a sin, and therefore never morally the right thing to do. Each of the adolescents in these clips also feel that the punishment—jail time—for this man is justified, but should be mitigated because his intentions were noble.

- Finally, Clip E represents a response typical of the post-conventional level of moral reasoning. The young woman in this clip believes that the man was morally right in taking the drug because an individual's right to life should be upheld above all else. She mentions social contracts, laws and rules that can bend to uphold individual and universal rights.

Placement

Kohlberg's work is an important part of any series of lectures pertaining to cognitive development. Kohlberg was a student of Piaget, who had previously put together his own framework on moral development. Kohlberg furthered his mentor's work with a more elaborate scheme for the development of the understanding of how rules are determined, and how and when they are to be adhered to. The Heinz dilemma is the most-often-used example from Kohlberg's methodology. Differences in the answers elicited from the experimental participants gives a view into how humans think about authority and conformity.

Discussion Questions:

1. How/Where do you think each child in this segment learned the morals they cite when explaining their answer to the Heinz Dilemma?

2. How is Kohlberg's theory of moral development related to Piaget's theory of cognitive development?

3. Who makes the moral "rules" cited by each child in these clips? How does the personification of authority change with each stage of moral development?

4. Which stage do you think you are in? Why?

Sensation and Perception
The Visual Cliff

Segment	Length:	File Name:
10a	02:06 min	10a_SensPer_VisCliffA.mpg
10b	00:22 min	10b_SensPer_VisCliffB.mpg
10c	01:15 min	10c_SensPer_VisCliffC.mpg

Description

This segment on perception development demonstrates Campbell's visual cliff, a design which explores whether the fear of heights is innate or learned in young infants. The visual cliff is a Plexiglas board, painted on one side and left clear on the other, giving the illusion of a large drop. The parent places the infant on the painted side and calls to them from the opposite end.

An infant who has just begun to crawl will cross the "cliff" without any fear and seemingly without any awareness of the apparent drop at all. In contrast, an infant who has been able to crawl for a month or more will show an interest in reaching the parent but will not cross the drop. A fear of heights is now apparent.

- In Clip A, Campbell himself explains the visual cliff and his theory. He suggests that beginning to crawl activates an innate but latent fear of heights in infants.

- Clip B is another demonstration of a child crossing the visual cliff without fear.

- Clip C shows another demonstration of a child now afraid to cross.

Placement

The work done using the visual cliff is classic research in the field of perceptual development. This topic area is often found in a chapter on cognitive development because perceptual abilities are subsumed under that more general heading. This segment gives the student insight into the development of depth perception in humans.

Discussion Questions:

1. What does the visual cliff phenomenon suggest about the nature versus nurture debate in human development?

2. Why is this "latent fear" expressed only upon learning to crawl?

3. What special considerations must psychologists make in performing research with infants and young children?

4. Using your knowledge of human visual perception, what cues, signaling a drop in height, have the crawling children in this segment learned to avoid? (Hint: The "floor" is a checkered pattern.)

Sensation and Perception
A Variety of Visual Illusions

Segment	Length:	File Name:
11a	00:33 min	**11a_SensPer_CafeWall.mpg**
		11a_SensPer_CafeWall.swf
11b	00:34 min	**11b_SensPer_LilacChaser.mpg**
		11b_SensPer_LilacChaser.swf
11c	02:04 min	**11c_SensPer_Mask.mpg**
11d	00:37 min	**11d_SensPer_MotionBlind.mpg**
		11d_SensPer_MotionBlind.swf
11e	00:35 min	**11e_SensPer_Spoke.mpg**
		11e_SensPer_Spoke. swf
11f	00:38 min	**11f_SensPer_Stepping.mpg**
		11f_SensPer_Stepping. swf
11g	00:37 min	**11g_SensPer_Thatcher.mpg**
11h	00:38 min	**11h_SensPer_Waterfall.mpg**
		11h_SensPer_Waterfall. swf

<u>Source</u> Illusions from Michael Bach's Visual Illusions Web site: <u>www.michaelbach.de/ot/index.html</u>

Description

The clips in this series are from Michael Bach's Visual Illusions Web site. These visual illusions, which often seem like malfunctions of the visual system, are actually the result of adaptations of our visual pathways to efficiently process typical, everyday visual stimuli. Each illusion not only provides insight into visual processing in humans, but also lends insight into the features of our environments that are most common and most important to human life, leading to the evolutionary development of these visual heuristics.

Café Wall Illusion (courtesy of Michael Bach <u>www.michaelbach.de/ot/index.html</u>)

This clip shows several rows of black and white checkered tiles. Each alternating row of tiles is moving in the opposite direction. When the tiles are "half-shifted," the horizontal lines between tiles appear skewed, so that each row looks wedge-shaped. When the tiles align top-to-bottom, either to create columns of black and white or to alternate in a checked pattern, we see that the rows are actually completely horizontal, with all tiles the same size.

Lilac Chaser (courtesy of Jeremy Hinton)

This illusion consists of a circle of lilac-colored dots. The participant must look at the X in the center of the circle as the lilac dots disappear and return, one at a time, in order around the circle. While staring at the X, the participant begins to see the missing lilac dot as a green dot, which then appears to be moving around the circle. If you hold your gaze at the center, the lilac dots will disappear all together, leaving only the appearance of the green dot rotating around the now empty circle. This effect illustrates a "negative retinal after-image," where we begin to see a color's complement after keeping our gaze steady.

Shading and Faces (courtesy of Richard Gregory www.richardgregory.org)

This clip shows a hallow face mask rotating on a rod. When the mask turns, revealing the back of the mask, the negative image instantly becomes a positive image, looking exactly like the face on the front. This illusion is related to our extreme sensitivity to facial stimuli. Because the face in its normal configuration is such a salient and common stimulus for humans, any stimuli which approximate a face in its normal configuration will often be processed as a face.

Motion Blindness (courtesy of Michael Bach www.michaelbach.de/ot/index.html)

This clip shows a square grid of blue Xs. There is a flashing green dot in the center (observers should look here) and three yellow dots in a triangle around it. The grid of blue Xs spins around the center, and as observers attend to the flashing green dot, the yellow dots seem to disappear. This effect is related to the Troxler Effect, a phenomenon in which objects in our visual field seem to disappear when we hold our gaze steady.

Reverse Spoke (courtesy of Michael Bach www.michaelbach.de/ot/index.html)

This clip shows a circle with gray, wheel-like spokes which divide the wheel into sectors. Each sector is on a grayscale from light to dark, and this gray scale moves clockwise. The clockwise change in contrast makes the spokes appear to move counterclockwise, although in actuality they remain stationary. The apparent movement of each spoke in this illusion occurs when the matching gray sector blends with that spoke on its clockwise rotation. When we look at the wheel as a whole, we see each spoke blending and then contrasting (thus, appearing to move) together, in Gestaltist fashion, creating the illusion of movement.

Stepping Feet (courtesy of Michael Bach www.michaelbach.de/ot/index.html)

This illusion is related to luminance or how bright a stimulus will appear to the eye. The clip begins with one blue and one yellow bar moving at a constant and equal speed across a gray screen. Observers should not look directly at the bars. The gray background then becomes a black and white grid. The motion of the blue and yellow bars does not change. However, with the black and white striped background, an effect called isoluminance occurs in which the blue bar and the black stripe, and the yellow bar and the white stripe have equal luminance. Therefore, when the edge of the yellow bar crosses that of the white stripe, the visual cues for motion are no longer present, making the blue bar appear to continue moving while the yellow bar is at rest. The same is true for the blue bar crossing the black stripe. This creates the appearance of "feet" walking across the screen.

Thatcher Illusion *(original illusion created by Peter Thompson and animated illusion by Michael Bach)*

This illusion shows two faces side-by-side which, at first, appear identical. However, upon rotation, we see that the eyes and mouth of the face on the right have been inverted. This effect illustrates our visual preference for faces shown in their natural orientation.

Motion Aftereffect (aka Waterfall)
(courtesy of Michael Bach www.michaelbach.de/ot/index.html)

In this illusion, the participant must begin by keeping a steady gaze on a central X. This X is surrounded by a black and white checked circle which appears to be sinking towards the center. After a short time observing the sinking motion, a stationary (non-animated) image of Buddha replaces the circle. Looking at the Buddha, it appears to grow larger and move toward the participant. This illusion is described as a "motion aftereffect" and involves fatigue of the visual processing of motion.

Placement

Visual illusions are an important aspect of the topic of perception, particularly visual perception (obviously). These illusions give us hints as to how the perceptual system works by fooling us, or getting around our perceptual mechanisms. The illusions help students to understand that our awareness of our environment is based on more than simple sensory information. The necessity to process sensory information in order to make sense of the world is highlighted.

Technical Information

Note that many of the files are supplied in both MPEG (.mpg) and Shockwave (.swf) file formats. The MPEG files can be played on any computer video player (for example, QuickTime, Windows Media Player, or Real Player). They can also be imported directly into PowerPoint (see "Video Support: Using MPEG files in PowerPoint" on page 253). As MPEG files, you can play the videos but you cannot manipulate, or change, the illusions.

If you would like the ability to manipulate the illusions (for example, change their speed, color, or direction) you should use the Shockwave (.swf) files. To open the Shockwave files, you will need to have a Web browser like Internet Explorer or Safari installed on your computer—though you do *not* need a live Internet connection.

To open the Shockwave files:

1. Open a new Web browser window.

2. Navigate to the folder with the .swf file you would like to open.

3. Drag the file onto your Web browser window.

4. The .swf file will begin to display.

5. Use the controls on the left- or right-hand side of the screen to change the features of the illusions.

Discussion Questions:

1. What areas of the brain and/or visual sensory system result in each of these illusions? In other words, what do these apparent "malfunctions" in visual perception tell us about how our visual system operates?

2. How might the processes which lead to these illusions be adaptive in normal, everyday situations?

Consciousness
Consciousness and Artificial Intelligence

Segment	Length:	File Name:
12	04:58 min	12_Conscious_AI.mpg

<u>Source</u> *Mind over Matter: Advances in Brain Research,* 2004 (Films for the Humanities and Sciences)

Description

In this segment, we are shown a humanoid robot, COG, created by Dr. Rodney Brooks at the Massachusetts Institute of Technology. The roboticists working on this project hope to one day make COG or one of its descendents into a conscious machine. But what is "consciousness"? This is the fundamental question asked in this segment.

The first interview shown is with Dr. Daniel Dennett, a philosopher from Tufts University. Dennett notes the unease many people feel when confronted with COG. He believes the reason is that humans, in general, underestimate how easily we equate the speed and grace of human movement with our sense of conscious thought. Therefore, COG *appears* to be conscious, and we find this unnerving.

The second interview is with Brooks himself. He attempts to define their goals in making COG "conscious." In a few years, he hopes that people will feel badly about turning COG off, and this empathy for the robot will equal "consciousness." To Brook most humanlike is the meaning of consciousness. When questioned, he explains that humans and animals are just extremely complex chemical machines and we have created this idea of "consciousness" to more easily explain this level of complexity. Therefore, if COG can reach a level of speed and grace rivaling that of a human (as Dennett suggests), then we can only describe this as being conscious.

Placement

This segment is appropriate for use with material on thinking and consciousness. The issues addressed in this segment question the definition of consciousness. It might also prove useful in fostering discussion regarding ethics in psychological research, particularly regarding what it means to be "human" and defining the limits of acceptable research.

Discussion Questions:

1. What is your definition of consciousness? Do you agree with Dennett and Brook, that robots can someday be "conscious"? Why or why not?

2. What are some characteristics of humans that a robot would need to achieve or imitate for you to consider it "conscious"?

3. Are there any ethical issues in this area of research? If so, what are they?

Consciousness
Narcoleptic Dogs

Segment 13	Length: 01:18 min	File Name: 13_Conscious_Dogs.mpg

Description

This segment illustrates narcolepsy in two different dogs. In the first segment, a longhaired dachshund is shown being taken for a walk. Out of nowhere, the dog falls to its side, asleep. Very soon following, the dog awakens and gets up as if nothing has happened.

In the second segment, an English cocker spaniel is shown being fed. Soon after it begins eating, the dog falls asleep with its head in its food dish. The owner tries to wake the dog, but it remains asleep until finally awoken by the smell of food.

Narcolepsy is a neurological disorder caused by the brain's inability to regulate the sleep cycle, and REM sleep in particular. In dogs, narcolepsy and cataplexy are often induced by excitement—in the case of this segment, by the prospect of going for a walk or food.

Placement

Narcolepsy is a form of sleep pathology and thus this segment is best used with material about sleep and dreaming. The comic nature of this segment belies the serious nature of this disorder. The use of amphetamines to treat narcolepsy makes this segment useful to some degree with lectures on drugs and behavior.

Discussion Questions:

1. How can we utilize this research on narcolepsy in dogs to better understand and treat the disorder in humans?

2. Why do we need a regular sleep cycle? What effect might its disruption have on your body's mental and physical well-being?

3. What is the function of REM sleep?

Learning and Memory
Bandura on Social Learning with Clips from Original Experiment

Segment	Length:	File Name:
14	02:49 min	14_LearnMem_Bandura.mpg

<u>Source</u> Albert Bandura, Stanford University and Worth Publishers

Description

This segment is a video narrated by Bandura himself, from his research on learned aggression. The segment begins with the stimulus video used by Bandura which shows an adult playing with a blow-up "Bobo Doll." The adult in this stimulus video acts aggressively, hitting the doll with a toy mallet, punching, kicking, and throwing it. Each of the children in the experimental group of this study is shown this video modeling aggressive behavior. Following the video, the child is left alone in the room filled with all sorts of toys, including the blow-up doll.

The children exposed to the video imitate the aggressive behavior of the adult towards the blow-up doll. These children devised novel ways to attack the doll and included aggressive language and expressions not modeled in the stimulus video. In addition, exposure to aggressive behavior led to an increased interest in toy guns versus children in the control group.

Placement

Bandura's classic research on social learning in children has a host of uses. First, it is a natural for lectures concerning learning. The fact that others can learn by modeling another's behavior is an important factor in process of acculturation. Secondly, Bandura's research is an important part of developmental psychology, both cognitive and social development. Finally, the interaction of the adult and child in this scenario clearly shows the important role of learning in social psychology.

Discussion Questions:

1. Given these findings, what advice would you give new parents about disciplining their children?

2. Does Bandura's research support the hypothesis that exposure to violent television, movies, and/or video games increases violent behavior in children? Why or why not?

3. Are humans "naturally" predisposed towards aggressive behavior?

4. What do the results of this experiment tell us about learning, specifically as it applies to modeling behavior? How might we relate these findings to children's moral development?

Learning and Memory

The Research of Carolyn Rovee-Collier: Learning and Memory in Preverbal Infants

Segment 15	Length: 02:15 min	File Name: 15_LearnMem_RoveeColl.mpg

Description

This segment illustrates the research of Carolyn Rovee-Collier on learning and memory in young infants. Rovee-Collier narrates the segment as she leads you through one experimental trial. The participating infant is placed in a crib with two stands. One stand remains empty and the other holds the stimulus mobile. Rovee-Collier ties a ribbon to the infant's right ankle and connects the other end first to the empty stand. To create a baseline, Rovee-Collier counts the number of times the infant kicks (defined as a movement of the leg fully outward and back in) for two minutes. She then ties the end of the ribbon to the stand holding the mobile so that the stimulus is moved when the infant kicks her leg. Rovee-Collier then counts the number of kicks for nine minutes. The segment shows the infant increase the frequency and intensity of her kicking in order to move the mobile. Finally, Rovee-Collier once again ties the ribbon to the empty stand, this time to see if the infant displays the learned behavior.

Placement

The segment describing Rovee-Collier's research is very useful for discussion of operant conditioning, which is part of learning. The fact that the child learns to increase the rate of the kicking behavior when the ribbon is tied to the mobile shows, in a very similar way to Thorndike's cats, that behaviors that lead to a desired outcome increase in frequency. Also, this research is helpful in punctuating lectures on perceptual development, which as previously mentioned is a topic often found under the larger heading of cognitive development.

Discussion Questions:

1. What type of conditioning is exhibited by infants in Royee-Collier's experiment?

2. How did Royee-Collier operationalize learning and memory in preverbal infants? Do you feel this was an appropriate definition?

3. Why did the experimenter tie the ribbon to the empty stand again, following the nine minutes connected to the mobile?

Problem Solving in Genus Corvus (Crows, Ravens, and Magpies)

Segment	Length:	File Name:
16	01:34 min	**16_LearnMem_Crow.mpg**

<u>Source</u> Behavioral Ecology Research Group, University of Oxford

Description

This segment illustrates problem solving and insight in nonhuman animals. The segment involves birds of the genus Corvus, which includes crows, ravens, and magpies. This segment is a videotaping of several birds as they attempt to retrieve a small bucket of food from a long glass tube. It begins with several birds exploring the tube, but unable to reach the food. The video cuts to a single bird that retrieves a small wire stick and begins to poke at the food in the tube's bottom.

After several unsuccessful attempts to retrieve the food in this manner, the bird exhibits a clear display of insight; moving away from the tube in order to bend a small hook in one end of the wire stick. The bird then uses this hook to reach in and pull out the bucket of food.

Placement

This unusual footage details toolmaking abilities in the crow. This footage can be used in conjunction with lectures dealing with evolution of cognitive abilities as well as learning. The crow in the segment uses trial-and-error learning to eventually derive a tool from a piece of metal. This is much like the type of learning that Thorndike identified, but also adds in the amazing ability to manipulate an object to produce a desired end. Obviously, this ability in Corvids came as quite a surprise to many scientists and is an important benchmark in our understanding of the genesis of that ability.

Discussion Questions:

1. Did this video surprise you? Why or why not?

2. The ability to make and use tools was long considered a trait particular to humans and some human-like primates. How might the findings of this study alter our perception of what it means to be "human"?

3. What types of problem-solving strategies did you see exhibited by the bird(s) in this segment? At what point, if at all, did the bird(s) exhibit insight?

4. Is learning an instinct?

Learning and Memory
Retrieval: A Journey Into Memory
– Retrieval Cues: An Interview with Dr. Robert A. Bjork
– Bias: An Interview with Dr. Daniel Schacter
– Memory Retrieval and the Misattribution Effect: An Interview with Dr. Elizabeth Loftus

Segment	Length:	File Name:
17a	06:28 min	17a_LearnMem_Retrieval.mpg
17b	03:35 min	17b_LearnMem_RetrievalCues.mpg
17c	02:00 min	17c_LearnMem_Bias.mpg
17d	03:11 min	17d_LearnMem07_Misattribution.mpg

<u>Source</u> Xunesis (2005)

Description

Retrieval: A Journey Into Memory

This segment is a short theatrical film about a man whose daughter has mysteriously gone missing. The clip begins with Nick, the father, remembering his last conversation with his daughter, Amber, before her disappearance, in which they were fighting. Music plays as Nick is shown in a room surrounded by pictures, letters he has written, and Amber's things. We are shown his memory of the last conversation as it changes over time. Nick reworks the interaction to make it more positive, perhaps in an attempt to ease the guilt and sense of loss he is feeling.

Retrieval Cues: An Interview with Dr. Robert A. Bjork

This clip is an interview with Dr. Robert Bjork of the University of California concerning retrieval cues and memory. Bjork emphasizes the vast store of information that is retained in memory, a store he claims is almost unlimited, but cue-dependent. Memory retrieval often requires the presence of an environmental, social, or emotional cue which allows the memory to be brought to consciousness. Humans have developed an adaptation such that every time a particular memory is retrieved, that memory then becomes easier to retrieve in the future, while other memories, in competition for those cues, become less retrievable. In this sense, according to Bjork, our distorted memories may be even more truthful than the initial memory, the distorted composite more accurately reflecting the true feelings and relationships between people than any one verbatim memory could incur.

Bias: An Interview with Dr. Daniel Schacter

This clip is an interview with Dr. Daniel Schacter of Harvard University regarding memory bias and the video in clip A with Nick and Amber. Schacter states that the accuracy of our memories of past events is influenced by our current state of mind at retrieval. He cites marriage research showing that couples who are currently happy with their relationships will recall positive renditions of past events, while those who are unhappy tend to recall negative renditions. Thus, retrieval cues can be emotive. Regarding the video with Nick and his daughter, Schacter suggests that either Nick's state of mind when he reacalled the first rendition of his last conversation with Amber made that memory particularly harsh or, he postulates, Nick altered his rendition of that last conversation to reflect his state of mind later in the clip.

Memory Retrieval and the Misattribution Effect: An Interview with Dr. Elizabeth Loftus

This clip is an interview with Dr. Elizabeth Loftus of the University of California, Irvine, regarding the misattribution effect. She explains how post-event information can add to, or distort, recollection of that event. Loftus describes two studies in which she was involved. In the first, participants were shown a video of a car accident in which the car ran a stop sign. Then, experimenters used leading questions to suggest that the stop sign was actually a yield sign. Approximately 80% of participants then "recalled" seeing a yield sign.

In a later study, participants were convinced, through three suggestive interviews, that they had been separated from their parents and lost for an extended time in a mall as a child. Approximately 25% of participants were convinced and began to embellish memories of this false event.

Placement

This collection of clips is best used to help explain the process of retrieval in memory. All four clips make different points regarding the process of memory that is normally thought of as the recollection or remembrance of materials from long-term memory. Material is retrieved into short-term memory (the conscious portion of our memory systems) for use that is pertinent to the situation the person finds him/herself in.

Discussion Questions:

1. In the dramatization shown in the first clip, how did Nick's memory of his last interactions with his daughter change over time? Why was it distorted so?

2. Bjork posits that a distorted composite memory may be "more truthful" than an accurate account. How might this composite effect be adaptive?

3. Given Schacter's theory of bias in memory recall, how might we maximize our ability to recall stored information accurately?

4. How does research regarding the misattribution effect impact our evaluation of testimony in court? What other areas of social life might be impacted by this phenomenon?

Thinking, Language, and Intelligence
Learning Language: Language Development in Infants and Toddlers

Segment	Length:	File Name:
18a	00:38 min	18a_Thinking_Language1.mpg
18b	01:25 min	18b_Thinking_Language2.mpg
18c	00:25 min	18c_Thinking_Language3.mpg
18d	00:27 min	18d_Thinking_Language4.mpg
18e	00:41 min	18e_Thinking_Language5.mpg
18f	01:15 min	18f_Thinking_Language6.mpg
18g	01:10 min	18g_Thinking_Language7.mpg
18h	00:40 min	18h_Thinking_Language8.mpg
18i	00:30 min	18i_Thinking_Language9.mpg

Description

This segment contains a series of clips illustrating the development of language from infancy to three years of age.

- In Clip A, we see newborn infants using only crying to communicate their needs.

- In Clips B and C, with infants from two to four months of age, we can see a sense of the external world developing. Crying and laughter become a form of communication, an interaction with the environment. The mothers in these clips are using high-pitched voices to respond to their infants.

- Clip D, of 6-month-old infants, shows the beginning of monosyllabic sounds—"oohs," "ahhs," and "mmms." Their sounds are often made with inflections similar to adult speech, which allow the infants to communicate without words. These inflections become more complicated by nine months, shown in Clip E, where the infants begin speaking gibberish. They are often able to say common, simple words like "mama," but the clip focuses primarily on the strings of nonsensical sounds that the child makes even when alone.

- Clips F and G show toddlers now able to speak their first words and simple sentences. The string of gibberish and sounds is still present, but more frequently in these clips we hear simple word combinations such as "I do" and "where go." Much of these sentences contain a noun and verb only. It is apparent that the child understands adult speech with ease even if unable to mimic it entirely.

- Clips H and I show 2- and 3-year-old children. In Clip H, the toddlers' sentences are still simple and of few words, but the meaning becomes more complex with expressions such as "my toys" and "who are you?" In Clip I, a child is able to sing an entire song, clearly expressing nearly all of the words.

Placement

This segment on infant language development works either in the setting of cognitive psychology or developmental psychology since it is part of both of these topics. Language is a major topic in the field of cognitive psychology and is normally covered in some detail in an introductory psychology course. The development of children's speech is germane to this topic, especially when considering the conflicting views of language development proposed by Skinner and Chomsky.

Developmentally, it is pretty clear that the differences seen in the infants and children in these clips reflect developmental stages that are often covered under the topic of cognitive development.

Discussion Questions:

1. How do the parents' responses to their infants change as the infants' language develops? What effect might the parents' responses have?

2. What function might nonsensical sounds serve for the developing toddler, particularly those they make while alone?

3. In what ways does the acquisition of language as an infant/toddler differ from learning a language later in life?

Thinking, Language, and Intelligence

Hothouse Babies: Mother Tries to Teach Her Two-Year-Old Multiplication *(Pushing Children to Perform Tasks Beyond Their Level)*

Segment 19	Length: 01:52 min	File Name: 19_Thinking_Hothouse.mpg

Description

This segment shows the mother of a 2-year-old girl describing her parenting philosophy. Despite no knowledge that her child is gifted or of above average in intelligence or development, the mother is attempting to train her daughter to perform tasks beyond her level of development. In the segment, she shows us the multiplication flash cards she has just bought her 2-year-old in order to prepare her for advanced preschool programs. The mother describes the importance of "structuring" the majority of her daughter's day with learning tasks and displays obvious concern that her daughter will be missing out on an important opportunity should she not make it into the "best" preschool program.

Placement

This segment is useful for the topic of cognitive development. It portrays a parent who seeks to push her daughter to mature at a faster pace than normal children. This brings up the issue of normative development and how milestones are determined. It also brings up another developmental topic—parenting styles. Finally, the segment can also be used when discussing the effects of nature and nurture. This type of coverage can help to decide whether this parent's strategy should be successful.

Discussion Questions:

1. Is the mother helping her child by structuring her education and development in this manner? Even if she is not helping her child, is she causing harm? How do you know?

2. Do you think this mother considers intelligence to be due more to nurture or nature? Where do you think intelligence falls on that continuum?

3. What is "normal" versus "gifted" development? How do you know? Who created that definition?

4. What advice would you offer this mother? Why?

Thinking, Language, and Intelligence
Psychologist Ellen Winner Discusses "Gifted" Children

Segment 20	Length: 03:15 min	File Name: 20_Thinking_Winner.mpg

Description

This segment shows an interview with psychologist Ellen Winner of Boston College as she describes the characteristics of gifted children and some possible causes. She notes three characteristics shared by gifted kids: "Precocity" (showing early and more rapid development in their gifted area when compared to typical children), "Rage to Master" (an intrinsic drive to master the knowledge in their gifted area), and "Marching to Their Own Drummer" (the child is different, thinks in different and novel ways, and learns in different and novel ways). She describes these children, whether they are gifted in areas of math, literacy, the arts, athletics, etc., as typically learning on their own without a lot of adult support. These kids will choose to participate in their gifted activity without being coerced in any way.

Winner also addresses the nature versus nurture debate. Despite the merits of hard work and early education, she has noticed that gifted children display these characteristics in their gifted areas at a very young age, some earlier than one year old, before their skills can possibly be attributed to hard work alone. She describes one child with which she has worked who before the age of two would draw all the time, at the breakfast table, when friends came over to play, etc. This demonstrates, she claims, the "Rage to Master" trait. Thus, in contrast to the mother of the previous segment, Winner feels that being gifted is primarily innate.

Placement

This film segment can be used in conjunction with nature/nurture material. The question of how genius develops is addressed by Winner in this segment. Most of her data suggest that superlative mental abilities are the product of genetic inheritance. The segment is also useful for coverage of cognitive development. The pattern shown by Winner's gifted children is somewhat different than that seen in other children.

Discussion Questions:

1. Do you agree with Winner's definition of "gifted"? Why or why not?

2. How might the cognitive development of "gifted" children differ from that of other children? How might their social development differ? Moral development?

3. Where would Winner place being "gifted" on the spectrum of nature versus nurture? Where would you place it? Why?

Emotion and Motivation
The Brain's Reward Center

Segment 21	Length: 04:52 min	File Name: 21_EmotMotiv_Reward.mpg

Source THE SECRET LIFE OF THE BRAIN
"The Teenage Brain: A World of Their Own"
David Grubin Productions

Description

This segment takes a physiological look at the effect of addictive drugs and alcohol on the brain's reward center. According to addiction research, drugs such as cocaine mimic the neurotransmitters of the brain that lead to feelings of pleasure. The segment takes a close look at the effect of dopamine which, in a normal brain, stimulates the dopamine receptors of a neuron in response to pleasurable stimuli. Computer graphics show dopamine being released into the synapse and then "vacuumed" back up into dopamine transporters. We are then shown the neural synapse in a brain on cocaine. Millions of cocaine molecules flood the dopamine transporters, preventing dopamine from being reabsorbed. Therefore, cocaine artificially floods the synapse with more dopamine and for a longer period than the body would ever experience naturally.

The segment then follows speaker James C. Berman, of the Caron Foundation, as he speaks with high school teenagers about the effects of drugs. He explains that cocaine raises the level of dopamine higher than even the most pleasurable natural experiences (i.e. orgasm, food, exercise, etc.). However, he also describes how repeated use of addictive drugs causes "down-regulation," where the things which made us feel good before no longer provide even natural pleasure. The segment interviews recovered teenage drug addicts about their experiences with cocaine. They describe how eventually nothing in their lives gave them pleasure except the drug. A few contemplated suicide.

Finally, the segment returns to the computer image of the reward center of the brain. With prolonged use, the brain begins to fight back against the unnatural surge of dopamine in its synapses by destroying the dopamine receptors. Without these receptors, dopamine can no longer elicit pleasurable sensations, even from natural pleasures. The segment ends with the suggestion that it is something in the genes and temperament of certain people which makes them vulnerable to addiction.

Placement

This segment can be used with a number of neuroscience topics, but is best suited to the topic of drugs and behavior which is often part of a chapter on consciousness.

The fact that drugs like cocaine and amphetamine cause excitation in the reward pathway makes this segment particularly important to the topic of drugs and behavior, however, the normal functioning of the reward pathway is of interest as well and that fits under the heading of the nervous system and motivation. Both of these topics would be well served by this graphic.

Discussion Questions:

1. Describe the normal reward pathway. How is this disrupted by drug use?

2. What is addiction? When is someone "addicted" to drugs or alcohol?

3. Is drug use a problem in our country? Why or why not? How might drug addiction be combated?

4. Is addiction a choice?

Emotion and Motivation
Ekman's Facial Expression Research: Detecting "Microexpressions"

Segment 22	Length: 02:48 min	File Name: No MPEG File Available

Source *The Human Face,* 2001 (BBC Worldwide Americas Inc.)

Technical Specification Please note that this segment is only available on the **VHS** and **DVD** versions of the ActivePsych: Video Teaching Modules.

Description

This segment shows Dr. Paul Ekman as he describes some of his research with facial expressions and lie detection. Ekman first shows a video of a previous experiment in which he attempts to discover if people are good at detecting liars. He explains how he showed nursing students a very gory medical video and asked them to convince participants that they had watched a nature film. In the control group, nurses were shown a nature film and asked to honestly describe the experience to participants. The participants were unable to see the film the nurses were watching themselves.

Ekman then shows us a more recent experiment in which participants held strong beliefs about a particular issue (in this case, the participant shown is strongly against capital punishment). These participants were then asked to act as if they believed the opposite (in this case that the participant believes capital punishment should be utilized). In this segment, Ekman isolates what he calls "microexpressions." These are fleeting facial movements which signal that the person is lying. An upturning of the inside corner of the eyebrows and minute forehead wrinkles signal distress, and thus lying behavior. Ekman explains that he can teach people to interpret these microexpressions in 30 minutes. This segment ends with President Bill Clinton on the witness stand testifying that he did not have sexual relations with Monica Lewinsky. He is showing the same microexpression signaling deceptive behavior.

Placement

This film of Ekman's work is suitable for coverage of both emotion and, to a lesser degree, perception. Facial expressions are an important part of coverage of emotions and this segment illustrates the lengths that Ekman has gone to identify the facial movements that make up our expressions. Reciprocally, the segment also provides coverage of our ability to recognize facial expressions, which is a topic sometimes considered in an introductory psychology course.

Discussion Questions:

1. How can this research be applied beyond the laboratory setting? (Hint: Consider areas of law, counseling, parenting, acting, etc.)

2. How is this research related to emotion? What emotions might we be experiencing when we lie?

3. Are humans generally good at detecting liars? Why or why not?

4. Are facial expressions innate? Are they universal across cultures? Are there any exceptions?

Stress and Health
The Development of Tangles and Plaques in Alzheimer's Disease

Segment	Length:	File Name:
23	01:20 min	23_StressHlth_Tangles.mpg

<u>Source</u> THE SECRET LIFE OF THE BRAIN
"The Aging Brain: Through Many Lives"
David Grubin Productions

Description

This segment shows a computer-generated image of the ill effects of Alzheimer's disease on the brain. The segment describes the long chain of molecules which carry nutrients across the cell. These chains depend on a protein called TAU for stability. In Alzheimer's, these proteins twist and become tangled, breaking these necessary molecule chains apart.

In addition, an Alzheimer's brain contains a suspicious protein molecule called Beta Amaloid. This molecule is sticky and clumps together to form plaques. These plaques attach themselves to neuron cells like barnacles. The neurons fight back by releasing powerful chemicals, but these chemicals set off a series of reactions which eventually destroy the neuron. In this way, the brain of an Alzheimer's patient deteriorates with time, affecting memory, thought, and speech.

Placement

This segment is useful when lecturing on adult development. In particular, when covering illnesses that are particular to older adulthood. The fact that the information in the film segment has much to do with neurons and the pathology that occurs to them in patients with Alzheimer's also makes it useful for coverage of the nervous system, particularly the cellular level analysis.

Discussion Questions:

1. What did you learn about the normal adult brain from watching this segment?

2. What types of research tools and technology are being used in research involving Alzheimer's disease?

3. What special considerations might be needed when doing research with Alzheimer's patients, in order to meet IRB and ethical guidelines?

Can the Immune System Be Used to Combat Alzheimer's Disease?

Segment 24	Length: 02:14 min	File Name: 24_StressHlth_Immune.mpg

Source THE SECRET LIFE OF THE BRAIN
"The Aging Brain: Through Many Lives"
David Grubin Productions

Description

This segment takes a look at research being done to find a cure or preventative measure for Alzheimer's disease. The segment begins with an interview with Dr. Dennis Selco, who has begun research based on the hypothesis that lowering the amount of Beta Amaloid (the protein that leads to plaque formation) in the brain may help reduce the effects of Alzheimer's, much like lowering cholesterol can prevent heart disease.

The second section of this segment leads us to San Francisco where neuroscientist Dale Shank is using research with rats in an attempt to utilize the immune system to lower the amount of Beta Amaloid in the brain. He created a vaccine which reduced the amount of plaque formations in adult mice to near-normal levels when treated with the vaccine throughout their development. These promising findings led him to treat adult mice with the vaccine, which also caused a significant decrease in the amount of plaque formations compared to rats in the control group.

The next step in this process might be to test this vaccine on human subjects with Alzheimer's. However, reducing Beta Amaloid to cure Alzheimer's is still only a hypothesis and, as Selco warns, there could still be potentially dangerous unknown side effects.

Placement

As with the previous segment, this segment is also useful with lectures that cover the topic of adult development, but this one goes into detail regarding the putative cause of the illness. The physiological details are thoroughly covered, and for that reason it might also be useful in lectures about the nervous system.

Discussion Questions:

1. How does a vaccine, like that developed by Shank, work?

2. What struggles might Shank and Selco come across when moving from testing their hypothesis on rats to testing with human subjects? How might the experiment be designed?

Disorders and Therapy
The Therapeutic Effect of Antipsychotic Drugs

Segment 25	Length: 02:20 min	File Name: 25_Disorders_DrugsA.mpg

Source *The Brain:* Second Edition, Thirteen, WNET, and Worth Publishers

Description

This segment offers an example of a positive outcome from the use of antipsychotic drugs. The segment begins with a therapeutic session with a patient named Augustine who is not currently on medication. The patient appears unkempt, "down," and describes his frustration with nonsensical "thoughts going across [his] head." The therapist asks how he feels about beginning his new medication and Augustine expresses his anticipation to return to drug therapy even though he is unaware of the name or type of drug he will be taking.

We then see Augustine a month later, after having begun his regimen of antipsychotic medication. He is now clean-cut and shaven, and can easily talk about the way he felt when, as he says, he was suffering from delusions. The therapist asks him what he sees in store for his future and Augustine says he thinks he will get a job, a significantly more positive outlook than one month before.

Placement

This segment is useful in lectures on either abnormal psychology or treatments of mental disorders. It covers the symptoms of schizophrenia when the patient is without treatment and then shows the change in behavior after the onset of treatment with an antipsychotic drug. Thus both the mental disorder of schizophrenia and its treatment are portrayed.

Discussion Questions:

1. The development of antipsychotic medication has created a number of changes in the way we treat schizophrenia, as well as in the way we view mental disorders in general. Describe these changes.

2. Is the overuse of drug therapy in treating psychotic patients a problem in our country today? Why or why not?

3. Do you think Augustine's experience with antipsychotic drugs is realistic? Typical? Why or why not?

Disorders and Therapy

Undesired Effects of Conventional Antipsychotic Drugs

Segment 26	Length: 01:00 min	File Name: 26_Disorders_DrugsB.mpg

Source *Madness: Brainwaves* (BBC Worldwide Americas, Inc.)

Description

In contrast to the previous segment, this segment illustrates the potential problems with the use of drug therapy. It begins with an interview with the author of *The Loony Bin Trip*, Kate Millet. Millet describes the negative side effects of Thorazine and the mind-numbing feeling when taking the drug. The segment continues with a look at the permanent effects of long-term use of antipsychotic drugs, including severe disorders of muscular coordination.

This segment mentions the overuse of drug therapy with psychotic patients, particularly in mental hospitals. A comparison of this segment with the last illustrates the two sides of the debate for the use of antipsychotic drugs in treating mental illness.

Placement

This segment is useful for lectures on the treatment of mental disorders. It portrays the negative side effects of the use of antipsychotic drugs. These side effects are very important to note since many schizophrenic patients stop taking their medication while they are living outside of the hospital setting and lose their ability to cope with everyday responsibilities and become homeless.

Discussion Questions:

1. In the early 1900's, lobotomy was a typical treatment for schizophrenic patients. We know today that it was, in most cases, ineffective and even harmful. Today, the introduction of a new drug or treatment evolves under much more scrutiny. How is a new drug or treatment introduced and proven?

2. What are some alternatives to drug treatment for schizophrenics? Are they effective? Why or why not?

3. What role should the schizophrenic patient have in making decisions regarding their own treatment? Are they typically given that authority?

Disorders and Therapy

Therapy in the Real World: The Use of Real-Life Exposure to Treat Phobias

Segment	Length:	File Name:
27	02:16 min	27_Disorders_Exposure.mpg

Source: "Phobias," *48 Hours,* 7/29/92 (CBS News)

Description

In this segment, taken from a CBS News clip, a therapist is providing group therapy to a number of phobia patients. The interview follows one patient, Bill, who is afraid to ride an elevator and has not ridden on one in eight years. We see the therapist challenge Bill to ride the buildings elevator once, with his supportive therapy group cheering him on. The camera takes us inside the elevator as we watch Bill succeed. Upon exiting, his fear is apparent, but his elation at successfully completing the challenge suggests that he is on his way to recovery.

The segment ends with a brief interview with the therapist providing real-life exposure therapy. This has proven a very effective method for the treatment of phobias. Although Bill's experience on the elevator may be rather mild compared to the reactions to exposure many phobia patients experience, his success is not atypical.

Placement

The segment is equally useful in both the learning chapter and the treatment of mental disorders chapter. The exposure therapy depicted is part of the therapeutic intervention known as behavior modification. It is the outgrowth of work done on classical conditioning, particularly the extinction phase of classical conditioning. Exposure therapies seek to bring clients into proximity of a phobic situation or object and for the client to experience no harm while confronting this. After a number of exposures the connection between the phobic object and the original aversive stimuli will be broken.

Discussion Questions:

1. Why might the therapist in this segment have chosen group therapy for the treatment of her phobic patients, versus individual sessions?

2. In many cases, someone in Bill's position would not be ready for full exposure therapy immediately after entering treatment. What are some methods the therapist might have used to build up to the elevator ride?

3. Everyone is afraid of something. Common fears include spiders, snakes, heights, or darkness. When does a fear become a phobia, in need of treatment?

4. Why are many fears, such as spiders or snakes, so prevalent among humans? How might certain phobias be adaptive?

Disorders and Therapy
A Case Study in Schizophrenia

Segment 28	Length: 09:25 min	File Name: 28_Disorders_Schiz.mpg

Source *Schizophrenia: New Definitions, New Therapies*, 1999 (Films for the Humanities and Sciences)

This segment is a case study in schizophrenia. As the segment informs, schizophrenia is a collection of many diseases that manifest themselves differently in different patients. It is an organic, physical brain disease caused by both genetic and environmental factors. The segment cites recent research which has found a correlation between the likelihood of developing schizophrenia later in life and damage to the patient while still a fetus, particularly during the second trimester. There is evidence of schizophrenia even in infancy, with likely schizophrenics having smaller brains and larger brain ventricles than their healthy counterparts.

The next segment includes an interview with researchers, Dr. Ruben Gur and his wife, Dr. Roehl Gur. They worked together to testify in the case of Russel Weston Jr., a 41-year-old man who killed two guards in a shooting at the U.S. Capitol Building in 1998. Weston was declared a paranoid schizophrenic. They discuss the difference between MRI scans of "normal" brain function, versus that of a schizophrenic. It appears that schizophrenic brains don't activate certain regions in response to environmental stimuli and often activate the wrong regions instead. In general, schizophrenic patients are not violent. Only in cases of paranoid schizophrenia, like that of Russel Weston Jr., is violence more likely.

The segment continues with a description of the symptoms of schizophrenia, which can be divided into two categories: positive and negative. Positive symptoms are those that schizophrenics exhibit, but normal people do not. Examples of positive symptoms include hallucinations, delusions, and disorganized speech. Negative symptoms are characteristics that represent a loss of normal function. Examples include social withdrawal, loss of pleasure, and lack of speech capability. One patient describes his experience with schizophrenia.

The segment ends with a description of the history of treatment for schizophrenia. The first popular antipsychotic drug was Thorazine. Thorazine treated positive symptoms and led to waves of schizophrenic patients being released from mental institutions. However, the side effects, such as severe motor disturbances and impotence in men, were often considered worse than the schizophrenia itself. New drug treatments, such as Clozapine and Olanzapine lack these side effects, but are better for the treatment of negative symptoms.

Placement

This segment is another look at the mental disorder known as schizophrenia. It is useful with lectures on abnormal psychology. This mental disorder has a number of different symptoms but the defining symptoms are hallucinations and delusions. These individuals evince a clear break with reality.

Discussion Questions:

1. Given the research discussed in this segment, what are some ways that we might prevent or reduce, early in life, the development of schizophrenia in adulthood? Are there certain demographics which might be at higher risk for schizophrenia? Why?

2. How do we determine who is capable of being held accountable in a court of law? Should paranoid schizophrenics be able to plead insanity? Why or why not?

3. The advancements in drug therapy have certainly been beneficial to schizophrenic patients in a number of ways. What are some of the problems or complications of the drug treatment trend?

Disorders and Therapy
Overcoming Schizophrenia: John Nash's Beautiful Mind

Segment 29	Length: 04:54 min	File Name: 29_Disorders_Nash.mpg

Source "John Nash's Beautiful Mind," *60 Minutes,* 3/17/02 (CBS News)

Description

This segment is another CBS News clip, this time an interview with John Nash, the famous mathematician whose life is the basis for the movie *A Beautiful Mind.* In 1958, after being named a "mathematical star" by *Fortune* magazine, John began to become paranoid. Like many schizophrenics, he heard voices, and these voices led him to fear conspiracies. He frankly describes these feelings and his experiences in the psychiatric hospital. The segment finishes with a discussion of the movie *A Beautiful Mind* and an interview with Nash's son, who is also a mathematician.

Schizophrenia affects up to 1% of adults and has no cure. John Nash claims to have "reasoned" his way out of the irrational thinking caused by the disease, but most patients find themselves in and out of psychiatric hospitals like the one shown. Amazingly, Nash's life and behavior seemed to make a drastic turn for the better following his receipt of the Nobel Prize for Economics in 1994. His experiences, described in this segment, offer insight into the workings of the schizophrenic mind and inspire empathy for patients suffering from the disease.

Placement

This segment is useful in either the abnormal psychology chapter or the treatments of mental disorders chapter. The topic of schizophrenia is a major component in any discussion of mental disorders due to the complexity and severity of the impairment. Treatment of schizophrenia is mentioned in this segment—both traditional treatment and John Nash's 'reasoning' therapy.

Discussion Questions:

1. In this segment, John Nash describes how he overcame the symptoms of schizophrenia with reasoning. Is this a practical solution for schizophrenics in general?

2. What insight into the disorder schizophrenia can we gain from John Nash's experiences?

3. Do you think that the media buzz surrounding John Nash and the movie *A Beautiful Mind* has realistically represented schizophrenia and the struggles faced by schizophrenics? Has this buzz been beneficial to the community of schizophrenics? Why or why not?

Disorders and Therapy
Experiencing Anxiety

Segment 30	Length: 01:14 min	File Name: 30_Disorders_Anxiety.mpg

Source *Phobias...Overcoming the Fear,* 1991 (Producer, Lalia Gilmore-Madriguera; Connecticut Public Television)

Description

In this segment, an interview with a young man named Julio provides insight into the experience and causes of anxiety. Triggering his anxious feelings, Julio lost two close friends to cancer. In addition, his schoolwork and daily life had become increasingly stressful. He describes his symptoms as being "edgy" all the time, and waking up in the middle of the night, fearing he, too, had brain cancer. His girlfriend, Nancy, briefly describes Julio's anxiety attack, which led to his hospitalization.

Placement

This segment is germane to material touching on abnormal psychology, particularly anxiety disorders. Anxiety disorders form a subclass of mental disorders which are very amenable to psychotherapy. They are the most common psychological disorder reported.

Discussion Questions:

1. Stress and anxiety are a part of life for every human. When does anxiety become a disorder in need of treatment? What were some clues that anxiety was becoming too much for Julio?

2. What types of therapy might be used to treat anxiety disorders? Why do you think these would be effective?

3. What characteristics might make someone more susceptible to anxiety? Why?

Social Psychology
The Actor-Observer Difference in Attribution: Observe a Riot in Action

Segment 31	Length: 00:44 min	File Name: 31_Social_Riot.mpg

<u>Source</u> Footage From the March 20, 2003 Antiwar Protest, San Francisco—Lisa Rein

Description

This segment is a handheld video of a street riot. Police officers are attempting to control the crowd and have weapons at the ready. One policeman hits an approaching woman with his club and moves away. Some crowd members are yelling "peace" or holding up peace signs. We should attempt to take the point of view of the different observers of this scene, in order to illustrate the actor-observer bias.

Placement

This segment is useful with lectures dealing with social cognition. Particularly with coverage of the actor-observer bias which is a interesting exception to the fundamental attribution error. This error is a well-reported social psychology phenomenon in which observers are more likely to ascribe someone's motives to his/her character rather than the situation the individual finds him/herself in.

Discussion Questions:

1. What is the actor-observer bias? What is the fundamental attribution error? How do these two phenomena play out in the segment you just saw?

2. Think of a time when you might have performed the fundamental attribution error. How might you have looked at the situation differently?

3. How do these phenomena affect our social lives and our society? Give two examples.

Social Psychology
Zimbardo's Stanford Prison Experiment

Segment	Length:	File Name:
32	08:19 min	32_Social_StanfordPrison.mpg

Source *Quiet Rage: The Stanford Prison Experiment,* 1988–2004 (Philip G. Zimbardo and Stanford University)

Description

This segment follows the events of Dr. Philip Zimbardo's 1971 Stanford Prison Experiment. Zimbardo created a mock prison in the lower basement of Stanford University and divided participants into guards and prisoners by the flip of a coin. Those participants who were made prisoners were arrested and given prison garb, a number, and a crime for which they were supposedly jailed. Those labeled guards were given khaki uniforms, dark glasses, and a nightstick, and were asked to do frequent "counts" in order to tally the inmates and initiate interaction. The segment shows video footage at various stages of the experiment and interviews with participants and Zimbardo himself.

The prisoners attempt several ways of dealing with their increasing sense of helplessness and despair. It begins with rebellion and solidarity. Some then passively rebel by breaking down emotionally until they are released from the experiment. Some become model prisoners, quickly obeying whatever the guards ask.

The guards, too, quickly take to one of three roles. Some are incredibly sympathetic to the prisoners, doing them favors. Others are tough, but fair—sticking to the rules. Some, however, become sadistic, punishing the prisoners with solitary confinement, strip searches, strenuous physical exercise, and verbal abuse.

One prisoner is removed after only 36 hours in the experiment when he falls into an uncontrollable rage. His replacement attempts to rebel, but finds no support from his fellow prisoners, now fearful of the guards' punishments. One guard describes how quickly he began to see the prisoners as inferior beings who need to be controlled.

Even Zimbardo himself describes how easily he was drawn into the drama, forgetting that it was a simulation and not reality. Not until a female graduate student spoke out against the treatment of the prisoners did he realize that the experiment needed to be stopped, only six days after it began.

The participants in this experiment, guards and prisoners, were brought together two months later to discuss what had transpired. This segment ends with a brief video of the postexperiment discussion between a particularly sadistic guard and one of the prisoners. The guard emphasizes the uniform and his orders as symbols of the role he felt he must fulfill. The prisoner expresses his discomfort with "knowing what [the guard] can do" given these circumstances.

This segment illustrates the sometimes horrifying effects of dehumanization and social conformity. The prisoners were given numbers, not names. They were quickly viewed as inferior. The guards were given uniforms to denote power and authority. They were no longer individuals, but members of a team whose duty was to keep the prisoners under control. Under these circumstances, "good" people took on the roles they were assigned. Very similar results can be found in modern-day prison scenarios, such as the conditions leading to the events at the Abu Ghraib Prison in Iraq.

Placement

Zimbardo's prison study is a classic in the field of social psychology. It is best used with lectures on social influences. This study exemplifies the way in which the social role that a person takes on can change an individual's behavior. In this case being either a "guard" or an "inmate" changes the behavior of a group of college students. Eventually, events get out of hand. This result was alarming and eye-opening for psychology community in the 1970s.

Discussion Questions:

1. If you were chosen as a participant and made a guard, which of the three types do you think you would have become? What if you were a prisoner?

2. Given these findings, how might we change our prison system and/or police arrest procedures to avoid some of these situations occurring?

3. How do the attribution bias and/or the fundamental attribution error play a part in this experiment?

4. Many of the situations that occurred during Zimbardo's experiment would not have passed the Human Subjects Review Board today. Were the findings worth it? How might the experimental design be changed to explore these issues safely?

5. Many have compared the events in Dr. Zimbardo's prison experiment with the torture and abuse that occurred in the Abu Ghraib Prison in Iraq in 2003. What about these two situations is similar? What is different? Do you feel that it was the prison situation that led to these events?

Being Gay: Coming Out in the 21st Century

Segment	Length:	File Name:
33	06:10 min	33_Social_BeingGay.mpg

Source *Being Gay: Coming Out in the 21st Century,* 2005 (Cambridge Educational, A Films Media Group Company)

Description

This segment is a composite of interviews with homosexual teens and teen counselors, as well as some facts and a brief history of homosexuality in the United States. In the early 20th century, homosexuality was legally a criminal offense and the APA considered homosexuality a mental disorder until 1973. And yet, homosexuality has been around since history began.

There is still much to be understood about homosexuality. However, it is not a disease and it is not a choice. Sexuality is a continuum, but society has created ever-changing definitions and labels by which we define who is homo- and who is heterosexual. "Coming out," or revealing publicly that one is homosexual, is a difficult and at times dangerous event in a homosexual's life.

The segment then turns to an interview with Ian Enriquez, a homosexual youth counselor, who describes the six recognizable stages of coming to terms with one's sexuality: Confusion, comparison, tolerance, acceptance, pride, and finally, synthesis. It concludes with a series of homosexual students speaking about their experiences coming out in the 21st century and information for urban centers that can offer free advice and support for homosexual teens.

Placement

This segment is useful with certain topics in developmental psychology, particularly gender identity. The topic of homosexuality is not often covered in much detail, and psychology is even considered culpable by some in the gay community for the fact that earlier versions of the DSM diagnosed homosexuality as a mental disorder. This segment attempts to identify the experience of a young person's growing understanding of their sexual orientation.

Discussion Questions:

1. What are some of the unique struggles faced by homosexuals in society? If you were a therapist or counselor, what special considerations might you make in your practice to account for these unique struggles?

2. How has the image of homosexuality in popular culture and U.S. society changed in the last century?

3. What are some steps that you can take, on a personal level, to help decrease homophobia and intolerance towards homosexuality?

***ActivePsych* CD 4 / DVD 3 / VHS 3:**

***Scientific American* Frontiers Video Collection for
Introductory Psychology, Third Edition**

Edited by Martin Bolt, Calvin College

Video Descriptions and Segment Lengths

Program 1: Brain and Behavior: Phineas Gage Revisited   (5:33 min)

Description

The program reviews the classic case of Phineas Gage. With Phineas's skull on display before him, narrator Alan Alda describes the day of the railroad worker's accident when a tamping iron exploded through his left cheek and out the top of his skull. Amazingly, Gage was immediately able to sit up and speak, and upon recovery, returned to work. However, as observers noted, he was "no longer Gage." He was impatient, obstinate, and unable to make plans for the future. Alda explains how this famous case was the first to explore the relationship between personality and the frontal lobes of the brain.

Jordan Grafman of the National Institute of Disorders and Stroke explains the specific nature of Gage's injury. Grafman notes that while Gage was able to return to work, he could no longer function as a foreman because of his loss of executive skills. Nineteenth-century thinking about the relationship between the brain and personality was unsophisticated. Grafman introduces a phrenology skull and describes how Sir Franz Gall attempted to link specific "faculties," or traits, to different parts of the brain. He mistakenly thought that bumps on the skull could reveal our mental abilities and traits.

The program concludes that although Gall was wrong in the details, he was right in suggesting that various brain regions have particular functions. Furthermore, no part of the brain is more important in distinguishing us from the rest of the animal world than the prefrontal cortex. Grafman notes that the frontal lobes serve as "the central executive, the chairman of the board" that helps us reason, plan, and achieve long-term goals.

Interpretive Comments

The program illustrates how everything psychological is simultaneously biological. Our study of the human brain is essential to understanding human behavior. The case of Phineas Gage illustrates the oldest method of studying brain–mind connections, that is, to observe the effects of brain diseases and injuries. Although Franz Gall was mistaken in arguing that bumps on the skull reveal our personality, his theory of phrenology correctly anticipated recent research findings that show that various brain regions have particular functions. The program also raises fundamental questions about biological contributions to personality.

Discussion Questions

1. Why is it important for psychologists to study the human brain? What other strategies do psychologists use in studying the brain?

2. What are the strengths and weaknesses of case studies in helping us to understand the causes of human behavior?

3. Does nature or nurture shape adult personality?

Relevant Topics: Neuroscience, Thought, Personality

<u>Program 2</u>: Neuroimaging: Assessing What's Cool   (6:36 min)

Description

How does our brain respond to objects "cool" and "uncool?" And what's the hidden motive behind the quest to be cool? Steven Quartz of Cal Tech describes his efforts to answer these questions through neuroimaging techniques. Using an MRI (magnetic resonance imaging) scan, Quartz peers into Alan Alda's brain as he views a variety of consumer products including purses, watches, and small kitchens appliances. Do our brains react differently to objects we rate as cool versus those not thought to be cool? Quartz argues that how we decide what is cool requires the most highly evolved parts of the brain.

After completing the 30-minute brain scan, Alda rates the objects he has just seen on a six-point scale from "not cool" to "very cool." Like most research participants, he rates relatively few as cool. In reviewing the results, Quartz suggests that the front of Alda's brain was significantly more active in response to objects he rated as "not cool" than in response to those he rated as "very cool." Interestingly, he indicates that a third of all his participants demonstrate this pattern and may be strongly oriented toward avoiding objects that are not fashionable. The next largest percentage of respondents show just the opposite brain pattern, that is, the front part of their brain responds very strongly to those objects they rate as cool. In addition, the part of their brain controlling movement becomes active, perhaps revealing the intended effort to reach out to favorite products.

The program concludes that the new efforts to peer inside our brain to study what we covet has captured the attention of marketers. The new field of "neuromarketing" is using brain imaging to understand our buying habits.

Interpretive Comments

Neuroimaging techniques enable researchers to look inside the brain without lesioning it. This program examines one of those techniques, namely, the MRI. More generally, the program highlights how the brain enables the mind. The mind, argues neuroscientists, is what the brain does. Individual differences in brain activity predict differences in emotion, motivation, and behavior. Finally, for some who watch this program, the new field of neuromarketing may raise questions about whether psychology is sometimes used to manipulate people.

Discussion Questions

1. What does this program suggest regarding the relationship between the brain and behavior?

2. What other strategies do psychologists use in studying the brain?

3. Is psychology potentially dangerous? Might its findings be used to manipulate people?

Relevant Topics: Neuroscience, Motivation

<u>Program 3</u>: Brain Plasticity: Rewiring the Visual Cortex   (6:53 min)

Description

The program provides a vivid example of the brain's capacity for modification. Michelle Geronimo volunteers to wear a blindfold for more than four days in Dr. Alvaro Pascual-Leone's experiment investigating whether, when we are temporarily blinded, our visual cortex will begin to process information coming through our fingertips. Prior research indicates that the visual cortex comes to process the sense of touch in people born blind.

The program shows that when the visual cortex of a blind person highly skilled in reading Braille is temporarily disabled through magnetic shock, his ability to read is significantly impaired. Clearly the brain has rewired itself to process touch in the area normally reserved for sight. Pascual-Leone's research asks whether a sighted person's brain will rewire itself in the same way.

Michelle spends much of the 100 hours that she is blindfolded studying Braille. At the end of the four days, an MRI reveals that when Michelle's finger is stimulated, her visual cortex lights up. And, as was true for the blind person, when Michelle's visual cortex is temporarily impaired, efficiency in reading Braille declines. Michelle's experience provides dramatic confirmation for Pascual-Leone's hypothesis that the brain can reorganize itself in a few days, let alone a lifetime.

Interpretive Comments

The program demonstrates that different brain regions have particular functions. Thus sight and touch are normally processed in different parts of the brain. Brain plasticity refers to the brain's capacity for modification as evident in brain reorganization following damage, as well as in experiments on the effects of experience on brain development. The brain is not as hardwired as once thought. You might note that our brains are most plastic when we are young children. If one hemisphere is damaged early in life, the other will pick up many of its functions. In extreme cases, an entire brain hemisphere has been removed and children function well, retaining both memory and personality.

Discussion Questions

1. What does this program tell us about the structure and function of the human brain?

2. What do the findings involving Michelle Geronimo suggest about the nature/nurture issue?

3. What are the implications of brain plasticity for those who suffer brain damage as a result of injury or disease?

Relevant Topics: Brain Reorganization, Sensation and Perception

<u>Program 4</u>: Achieving Hemispheric Balance: Improving Sports Performance (5:19 min)

Description

For decades, clinical observations have indicated that the brain's hemispheres serve different functions. Contemporary research on people with a severed corpus callosum has refined our understanding of each hemisphere's special functions. In this program Debbie Crews of Arizona State University explains how establishing balance between the left and right hemispheres may be one important key to success in sports. Her hypothesis is that the analytical, verbal left hemisphere which tells us what to do must be calm, while the right hemisphere which controls rhythm, timing, and balance must increase its activity. In the last second before we move, say, to swing a golf club, the two hemispheres achieve a balance.

Crews uses Alan Alda to illustrate her theory. After donning a cap that assesses his brainwaves, Alda begins to putt, rating his shots on a one-to-10 scale. Then Crews puts him on a board that forces him to balance his body and hopefully the activity in his cerebral hemispheres. An EEG reveals that Alda's use of imagery in which he imagines himself as a cloud helps him to establish the intended balance. Once he stops trying to figure out how to balance—a predominantly left brain activity—and lets his body take care of itself—aided by right-brain imagery—the task becomes possible. His putts show noticeable improvement.

In the final scene, Alda explains that the Crews' research program at Arizona State University is best known in professional golfing circles for its work on imaging. Crews gives Alda mental rehearsal instructions before he drives. After first picturing his golf ball reaching the intended target, Alda drives successfully.

Interpretive Comments

The program provides the opportunity to review the special functions of the cerebral hemispheres. Each makes unique contributions to the integrated functioning of the brain. Crews' research clearly illustrates how we have unified brains with specialized parts. The segment also highlights the value of thinking in images. Athletes in many different sports now supplement physical work with mental practice. Research indicates that such mental rehearsal can improve performance.

Discussion Questions

1. What are special functions of each cerebral hemisphere?

2. What does Debbie Crews' research suggest regarding the relationship between the hemispheres?

3. Can mental rehearsal improve academic as well as athletic performance? Why or why not?

Relevant Topics: Neuroscience, Thought

<u>Program 5</u>: Genes and Personality: Understanding Williams Syndrome   (5:51 min)

Description

The program opens at a picnic in La Jolla, California, attended by people with Williams syndrome, their friends and families, and researchers studying the rare genetic disorder. Willliams syndrome affects one in 25,000 children, and, as narrator Alan Alda notes, its most striking physical feature is an appealing elfin face. Its most characteristic psychological attribute, suggests Alda, is extraordinary friendliness. It is evident in the warm reception he receives at the picnic. Researcher Ursula Bellugi, who began investigating the disorder at the Salk Institute in the early 1980s, confirms that being "affectionate" and "sociable" best describe those with Williams syndrome.

Testing of Justin illustrates the limits of those with the syndrome. When queried, he answers that there are 24 months in a year and that the oldest woman on earth is likely 50, and that the average annual salary of a doctor is $8.45. Perhaps the most striking challenge for those with Williams syndrome, as is evident in additional testing conducted by Bellugi, is performing visual-spatial tasks. Although they get the details right, they have difficulty grasping the overall pattern or organization.

In the final segment, the specific genetic basis for Williams syndrome is described. As Alda explains, an abnormality in chromosome seven that involves a missing chunk of 25 genes underlies the disorder. Researchers hope to trace both the strengths and disabilities of those with the syndrome to just a few genes. Most remarkably, Bellugi describes the hunt to find the genetic basis for traits such as sociability in all of us.

Interpretive Comments

The program raises basic questions, not only about the basis of a rare and intriguing genetic disorder, but of personality traits we all share. Clearly the program suggests our defining characteristics have an important genetic component. In addition to raising the nature/nurture issue, the segment highlights how the study of disorders may enlighten our understanding of human nature and behavior more generally.

Discussion Questions

1. What does Williams syndrome tell us about the nature of intelligence?

2. How does the study of disorders enlighten our understanding of human nature and behavior?

3. How are our personality traits shaped by both nature and nurture?

Relevant Topics: Nature/Nurture, Intelligence, Personality

Program 6: Cognitive Development: Overcoming Attentional Inertia   (6:21 min)

Description

This segment opens with a 3-year-old learning to sort cards by color, ignoring shape, and then by shape, ignoring color. As she performs each task, a blue star appears above one sorting bin and a red truck above a second sorting bin. The researcher or child restates the rule before each card is presented and the 3-year-old performs flawlessly. Next, in a critical test, the child must reverse what she has just been doing (sorting by shape), and sort once again by color. Interestingly, she fails to make the reversal and continues to sort by shape, placing blue trucks into the bin under red trucks, and red stars into the bin under blue stars. Researcher Adele Diamond refers to the phenomenon as "attentional inertia," that is, the child is unable to redirect her attention from one dimension to another.

Narrator Alan Alda suggests that the tendency to stick with the "tried and true" is controlled by lower, more primitive regions of the brain. In adults, the prefrontal cortex overrides this tendency, enabling us to make correct choices. However, in young children, the prefrontal cortex is not fully developed. Adele Diamond hypothesizes that if the child verbalizes the categorizing rule before choosing, she may achieve greater accuracy. Such a strategy can provide a "verbal scaffold," suggests Diamond, that shifts attention to the relevant dimension.

In the final scene Alda is challenged with an adult version of the sorting game. He, too, has difficulty. However, in his case it is speed, not accuracy, that's the problem.

Interpretive Comments

The segment provides remarkable insight into the inner workings of the child's mind and provides a helpful extension of the text's description of cognitive development. As Piaget suggested, the mind of the child is not that of a miniature adult. This program also links cognitive development to physical development. It suggests that, to some extent, cognitive development is a matter of maturation and not merely experience. Finally, the laboratory demonstrations reveal the creative ways in which researchers study the child's thought processes.

Discussion Questions

1. What do these findings suggest about the nature of the child's thought process?

2. Is nature or nurture more important in understanding cognitive development?

3. What is the relationship between language and thought?

Relevant Topics: The Developing Person, Neuroscience, Thought and Language

<u>Program 7</u>: Moral Thinking and Emotion: A Challenging Dilemma (5:34 min)

Description

This program opens with a description of the structure and function of the anterior cingulate cortex, a structure above the corpus callosum. It plays a critical role in helping us to resolve inner conflict.

Joshua Greene of Princeton University poses the moral dilemma of a train headed for five people. All will be killed unless you throw a switch that diverts the train onto another track where it will kill one person. Should you throw the switch? Most people say yes. Now consider the same dilemma with this slight alteration. Your saving the five depends on pushing a large stranger onto the tracks where he will die but the five will live. What should you do? Although the logic is the same, most people say no.

When Greene's research team used brain imaging to study people's neural responses as they considered the second dilemma, they found that the brain's emotion areas lit up. The dilemma engaged emotions that lengthened the time people considered the dilemma and they changed their moral judgment.

The Princeton team also used the last episode of the popular television series *Mash* to study how people wrestle with moral dilemmas. As a bus load of people hides from enemy soldiers, a baby onboard begins crying. The mother, in trying to quiet the baby, smothers her. In such a case, is it all right to kill the baby? This dilemma also generates strong conflict between moral feeling and moral thinking. After studying neural processing while people consider such a dilemma, the research team believes that the anterior cingulate plays a critical role in receiving information from different parts of the brain to help us make a final judgment.

Interpretive Comments

The Princeton research program poses important questions about the role of the brain in moral decision making. It also raises questions about the relationship between moral thinking, moral feeling, and moral behavior. Clearly, moral judgment involves more than moral thinking. Sometimes moral feelings precede moral reasoning and our reasoning attempts to convince us and others of what we intuitively feel.

Discussion Questions

1. What is the relationship between moral thinking and moral feeling?

2. On what should parents and schools focus in fostering the development of morality?

3. Are people who suffer brain damage responsible for their actions? Why or why not?

Relevant Topics: The Developing Person, Neuroscience, Emotion

<u>**Program 8**</u>: **Childhood Disorder: Understanding Autism**   **(7:18 min)**

Description

Autism, reports narrator Alan Alda, is disturbingly common, affecting one of every 700 to 800 children born. Many children suffering from the disorder are mentally retarded and without language. Geraldine Watson of the University of Washington suggests that the key feature of the disorder is difficulty in social relationships.

Six-year-old Alex suffers from autism. An EEG assesses his neural responses as he views his mother's face and that of a stranger's. Most children show a very different response to a parent than to someone they do not know. Alex does not. He responds in the same way to both images. In general, notes Watson, autistic children do not show a normal response to social stimuli. One important therapeutic goal is to foster attention on such stimuli at a very early age in those suffering from the disorder. Failure to establish eye contact at critical times in the course of communicating with others, suggests Watson, is the most significant diagnostic sign of autism.

Andrew Meltzoff suggests that imitation is an even higher order activity than establishing eye contact. Typically children are great imitators of adults. Autistic children are not. Meltzoff suggests that this failure is symptomatic of the autistic child's inability to relate to others at a meaningful level. Very likely it is at the root of the difficulty that autistic children have in seeing other people as beings like themselves. Early intervention programs now aim to teach autistic children the simple skill of imitation.

Interpretive Comments

The program describes the variety of symptoms that mark the troubling disorder of autism. It explores how its central characteristics may have a neurological basis. The segment also shows the goals and strategies of therapy with children suffering from the disorder. The program suggests that early intervention is critical, perhaps even in shaping the course of brain development, thus highlighting the interaction of nature and nurture.

Discussion Questions

1. What does this program suggest about the causes of autism?

2. Why do you think those with autism are typically unable to infer others' states of mind and what are the likely consequences of this difficulty?

3. What does the study of autism presented in this program tell about the relationship between nature and nurture?

Relevant Topics: The Developing Person, Neuroscience, Personality, Nature/Nurture

<u>Program 9</u>: Memory Loss: A Case Study   (7:28 min)

Description

E.P. is a spry, sociable 82-year-old who is retired from a career in electronics. In 1982 he suffered an acute virus infection that destroyed his hippocampus, a brain structure that is critical to memory. Psychological testing reveals that most of his thinking skills remain intact. His limitations, however, become apparent as he forgets what he has just said and spontaneously repeats the same story several times to his tester within a few minutes.

Researchers Larry Squire and Jennifer Frascino of the University of San Diego indicate that, although they have visited and tested E.P. several times, he is unable to remember their names. Anything new that happens to him is simply not stored and thus he lives in a state of "permanent present." Although new memories are not recorded, old memories from decades back remain strong. Remarkably E.P. can accurately describe the route from his boyhood home to the town library but cannot remember the names of any of the streets in his current neighborhood.

E.P. remains jovial, optimistic, and outgoing. He genuinely enjoys life in spite of his his inability to store new memories. Narrator Alan Alda concludes by noting that, while the hippocampus is important in processing new memories, clearly it is not where memories are permanently stored. E.P has vivid and accurate recollections of his distant past.

Interpretive Comments

The program provides an excellent illustration of the oldest method of studying mind–brain connections, namely to observe the effects of brain diseases and injuries. More generally, the program highlights the importance of case studies in understanding human behavior. The effect of E.P.'s illness provides valuable insight into the role of the hippocampus in processing memories. Showing this program is also useful for distinguishing between short-term and long-term memory as well as the processes of encoding, storage, and retrieval. You might also note that studies of people with brain damage reveal that we have two types of memory—explicit (declarative) memories processed by the hippocampus, and implicit (nondeclarative) memories processed by the cerebellum and the amygdala.

Discussion Questions

1. Explain the claim, "We are what we remember." Do you agree or disagree?

2. Distinguish between the processes of encoding, storage, and retrieval.

3. E.P remains remarkably upbeat in spite of his limitation. Had the illness occurred before his retirement, do you think he would have been able to continue his work in electronics?

Relevant Topics: Memory, Neuroscience, Research Methods

<u>Program 10</u>: Enhancing Memory: The Role of Emotion   (7:38 min)

Description

The program opens with Jim McGaugh of University of California, Irvine, reflecting on the question of why memories of some events remain vivid while others seem to fade. Clearly, events that arouse emotion are more likely to stick than those that are mundane. For example, Nobel Peace Prize winners as well as actors and writers who receive negative reviews never forget the events.

In a laboratory experiment designed by Larry Cahill, research participant, Malina, watches slides of scenes having varying emotional content. Immediately after she views the slides, she is asked to immerse her hand in a tub of ice water, holding it there as long as she can. Cahill's hypothesis is that the immersion triggers a stress-hormone response which in turn enhances memory of the slides. Presumably, the stress hormones work to consolidate the scenes into storage. Indeed, when participants like Marina are tested a week later for their memory of the slides, they remember the emotional slides more clearly than do control participants who have not received the ice-water treatment.

Cahill explains that the stress hormones activate the amydala, a small almond-shaped region of the brain near the hippocampus, which is responsible for the enhanced memory. Learning can occur, explains McGaugh, without activation of the amygdala but the memory will not be as strong.

The program concludes with a consideration of possible gender differences in the memory of emotional events. When Cahill had participants watch movies of emotionally arousing events, he found that they activated the right amygdala in men and the left amygdala in women. Given the specialized functions of the two cerebral hemispheres, Cahill speculates that this finding may mean that men may be more likely to remember the gist of an emotional event and women may be more likely to remember its details.

Interpretive Comments

The program highlights emotion as one of the important factors that impacts memory. It can provide a good introduction to the interesting phenomena of flashbulb memories, which represent clear memories of emotionally significant moments or events. You might ask your students if they remember where they were and what they were doing when they heard the tragic events of 9/11. Do they have other flashbulb memories?

Of course, emotion enhanced remembering has its limits. Prolonged stress (e.g., sustained abuse or combat) can corrode neural connections and shrink the hippocampus that is vital for storing memory. Stress hormones can also block retrieval of older memories. Have any of your students had the experience of their minds going blank while speaking in public?

Discussion Questions

1. In what ways is it adaptive that emotional events are remembered better than the mundane?

2. What might be the relevance of this research for the controversy over repressed and recovered memories?

3. What are some of the implications of this research for improving memory?

Relevant Topics: Memory, Learning, Emotion, Gender

<u>Program 11</u>: Aging and Memory: Studying Alzheimer's Disease   (6:53 min)

Description

Lola Crosswhite is in the early stages of Alzheimer's, a devastating illness that gradually robs its victims of their memory. It affects 4 to 5 million Americans. Lola reports that the first indication of a problem came when she had completed a telephone conversation and moments later was unable to recall any of its content.

Mark Tuszynski of the University of California, San Diego, reports that in the early stages of the illness, sufferers have problems forming new memories. Lola reports that she would often become confused in the course of performing simple daily activities. This problem, continues Tuszynski, is often followed by an inability to recognize the familiar, by impairment in speech, and by difficulty in manipulating common objects. The middle stages of the illness often last a few years until a final, more global decline in cognitive functioning occurs.

Neuroimaging of the progression of Alzheimer's clearly indicates deterioration of the brain which initially involves destruction of the hippocampus followed by the neural areas involved in emotion and reasoning. Spared to the very end are those centers controlling sight, hearing, and touch. Gary Small of UCLA demonstrates how Positron Emission Tomography (PET) technology is detecting subtle changes in the brain before Alzheimer's symptoms occur, thereby enabling earlier treatment.

Dennis Selkoe of Harvard Medical School explains that the clustering of the molecule amyloid beta is likely responsible for the illness. Indeed, an antibody that removes this molecule has been effective in preventing Alzheimer's in mice. However, when tried in humans, the vaccine was stopped after one patient died from a brain inflammation. The Selkoe research team is hopeful that administering the vaccine nasally will be less dangerous and more effective.

Interpretive Comments

The program vividly demonstrates why Alzheimer's is the most feared of all brain ailments. It also illustrates what many regard to be the discipline's most important principle, namely, that everything psychological is simultaneously biological. Recent developments in neuroscience foster hope that Alzheimer's can be effectively treated and even prevented. You might note that other lines of research suggest that we can all decrease our risk of Alzheimer's by eating well, reducing stress levels, and engaging in significant physical and mental exercise.

Discussion Questions

1. What are potential benefits and limits of animal studies in psychology?

2. How does this program illustrate the important principle that everything psychological is simultaneously biological?

3. Apart from physical intervention, what might be some behavioral strategies for decreasing the risk of getting Alzheimer's?

Relevant Topics: The Developing Person, Memory, Neuroscience

Program 12: Experience and Exercise: Generating New Brain Cells   (6:17 min)

Description

In order to practice their occupation, London cabdrivers must first demonstrate a mental map of the city's mazelike streets. Recent brain scans of 16 volunteer cabbies revealed an unusually large hippocampus, the brain area used for packaging memories before they are stored.

Fred Gage of the Salk Institute reported the even more astonishing finding of new neurons in the hippocampus of Swedish cancer patients. This finding overturned scientists' long-held belief that mature brains lose cells with age but never gain them.

Studies of rats at the University of Illinois had indicated that when the animals were raised in enriched environments their brains formed many more neural connections. However, there had never been any evidence of the formation of new neurons until Gage's research team set up a similar study with mice and found that a challenging, enriched environment generated new neurons. Henriette van Praag reports that subsequent research found that merely providing mice with a running wheel for exercise produced new brain cells. Mice who had exercised proved smarter than mice housed in standard cages.

Van Praag hopes physical exercise in humans may produce similar beneficial effects. Furthermore, researchers continue to explore the possible implications of this research for those suffering diseases such as Parkinson's and Alzheimer's which involve the loss of brain cells.

Interpretive Comments

Recent findings indicate that the brain is not as hardwired as scientists once thought. The scientific attitude of curiosity, skepticism, and humility is illustrated in the work that shows nature and nurture sculpt neural tissue throughout life. Research challenges existing claims and extends prior findings. You might note that physical exercise both lifts mood and increases heart and lung fitness. Studies indicate that even moderate exercise extends life.

Discussion Questions

1. How does this research highlight the key characteristics of the scientific attitude?

2. What do these findings tell us about the relationship between nature and nurture?

3. What are other potential benefits of physical exercise on physical and psychological well-being?

Relevant Topics: Health, Neuroscience

<u>Program 13</u>: Stress Management: The Relaxation Response   (6:58 min)

Description

In the opening scenes of this program, Herbert Benson of Boston's Mind/Body Medical Institute teaches Alan Alda the "relaxation response." He instructs Alda to close his eyes, and then beginning with his feet, tells him to relax all the muscles of his body. He is to focus on his breathing while silently repeating to himself the mantra, "calm." Other thoughts will occur, suggests Benson, but each time he should come back to "calm." This attempt to elicit relaxation reflects a simple form of meditation and Alda responds well. Physiological measures confirm a significant reduction of muscle tension. Benson suggests that to the extent stress causes or worsens any disorder, the relaxation response is therapeutic.

Indeed John Goddard benefits greatly from relaxation therapy. Once a victim of panic attacks, depression, and high blood pressure, he is now mentally stable and off his blood pressure medication. He states that his daily meditation is responsible: "It's given me my life back."

In 1981, Benson led expeditions to northern India to study Tibetan monks who practice Tummo yoga as part of their spiritual practice. Vintage film footage dramatically demonstrates how the monks are able, through meditation, to dry (within three to five minutes) ice-cold, wet sheets that have been wrapped around their bodies. Benson reports that they are able to raise the temperature of their extremities by 15 degrees. At the same time they do not increase their heart rate.

Benson reports that the relaxation response counteracts stress hormones and thus raises body temperature. Normally the flight-or-fight stress response occurs automatically and is beyond our conscious control. Meditation brings that stress response under control, and, as Alda concludes, "you don't have to be a Tibetan monk to do it."

Interpretive Comments

As a classroom exercise, you may want to ask students to close their eyes and follow the instructions that Herbert Benson gives Alan Alda at the beginning of the program. Interrupt the program to ask students to relate their experience (before Alda reports his!).

Research indicates that Tibetans in mediation report a diminished sense of self, space, and time. Brain scans indicate that a part of the parietal lobe that monitors our location becomes less active than usual while a frontal lobe involved in focused attention becomes more active. Numerous studies document the benefits of relaxation therapy. For example, it has been shown to alleviate headaches, hypertension, anxiety, and insomnia.

Discussion Questions

1. What physical and psychological disorders are most likely to benefit from relaxation therapy?

2. What does this research suggest about the relationship between mind and body?

3. In addition to relaxation, what other effective ways have you found to manage stress in your own life?

Relevant Topics: Stress and Health

Program 14: Therapeutic Effectiveness: The Placebo Effect (6:59 min)

Description

In the 1960s, Cedric had great success racing automobiles in his native England. After he emigrated to Canada 20 years ago, Parkinson's disease struck. Movement became difficult and he now takes 16 to 20 pills daily to regain control of his body.

Cedric was one of the volunteers in Jon Stoessl's studies of medication for Parkinson's sufferers at the University of British Columbia. The standard treatment for the illness is a drug that stimulates the brain to release dopamine, a brain chemical that helps control movement. Each patient in Stoessl's study received three or four injections, one of which was an inert substance, a placebo. Patients knew that one of the injections was inert but not which one it was. PET scans assessed the brain's response to each injection.

In some patients, including Cedric, Stoessl was amazed to find that the release of dopamine to the inert substance was as strong as it was to the regular medications. Stossel explains that dopamine is intimately involved in reward mechanisms in the brain and the placebo effect involves a strong expectation of benefit. Thus, on careful reflection, its association with dopamine release is not so surprising.

Interestingly, in Cedric's case, the placebo released dopamine in precisely the same place as the standard medication, that is, in the part of the brain that controls movement. Indeed careful testing found that in response to the placebo, Cedric's major symptoms were relieved.

Interpretive Comments

The placebo effect is well documented with pain, depression, and anxiety. The research findings covered in this program indicate that placebos can affect not only human experience and behavior but the brain itself. They provide an extraordinary example of the mind controlling the body as expectations materially affect the physical outcome. Remarkably an inert substance has the same physiological and behavioral effects as standard medication. You may want to remind students of how investigators control for the placebo effect in their research by using the double-blind procedure.

Discussion Questions

1. Can you share any examples of how your expectations, either positive or negative, have impacted your behavior and/or outcomes?

2. Why is knowledge of the placebo effect important in conducting scientific research? How do investigators control for its effect?

3. How important do you think the placebo effect is in understanding the effects of psychotherapy?

Relevant Topics: Therapy, Research Methods, Neuroscience

Program 15: Hidden Prejudice: The Implicit Association Test   (6:10 min)

Description

In the Harvard lab of Mahzarin Banaji, Alan Alda takes a test designed to measure his attitudes toward women in the workplace. Having always thought of himself as a feminist, Alda anticipates the outcome of his own performance. Banaji's test is the Implicit Association Test which measures the strength of associations we have often unconsciously formed between such things as men and career versus women and career. Actually, as the program explains, the key to assessment is the time it takes to make the association. Results of Alda's test suggest that he harbors a slight bias against the association of women and career. Surprisingly, Mahzarin admits that the test shows that she has an even stronger bias again women in the workplace.

Next Brian Nosek, one of the creators of the test, assesses his own associations between Europeans and African Americans with the characteristics of "good" and "bad." In spite of his conscious and expressed tolerance of all ethnic groups, he shows a hidden bias against African Americans.

While admitting his hidden bias, Nosek suggests that it need not control his actions. He also notes that when he thinks about positive African American exemplars such as Michael Jordan and Colin Powell, his performance on the test improves. Banaji also suggests that exposure to positive models is one way in which we can effectively combat implicit prejudice. In short, our environment can successfully intervene in combating bias whether it is overt or hidden and automatic.

Interpretive Comments

The program provides an excellent opportunity to introduce current information-processing research that indicates that access to all that goes on in our minds is very limited. Consciousness is only the tip of the information-processing iceberg. Prejudice can be blatant and overt but also subtle and automatic. People who deny harboring gender or racial prejudice still may carry negative associations. Researchers must continue to study strategies for reducing prejudice at both levels.

Discussion Questions

1. Do you think the test is a reliable and valid measure of prejudice? How would researchers determine its validity and reliability?

2. What do you believe may be the sources of subtle, automatic prejudice?

3. Do you share the researchers' optimism that subtle, automatic prejudice can be reduced or even overcome? Why or why not?

Relevant Topics: Social Psychology, States of Consciousness, Personality

PART III: Video Support *(using MPEG files in PowerPoint)*

Integrating Video into Your PowerPoint Lectures

Importing videos into PowerPoint on a PC...

...in Windows 97/2000:

1) In slide view, display the slide to which you want to add the video.
2) On the **Insert** menu, select **Movies and Sounds**.
3) To insert a video from the Media Gallery, select **Movie from Gallery**, and then double-click the video you want.
4) To insert a video from another location, select **Movie from File**, locate the folder that contains the video, and then double-click the video you want.

   Tip: By default, the video will start when you click it during a slide show. To change how you start a video—for example, by positioning the mouse over the icon instead of clicking it—click Action Settings on the Slide Show menu.

...in Windows XP:

1) Display the slide to which you want to add a movie or animated GIF.
2) On the Insert menu, point to **Movies and Sounds**, select **Movie from File**. Locate the folder that contains the file you want and then double-click the file.

   Note: A movie or GIF file that you've added to the Clip Organizer is found in the **Clip Organizer** folder within the **My Pictures** folder on your hard disk. Or, you can go to the original location for these files.

3) When a message is displayed, do one of the following:
   a) To play the movie or GIF automatically when you go to the slide, click **Yes**.
   b) To play the movie or GIF only when you click it, click **No**.

If you try to insert a movie and get a message that Microsoft PowerPoint can't insert the file, try inserting the movie to play in Windows Media Player, as follows:

1) In Windows, launch **Windows Media Player** (from the **Start** button, on the **Accessories** submenu).
2) On the **File** menu in Windows Media Player, click **Open**, and then type the path or browse for the file you want to insert, and click **OK**.
3) If the movie opens and plays, go to step 5 in this task.

4) If the movie cannot play, then it won't play when you open the Windows Media Player in PowerPoint, so don't complete this task. You can consult Windows Media Player Help to try to troubleshoot the problem. Also, in PowerPoint, search on "Troubleshoot movies" in the **Ask a Question** box on the menu bar to get more suggestions.

5) In PowerPoint, display the slide on which you want the movie to reside, and from the **Insert** menu, select **Object**.

6) Under **Object Type**, click **Media Clip**, and make sure **Create new** is selected. If you want the movie to display as an icon, select the **Display as icon** check box.

7) Click **OK**.

8) On the **Insert Clip** menu in Windows Media Player, click **Video for Windows**.

9) In the **Files of type** list, select **All Files**, select the file, and then click **Open**.

10) To play the video, click the **Play** button just below the menu bar, on the upper left; to insert it onto your slide, click outside the movie frame.

To add a motion clip from Microsoft Clip Organizer:

1) On the **Insert** menu, point to **Movies and Sounds**, and click **Movie from Clip Organizer**.

2) In the **Insert Clip Art** task pane, scroll to find the clip you want, and click it to add it to the slide.

3) If a message is displayed, do one of the following:
   a) To play the movie or GIF automatically when you go to the slide, click **Yes**.
   b) To play the movie or GIF only when you click it, click **No**.

Tip: To preview a clip go to the **Insert Clip Art** task pane. In the **Results** box that displays the clips available, move your mouse pointer over the clip's thumbnail; click the arrow that appears; and then click **Preview/Properties**.

Notes:
■ Clip Organizer initially includes a collection of animated GIFs. Other GIF files and movie files you add to Clip Organizer will also appear in the task pane.

■ To do a search for clips in Clip Organizer, click **Modify** and select criteria for a search. To get more information about finding the clip you want, click **Tips for Finding Clips** at the bottom of the task pane; it gives details on finding files using wildcards and adding your own clips to the Clip Organizer.

Importing videos into PowerPoint on a MAC…

…in MAC OS/9:

1) In slide view, display the slide to which you want to add the video.

2) On the **Insert** menu, go to **Movies and Sounds**.

3) To insert a video from the Clip Gallery, click **Movie from Gallery**, then double-click the video you want. To insert a video from another location, click **Movie from File**, locate the folder that contains the video, and then double-click the video you want to insert.

Tip: By default, the video will start when you click it during a slide show. To change how you start a video—for example, by positioning the mouse over the icon instead of clicking it—click **Action Settings** on the **Slide Show** menu.

...in MAC OS/X:

1) In slide view, display the slide to which you want to add the video.
2) On the Insert menu, point to **Movies and Sounds**.
3) Do one of the following: To insert a video from the **Clip Gallery**, click **Movie from Gallery**, and then locate and insert the video you want. To insert a video from another location, click **Movie from File**, locate the folder that contains the video, and then double-click the video you want.
4) A message is displayed. If you want the movie to play automatically when you display the slide, click **Yes**; if you want the movie to play only when you click the movie during a slide show, click **No**.
5) To preview the movie in normal view, double-click the movie.

** *Please understand that these instructions will not work with every version of PowerPoint, or every computer operating system, as all systems are different. If you have problems importing the video clips into your presentations, please see your PowerPoint Help menu, or visit Microsoft's PowerPoint home page at: http://office.microsoft.com/en-us/FX010857971033.aspx*

You can also contact BFW TechSupport at (800) 936-6899 or techsupport@bfwpub.com.